CITY TAVERN
COOKBOOK

200 YEARS OF CLASSIC RECIPES
FROM AMERICA'S FIRST
GOURMET RESTAURANT

By WALTER STAIB
WITH BETH D'ADDONO

RUNNING PRESS
PHILADELPHIA · LONDON

9   8   7   6   5   4   3   2   1
Digit on the right indicates the number of this printing

Library of Congress Cataloging-in-Publication Number 98-68464

ISBN 0-7624-0529-5

Cover photograph by Bill Deering
Picture research by Susan Oyama
Cover and interior design by Bill Jones
Edited by Mary McGuire Ruggiero
Copyediting by Spectrum Communication Services, Inc.
Typography: Adobe Garamond and Caslon Antique

This book may be ordered by mail from the publisher.
Please include $2.50 for postage and handling.
But try your bookstore first!

Running Press Book Publishers
125 South Twenty-second Street
Philadelphia, Pennsylvania 19103-4399

Visit us on the web!
www.runningpress.com

I dedicate this book
to the memory of my grandparents,
Ernst and Karoline, from whom I learned
my true and lifelong passion for food.
And to my family, Gloria, Patrick, and Elizabeth,
for their inspiration.

Acknowledgments

First, I would like to thank the United States Department of the Interior, National Park Service for their unwavering trust and confidence in me as the operator of this unique, historic restaurant.

I also wish to thank the Independence National Historical Park, especially Superintendent Martha Aikens, Museum Branch Chief Karie Diethorn, Museum Curator Bob Gianinni, and Chief Interpretive Specialist Mary Reinhart.

I am truly grateful for the invaluable assistance of my literary agent, Linda Konner, as well as Dr. Lorna Sass, Barbara Kuck, and the Chief Archivist at Johnson & Wales University. I would also like to thank Beth D'Addono for her diligent assistance in writing this book.

Special thanks to my Chef de Cuisine, Peter Chan; my Pastry Chef, Kelly McGrath; and to my Public Relations/Marketing Coordinator, Karina Kachurak.

Most of all, I want to thank the entire staff of City Tavern for their daily commitment to the accurate recreation of the history that makes us one of a kind. My most heartfelt thanks to all of you for making my vision become a reality!

Contents

City Tavern Timeline

1772 to 1773: Fifty-three prominent citizens commission the building of the City Tavern, which is to be "a large and commodious tavern" that will be worthy of Philadelphia's standing as the largest, most prosperous city in the colonies.

December 1773: City Tavern opens for business. The building has five levels and includes kitchens, a bar room, two coffee rooms, and three dining rooms; the second largest ballroom in the New World; five lodging rooms and servants quarters. Daniel Smith, its first proprietor, leases the Tavern for £300 per year, an amount roughly equivalent to five years of wages for the common man. He resides there from 1774 to 1778.

May 1774: Paul Revere arrives at the Tavern to announce Parliament's closing the port of Boston. The next day, two to three hundred prominent Philadelphians meet at City Tavern to select a committee of correspondence to draft a letter of sympathy for Revere to take back to Boston.

September to October 1774: City Tavern is the unofficial meeting place of the delegates before and after sessions of the first Continental Congress, convened at nearby Carpenters' Hall. George Washington, Thomas Jefferson, John Adams, Richard Henry Lee, and Peyton Randolph are among the participants.

1776 to 1777: Continental and British troops use City Tavern to house prisoners of war. Military courts-martial are also held there.

July 4, 1777: America's first Fourth of July celebration is held at City Tavern.

August 3 to 5, 1777: General Washington and his aides-de-camp share table and quarters at City Tavern, making the Tavern the official headquarters of the Continental Army for three days.

1778: On December 10, politician John Jay is elected president of the Continental Congress, while staying as a guest at the Tavern.

1783: The Pennsylvania Society of the Cincinnati is formed at City Tavern in the second floor northwest dining room.

1784: Original subscribers sell City Tavern to Samuel Powel, a prominent Philadelphian and former mayor of the city.

January 1789: City Tavern's two front rooms become headquarters of the Merchants' Coffee House and Place of Exchange.

April 1789: City Tavern hosts a banquet for George Washington as he passes through Philadelphia on his way to New York for his inauguration.

March 1834: City Tavern's roof catches fire, the building is heavily damaged.

1854: The surviving structure is razed.

1948: Congress authorizes Independence National Historical Park to preserve certain important buildings and sites of significant national importance, encompassing more than forty buildings on forty-two acres, including the site of the original City Tavern.

1975: Historically accurate replication of the original Tavern is completed according to period images, written accounts, and insurance surveys.

1976: The newly rebuilt Tavern opens in time for the bicentennial. The restaurant is managed by a large food service company.

December 31, 1992: The restaurant concession at the Tavern closes.

1994: Walter Staib wins congressional approval as operator of the Tavern, which re-opens for business on July 4, featuring eighteenth-century style gourmet cuisine.

Forewords

The decision to publish Walter Staib's *City Tavern Cookbook* in the autumn of 1999 could not have been more fitting, timely, or meaningful. With a new millennium poised to slam shut an epochal door, Americans are pausing to reassess their national past and present, in hopes of learning from what went wrong and, whenever possible, preserving what went right.

With the end of World War II, another closing of an epochal door, Congress authorized the preservation of landmark sites and buildings intrinsic to the nation's history, among them City Tavern. In 1975, under the aegis of Independence National Historical Park, and borne on bicentennial winds, the line-by-line replication of City Tavern arose from its original footprint. Years went by however, and the food operation languished.

In 1994 the concession was triumphantly rescued by Walter Staib. Of mixed German and Burgundian lineage, with adopted American roots, Staib is today's General von Steuben of American colonial cuisine. The comparison is apt: like a triumphant general, Staib's blouse is heavy with campaign medals, including the French Republic's *l' Ordre du Merite Agricole* and *Food Arts'* Silver Spoon award for sterling performance.

It is tempting to draw further parallels between Walter Staib and figures of the colonial past. City Tavern's first lessee, Daniel Smith, was also born on the other side of the Atlantic; as described by eighteenth-century Philadelphia tavern-going and public life scholar Peter Thompson in his recent book *Rum Punch and Revolution*, Smith "was probably the first American ever to be interviewed for a position as tavern keeper," a measure taken to ensure the protection of the Tavern's tone and reputation, a provision outlined in the lease. Staib, too, was obliged to apply for congressional approval as operator of City Tavern, which he won in the spring of 1994, giving him precious few weeks to totally refurbish the property in time, appropriately enough, for a bang-up Fourth of July opening. This, characteristically, he was able to do successfully.

For Smith to win his lease from the Tavern's charter members, he had published a letter of intent stating the exquisite degree to which he was willing to go to furnish the place in elegant style. Staib, too, shot aesthetically high, commissioning not only the reproduction of the original china's decorative rim, but also hefty colonial-sized silverware, and Madeira glasses from the same outfit that had hand-blown them for Thomas Jefferson's epicurean Monticello table.

Staib's mining of recipes has delved equally deep and wide, effectively dismissing the popular delusion that Puritan-fathered American cooking was shy of bold and complex flavors (indeed, our own research once turned up the fact that Oliver Cromwell's wife herself had written a cookbook, with some recipes reading like inventories of a spice caravan). Staib's City Tavern recipes are real page-turners for active and armchair cooks, all the favorite flavors of the young Republic intermingling irresistibly—sorrel and marjoram, Madeira and ale, bacon dressing, and oyster stuffing, cornmeal crusts, and pungent chutneys, just to start. However, this being the city of the Liberty Bell, here and there Walter Staib has taken some reasonable liberties; just as his faithful replication of City Tavern may now be viewed at night by soft electric light, he has discreetly electrified the menu with such modern amenities as mallard duck sausage and salmon carpaccio. But as salmon had once been so overabundant in Pennsylvania that farmers used it for fertilizer, I believe Philadelphians would have welcomed Staib to colonial times to show them such a delicious extra thing or two.

The word "tavern," according to the dictionary, has cousinly roots with "tabernacle," a sanctuary. Walter Staib's City Tavern and *City Tavern Cookbook* succeed in serving as cultural sanctuaries and living connective tissue with our past.

—Michael Batterberry
1999

It is wrongheaded to say that American gastronomy is so much younger than those of Europe and Asia, for it was the Americas that gave the world so many of those ingredients that help to define what we think of European and Asian food. What would India's or Thailand's or China's gastronomies be without chile peppers? What would Italian cooking be without the tomato? What would Europe do without the potato, which kept many a soul in Ireland and Germany alive in the eighteenth and nineteenth centuries? Corn and chocolate are staples of world cuisine, yet they didn't exit outside of the Americas before 1492.

Indeed, the story of American food is one that was already rich in native ingredients, made more so by the arrival of European settlers who brought everything from chickens to pigs. By the beginning of the seventeenth century, American gastronomy was already more diverse and more consistent than most of what the masses had to eat in the rest of the world, and by the next century the American bounty for meat, vegetables, and fruit astonished Europeans who visited and saw how well fed Americans were, even in the backwoods of the western territories. That these same Europeans sometimes criticized American tables for their lack of culinary finesse, none came away anything but impressed by the abundance that had become an American birthright by the time of the Revolutionary War.

The Tavern was one of these eateries where men of various social classes came to feast on wild game, fish from local waters, the freshest seasonal fruits and vegetables, and wines made from native grapes.

American taverns were not all rough and roustabout, though few were very genteel, and they gave the first indication of what American hospitality would always be—a comfortable, fairly casual attention to service and to eating and drinking that fit perfectly with the national spirit.

In those days, taverns were usually common eating places, where there were no menus as such and eating at long tables stacked with plates or soup and poultry and meats and tankards of ale was part of the bonhomie of the place. Only after 1837, when Delmonico's in New York copied the new French model of restaurants, did the set, well-appointed table with its own menu and waiter make its appearance in American cities, though the taverns continued to be the prime social center for the men of the nineteenth century. (Women would not be allowed to dine alone in any kind of eating establishment until well into the 1890s.)

Walter Staib, like almost every one of us in America, is an immigrant who is enthralled by American largess and food. At the City Tavern, he has sought to rescue the traditions of the true tavern from the gimmicky, adulterated quaintness of so many other taverns, preserved, rebuilt, or otherwise, in eastern cities dating to the colonial period. His dedication to both the authentic architecture and decor of the rooms has provided City Tavern with museum-quality reproductions, and the menus, as evidenced in this fine cookbook, show how varied, how remarkably well thought-out, and how delectable tavern food and drink were more than two centuries ago. From the rich seafood chowders to the fruited desserts, this is wholesome, good cooking. City Tavern's menu brings back an appreciation for cooking with Madeira wine, walnuts, pumpkin, and brings back savoriness of pot pies and casseroles we haven't seen in decades on American menus.

No one even vaguely interested in what the American larder once was and how Americans once ate can help but be fascinated by reading through every page of this cookbook. The home cook will also be rewarded with good recipes that link us all to our heritage, wherever we may have come from.

—John Mariani
1999

Preface

As a child growing up with my grandparents in Pforzheim, Germany, a small town located at the entrance to the Black Forest, I always loved and appreciated food. My grandfather's roots were in Burgundy, France, and he was an avid culinarian. My mother was a chef, and the entire family had a passion for cooking, gardening, and raising livestock. We made our own preserves, canned fruits and vegetables, and sausage and smoked meats—all the techniques that mirrored what the early Americans did back in 1773.

At age six, I worked in my uncle's restaurant, Gasthaus zum Buckenberg, complete with its own huge butcher shop. I started out doing odd jobs, and was soon learning about food and developing cooking skills. I loved the restaurant environment from the beginning—to me, it was like a colorful carnival, always changing, always exciting. Food was my passion—there was never any question that I would pursue cooking as a professional career.

Over the next four decades, I worked at some of the finest hotels and restaurants in Europe and the United States. In 1979, I moved to Philadelphia, taking over as president for the Davre's restaurant chain owned by ARA services. In 1989, I started my culinary consulting business, Concepts By Staib, Ltd. I heard about the City Tavern's closing on New Year's Eve, 1992, and couldn't get the Tavern out of my mind.

After inquiring with the National Park Service, which supervises the Tavern, I received a prospectus to apply for its operation. Although it seemed complex and too full of governmental jargon and red tape, I took it with me on a trip to Asia. It was on the return flight home from Tokyo that the project really captured my imagination. I couldn't believe the lifestyle and level of sophistication those early Philadelphians had. It quickly became clear to me that City Tavern had been, without a doubt, the greatest restaurant in eighteenth-century North America.

The more I learned about City Tavern and its special place in social, political, and gastronomic history, the more I started to believe in its potential. Realizing that, with the right management and cuisine, the Tavern could once again rival any restaurant in America, I began to feel like a culinary crusader, impassioned about keeping America's gastronomic heritage alive. I submitted a proposal.

The first hurdle in my quest was to win the approval of Congress as the Tavern's operator, a process which took six months. I was awarded the contract on April 15, 1994, and set about immediately undertaking extensive restorations to bring it back to its original elegance. The National Park Service's library and archives provided volumes of research material to assist me and my wife, Gloria, with this huge project.

Before we opened our doors on July fourth of that same year, we had completely renovated the kitchen, removed the freezers and the commercial laundry facility, and installed a pastry and bake shop. Independence Historical National Park chief curator, Karie Diethorn, worked closely with us to recreate the most authentic City Tavern experience possible, with slight adjustments to make room for the modern day context. The walls were painted in the Tavern's original colors, the rooms were decorated in reproduction furniture and fabrics, and we dressed our service staff in handmade eighteenth-century attire. We chose reproduction table settings, including candlesticks, plates with a china pattern based on one from 1793, and mid-eighteenth-century style lead-free pewterware for our tabletops. Even our glassware, which was imported from Italy or hand-blown by artisans in West Virginia, was selected to reflect styles used in the late eighteenth century. And for an authentic ambiance, we decided to commission colonial-period "characters" for special events, such as Thanksgiving, and to provide live harpsichord and violin music on weekends.

As critical as the setting was, the most important thing for me as a chef was to work diligently on the food and dining experience. I was fortunate enough to have a head start—a few years earlier, as a consultant to a restaurant of the same period in Richmond, Virginia, I had researched colonial culinary and dining traditions with New York food historian Dr. Lorna Sass. It became my mission to recreate the culinary heritage of City Tavern, a one-of-a-kind dining institution.

This experience turned out to be a delightful awakening as I discovered how close to "home" eighteenth-century food was for me. Having grown up in the Old World, where everything was done the old-fashioned way, the original City Tavern recipes were comfortably familiar. Many of them could have come right from my own grandmother's kitchen.

In keeping with Old World tradition, my food philosophy for the Tavern continues to be "from the farm to the table, as fresh as possible." Accordingly, our produce is delivered two to three times a day, breads and pastries are baked each morning, and we use no walk-in freezers—our meats are delivered daily and marinated in the same manner as they were in the early colonial era.

This philosophy is also reflected in our beverage selection. Our beers and ales are custom-brewed for us by a local microbrewery, free of all preservatives and additives, and are served in traditional 20-ounce British pints. City Tavern offers a unique selection of colonial shrubs, a beverage produced today in the same manner in which it was produced in the eighteenth century.

Thankfully, all our attention to detail has been rewarded with national and international press coverage. On June 29, 1994, days before we opened, City Tavern was the cover story, penned by Florence Fabricant, for the *New York Times Living Section*. That same year, John Mariani of *Esquire* magazine named City Tavern one of the best "new" restaurants in America, and we've continued to garner praise from food professionals and the public alike.

City Tavern is indeed more than a restaurant. It is a piece of history; a living culinary museum that offers diners an experience unavailable anywhere else—insight into our country's vast and underappreciated culinary heritage. I wrote this book to extend that experience to a larger audience, and to solidify City Tavern's place in American gastronomic history.

This collection of 200 recipes reflects the kind of food enjoyed by our country's Founding Fathers in the Tavern's heyday—which we faithfully recreate today.

Many of these recipes were inspired by those in *The Art of Cooking Made Plain and Easy*, written by Hannah Glasse in 1745, along with recipes penned by the first First Lady in her circa 1753 *Martha Washington's Booke of Cookery*. Although I strive to preserve the authentic nature of the colonial recipes we use, I have had to adapt some of them to modern tastes and equipment.

I hope you enjoy this delicious lesson in our country's culinary history.

Cheers! (Or as they would have said in colonial days, Huzzah!—a precursor of today's Hurrah!)

—*Walter Staib, Chef/Proprietor*

A Taste of History

Appreciating the Eighteenth·Century Tavern

A tavern in colonial days was much more than a place to drink a pint of ale. In smaller towns and cities where there were no office buildings or convention centers, taverns met all these needs. Taverns were a town's central place of meeting, a place where stock and ship cargoes were bought and sold, new companies organized, notices posted, and newspapers from home and abroad perused. Taverns were social focal points as well, the place where dinners for fraternal societies were held, political causes championed, and dances and live music enjoyed. Taverns, like eighteenth-century coffee houses, served food and drink, but also offered lodging for visitors passing through the area. City Tavern was the finest tavern of its day, the grandest of all taverns in the New World.

Eighteenth·Century Cuisine: America's Original Fusion

The uninitiated may imagine that the American cuisine served at Philadelphia's original City Tavern in the 1700s was dull, flavorless, and limited. That assumption couldn't be further from the truth. In reality, the nearby bustling port brought a dizzying mix of ethnic groups into the city, each arriving with the culinary tradition of their own heritage. From the British came hearty stews and meat pies, along with scones and breads. The Germans offered their country's tradition of sausages, soups, and baked goods. African and West Indian slaves who arrived in the New World brought with them a food culture that included curries, hot peppers, and exotic spices and fruits.

The French Revolution and the slave rebellion in Hispaniola delivered an influx of French immigrants, among them pastry chefs, confectioners, and a multitude of other food artisans and tradesmen. It was this French influence that brought Philadelphia's cuisine up to European standards.

City Tavern, separated from the Delaware River by just a few short blocks, was a magnet for the ship captains who came to barter their cargo. Depending on the route the captain sailed, he might be offering Madeira from the island of the same name (used as ballast), oranges from Seville, port from Portugal, Nürnberg gingerbread, dried plums, and cherries from Germany, rum, pineapples, and mangoes from Jamaica, or spices from the Spice Islands. Ships arrived about three times a week from the West Indies. Since modern refrigeration did not exist, cargo had to be disposed of quickly before it spoiled, so most goods were auctioned—often at shipside—to eager innkeepers and caterers. Drying, salt curing, and pickling were used to preserve foods over time.

Philadelphia, then the largest city in the New World, and the second largest city in the British Empire, was home to open-air markets that offered the bounty of the area. The Delaware River was brimming with fish and oyster beds. The area's rich agricultural land produced an abundance of natural foods, including wild fruits and berries, game, wildfowl, maple syrup, and honey. From the Indians, settlers learned to cultivate corn, along with sweet potatoes, squash, beans, and wild rice. Local farms produced eggs as well as grains and flour.

This is the stuff of City Tavern's menu, today, as well as then: a cuisine that represents an unparalleled and authentic gourmet dining experience.

City Tavern: A Pivotal Site in American History

The year is 1774. Storm clouds of revolution were ominously forming in the New World. The people who would become this country's shapers and leaders, men like Thomas Jefferson, Benjamin Franklin, John Penn, and John Adams, were laying the foundation for a document that would become the backbone of a new society. These men spent hours together in heated discussion, arguing, defining, and detailing the basis for this emerging nation.

All of this talk didn't happen on an empty stomach. The food that fueled these intellectual architects was provided by Philadelphia's City Tavern.

The "Le Cirque" of its day, modeled after the finest taverns in London, City Tavern was by all historical accounts considered the best restaurant in British North America. Opened in 1773 by fifty-three prominent Philadelphia businessmen and investors, including several signers of the Declaration of Independence, City Tavern was the setting for suppers "as elegant as was ever laid on a table," according to John Adams.

Yet, politics was the true main course on City Tavern's menu. Every Saturday, members of the Second Continental Congress would convene to dine on City Tavern fare. Eight delegates even formed their own "table," opting to frequent the Tavern on a daily basis. Despite such a glorious beginning,

> "No man can be a patriot on an empty stomach"
>
> —*William Cowper Brann* *(1855–1898)*

City Tavern fell out of favor with the Philadelphia elite in the early 1800s. After an ignoble end—the Tavern acted as a merchant's exchange before catching fire in 1834 and finally being razed in 1854—City Tavern remained a mere footnote in the history books for a century until it was rebuilt and finally reconstructed in its current, authentically beautiful state.

To understand the vigorous role that the Tavern played in eighteenth-century Philadelphia society, you really need to take a historical journey back in time. When City Tavern was conceived in 1772, the city's inns and taverns of the day were roughly hewn, serving primarily as meeting places for merchants to haggle over prices, tip pints of ale, and put up for the night.

The city's elite decided to take matters into their own hands. The original subscribers paid £25* per share to be charter members of the Tavern. Socially connected property owners, office holders, doctors,

---

*Translating the Tavern subscription cost into modern currency is challenging since dollars had not yet been "invented" at the time. However, the average laborer in 1762 annually earned £60, of which about £55 was used for food, housing, and other necessities; any colonist paying £25 for Tavern membership certainly lived comfortably.

(*Source: Billy Smith's Philadelphia's Laboring People*)

lawyers, and merchants were among charter members' ranks. Well traveled and schooled in London, these upper crust gents knew what they wanted, and went about getting it. Mixed among the more sober Quakers in the group were raconteurs and gamblers, men accustomed to high living, fine food, and wine. Collectively, the subscribers wanted a place to call their own.

A glance at the subscribers' ranks delivers a Who's Who of eighteenth-century Philadelphia. A few of the more well-known subscribers included Samuel Powel who later became mayor of Philadelphia; Thomas Mifflin, soon to be governor of Pennsylvania; Lt. Governor John Penn; and Samuel Meredith, acclaimed financier who worked tirelessly in government for more than twenty years.

City Tavern Trustee Henry Hill, patriot and Madeira wine importer, would also serve as trustee to Benjamin Franklin's estate when the great man died in 1790. George Clymer, a partner of Samuel Meredith, was among the first to advocate separation from Britain. John Wilcocks was perhaps the most public spirited of the group, serving as trustee of Bray Associates, which provided schooling for black children. John Nixon read the Declaration of Independence in public for the first time. Edward Shippen became a colonial chief justice of the Pennsylvania Supreme Court; Jared Ingersoll, Will Parr, and Benjamin Chew were lawyers and holders of public office. This group naturally sought to emulate the manners, interests, and style of living of their mother country—the Tavern fit perfectly into that picture.

The Tavern's location was prime—two short blocks from the port's wharves in one direction, two long blocks from the courthouse and markets in another, and fronting the city's main north/south thoroughfare, the "Old King's Road" with connections to all principal points.

The Tavern's design may have come from the subscribers themselves—many, including Hill and Powel, had studied architecture and even designed their own homes. It is certain that they networked among themselves and their friends to secure the finest workmanship available. Among the receipts of moneys paid to tradesmen during the building process was £5.12 to Martin Jugiez, a master carver who had also worked on the intricate carvings commissioned for Benjamin Franklin's house.

The Tavern's construction, which took just a year, was completed in November 1773, with the first recorded public event held on January 24, 1774. On that day, a meeting of the St. Georges' Society and the Society of Englishmen and Sons of Englishmen convened, societies established for the assistance of "Englishmen in distress," according to a notice in the *Pennsylvania Gazette*, the city's paper, published, coincidentally, by Benjamin Franklin.

Before City Tavern's arrival on the colonial scene, no place of public accommodation in America had assumed real distinction—the Tavern did for more than two decades. It was appropriate that City Tavern be built in Philadelphia—the colonial center for art, science, education, and commerce and boasting many paved streets lit with lamps, fine public buildings, three libraries, a college, and the first hospital in the New World. If you were active in public, civil, and military life during the Revolutionary period, you entered the Tavern's portals at one time or another. Despite its social status, it was not overpriced—one visitor in 1798 noted that City Tavern, although the "best in town, charges about the same price as the others."

Little is known about the first innkeeper, Daniel Smith, except that he was British and experienced at his trade. The tavern keeper of that day had to wear many hats, from overseeing the inn's physical upkeep and care to serving as room clerk, bookkeeper, and cashier.

Smith was the first of three innkeepers that tended to the Tavern during its heyday. During the Tavern's "Golden Age," where it was without peer and always at the center of the city's social and political activity, most occasions of note were held in the Long Room. These events included soirées held for heads of state, and more than one lavish dinner for General Washington, including the affair, complete with fireworks, held April 20, 1789, when Washington stopped in Philadelphia on his way to New York to be inaugurated President.

Important Events Held at the Tavern

City Tavern's role as the backdrop for the unfolding of American history is indisputable and well documented. When Paul Revere rode six days from Boston with news that the British had closed the port in retaliation for the famous tea party, he went directly to City Tavern to deliver the news. As the delegates of the first Continental Congress began to arrive in the Fall of 1774, they stopped first at City Tavern. In fact, when John Adams arrived in town, dusty and fatigued from the long ride, he went straight to the Tavern, "the most genteel one in America." George Washington did the same, not proceeding to his lodgings until first supping at City Tavern.

The delegates of the Continental Congress frequented the Tavern the entire time they were assembled, where they often conducted informal discussions outside of the more formal confines of Carpenters' Hall.

When the battles of Concord and Lexington were announced by a rider at City Tavern on April 24, 1775, it became the center of military activity during the war. As battles raged, the funerals of war heroes such as Colonel John Haslet of Delaware and General Hugh Mercer took place at the City Tavern, with full military honors.

In 1777, the nation's first Fourth of July celebration was held at the Tavern, "with festivity and ceremony becoming the occasion," according to John Adams. When Washington moved his headquarters to Philadelphia in August of the same year, his letters indicate that he used the Tavern as his informal headquarters—although he would not allow his troops entrance, for fear of their corruption.

When the British retook Philadelphia that fall, innkeeper Daniel Smith welcomed his countrymen with open arms—and an open till. The Tavern was commandeered as a center for officer recreation, including a weekly series of balls where Philadelphia's Tory belles were entertained. The fun was not always so wholesome—record of a horse theft from in front of the tavern was made in October 1777.

Soon after the Continental Army reoccupied Philadelphia in 1778, Smith returned to England. Gifford Dalley and then George Evans succeeded him as innkeepers. City Tavern once again hosted special events for the upper crust of America and abroad. During Dalley's tenure, the Coffee Room developed into an exchange room and seat of business. When the second Continental Congress convened, a series of dazzling balls and national affairs of state took place, often continuing until the wee hours of the morning. With the establishment of the new political order, Philadelphia was suddenly inundated by politicians needing entertainment,

room, and board—exactly the kind of trade most restaurants pray for.

The most lavish party held at the Tavern was most likely the election and installation of the state's chief executive, the president of the Supreme Executive Council in 1778. A party of 270, including ambassadors and ministers of France and Spain, attended. The bill was £2995—only £500 of that for food. The rest was for a stupefying amount of alcohol, including 522 bottles of Madeira, 116 large bowls of punch, nine bottles of toddy, six bowls of sangria, 24 bottles of port, and two tubs of grog for artillery soldiers. Understandably, the party turned boisterous—the bill also covered 96 broken plates and glasses, as well as five decanters.

In 1785, the Tavern was sold to Samuel Powel, one of the original proprietors, the former mayor of the city and a man of great wealth and social standing. When thirty-nine delegates, representing twelve of the thirteen states, approved a constitution for the United States of America, on September 17, 1787, they then adjourned, according to the record, "to the City Tavern, dined together and took a cordial leave of each other."

From 1785 to 1824, City Tavern served primarily as a hotel, merchants' exchange, and coffee house. The merchants' exchange, a forerunner of the Philadelphia-Baltimore-Washington stock exchange of today, was a bustling center of industry, a lively place where sea captains, insurance salesmen, and farmers haggled and exchanged gossip. The Tavern's fortunes gradually declined in the early 1800s, and in 1834 its roof caught fire, damaging the Tavern irreparably. In 1854, when City Tavern was demolished, The *Pennsylvania Gazette* wrote, "... nobody is going to miss this Tavern except those persons living in the past."

City Tavern Rises Again in the Twentieth Century

Fortunately, that period of the Tavern's obscurity ended when the U.S. Department of the Interior was authorized by the Truman Administration to create Independence National Historical Park, a surviving group of pivotal historic sites that formerly included City Tavern. Although that decision was made in 1948, it took more than twenty-five years of research to recreate the Tavern, brick by brick, according to historic documentation of the original structure. City Tavern finally opened in 1976, just in time for the country's bicentennial celebration.

While there are other restaurants on the Atlantic seaboard that attempt to recapture America's past, only City Tavern has faithfully revisited the high culinary standards of the day. City Tavern is clearly an American original, a restaurant famous both for its Revolutionary cuisine and its formidable place in our nation's history. This unique two-fold attraction appeals to tourists and locals alike and guarantees City Tavern a distinguished place in culinary history, both for its vibrant past and its utterly delicious present.

Touring the Tavern

In 1975, after painstaking research, the National Park Service rebuilt City Tavern. Today, the Tavern appears essentially as it did 200 years ago, even down to the front awning, which shades the Tavern from the direct summer sun. Every year, 12,000 to 20,000 guests are drawn to City Tavern because of its reputation for fine, authentic colonial dining, as well as for its historic élan. At the Tavern, they enjoy a taste of the past in the same atmosphere of gentility and good cheer enjoyed by our nation's founders. Here's a quick "guided" tour through the seven dining and public rooms of this accurately reconstructed inn.

The original City Tavern was comprised of five levels. The cellar housed the kitchens; the first and second floors contained the public areas; the third floor was devoted to lodging rooms; and the attic probably served as servants' quarters. The first and second floors, which we will tour in detail here, were the heart of the Tavern's operation.

First Floor

As you walk up a set of marble stairs into the Tavern from Second Street, you first enter a long hallway. On your right is the Subscription Room, so-called because the magazines and newspapers, ships' manifests, and letters of decree to which the Tavern subscribed were located there.

Behind the Subscription Room is the Bar Room, with its high-backed wooden booths and central fireplace. Although it doesn't have a "bar" as we know them today, per se, it does have a narrow, closet-sized room that can accommodate the bartender and, of course, the liquor. It has a window and a Dutch door that doubles as a shelf, with barred gate that slides down on top of it. In the 1700s, this was commonly used to separate the innkeeper and his liquor from the patrons. Since tempers and political arguments were often stoked by alcohol consumption, whenever the innkeeper felt threatened, he would lower and lock "the bar" to protect himself, thereby explaining the derivation of the modern-day term. Back then, the bar would have functioned as the Tavern's nerve center, where patrons would arrange to rent a room, order a meal, or hear the latest news.

Across the hallway from the Subscription Room is a Coffee Room. From the very beginning of the Tavern's history this Coffee Room was the place where merchants would discuss ship movements and other business over a cup of coffee or stronger drink—one reason why maps remain on the Coffee Room wall today.

In the room next door is a second Coffee Room

that is representative of the Tavern's public dining spaces.

Back in the main hallway, to our left is the back door, which leads out to the porch and garden area, and doubled as the entrance for the gentry class en route to balls and private parties commonly held upstairs.

Second Floor

The stairs in the main hallway lead to the second floor. At the top of the stairs, straight through the hallway, is the Long Room—the scene of countless elegant balls, brilliant musical performances, large meetings, and card games. In fact, it was in the Long Room that Congress held the first Fourth of July celebration in 1777.

Adjoining the Long Room are two private dining rooms. Originally, these rooms would have accommodated clubs or groups desiring privacy. On the left at the top of the stairs, is the Cincinnati Room (originally called the Northwest Dining Room), named in 1975 in honor of the Pennsylvania chapter for the Society of the Cincinnati, which helped refurbish this room. This organization is composed of direct descendants of the Revolutionary officers who founded the original Pennsylvania chapter at City Tavern in 1783.

Across the hallway is the Charter Room, named in honor of the fifty-three original Tavern subscribers and once reserved for their private use. This room also serves to honors the members of the national Home Fashions League, who contributed toward furnishing the present City Tavern.

Lower Level

The adaptation of City Tavern's cellar provides insight into the historical aspect of food storage, preparation, and service. From 1773 to 1848, the cellar served the vital purpose of being both a work and storage area. Fresh foodstuffs were delivered to the Second Street entrance. At the rear of the building, casks, barrels, and boxes were loaded into the cellar through the cobblestone alley. Because there was access to water pumps on the public street, this area also served for dishwashing.

The back cellar room was used for the long-term storage of bulk foodstuffs such as flour. The larder room located on the southeast corner was possibly used as a storeroom for prepared foods like pickled meat and preserved fruits. From the kitchen on the northeast corner, food was prepared and distributed.

In 1994, the cellar area was opened to the public for dining.

Part 1: First Plates

When City Tavern first opened, appetizers weren't served as they are today. Meals were organized as "first plates" and "second plates," with first plates including appetizers, soups, and salads. All first plate items were brought out at the same time and served family-style and in eclectic dishes of various shapes and sizes before the main course—second plates.

Appetizers

Appetizers would have been a foreign concept to colonial diners at City Tavern. The custom of the day was to serve a lavish first plate spread, with the foods we know as appetizers as just one part of that feast. Remember that dining at the Tavern was a one-of-a-kind experience—the average person at home didn't eat in this opulent style every day. Of course, this type of feast wouldn't fit into our modern lifestyle either, which is why I've selected these recipes for you to prepare as stylish starters for your parties.

Peppered Smoked Salmon on Potato Pancakes

Smoking was one of the main ways colonists had of preserving fish over the winter. Today, peppered smoked salmon is readily available at specialty gourmet stores and seafood markets. The style of potato pancake used here has its roots in Southern Germany, where I come from, and it is still made today in the Pennsylvania Dutch and Amish communities in Lancaster, Pennsylvania. This recipe differs from the all-potato pancakes made in Northern Germany in that it includes flour. If you prefer, make the pancakes ahead and reheat them.

Makes six 7-inch pancakes; Serves 4 to 6

4 medium red skinned potatoes

1 cup all-purpose flour

1 cup whole milk

2 eggs

5 ounces (1 stick plus 2 tablespoons) unsalted butter

1 teaspoon salt

1 teaspoon chopped fresh parsley

½ teaspoon freshly ground black pepper

2 pounds presliced, peppered smoked salmon (available at most delicatessens or gourmet shops)

1 medium red onion, thinly sliced, for serving

¼ cup small capers, drained, for serving

1 cup sour cream, for serving

6 lemon wedges, for garnish

1½ tablespoons chopped fresh parsley, for garnish

Potato pancakes also work well with other kinds of smoked fish.

1. In medium saucepan cook the potatoes in enough lightly salted boiling water to cover for 20 to 25 minutes or until fork-tender.
2. Drain potatoes, cool with cold water, peel and shred.
3. To prepare the pancakes, in a medium mixing bowl, combine the flour, milk, eggs, potatoes, 8 tablespoons of the butter, salt, parsley, and pepper. Whisk until there are no lumps.
4. For each pancake, in a 7-inch nonstick skillet, add 1 teaspoon of the remaining butter to coat the pan and ladle ½ cup of the batter into the skillet.
5. Cook over medium heat for 2 minutes on each side, until brown.
6. Transfer the pancakes to a plate and keep warm in a 275°F oven.
7. To serve, place 6 to 8 ounces (4 slices) of the salmon on top of each warm potato pancake. Top with the onion slices, capers, and dollops of sour cream.
8. Garnish each pancake with a lemon wedge and a sprinkling of parsley. Serve immediately.

Crab Cakes with Herb Rémoulade

Crab, like lobster, was so plentiful in the New World that it was used as bait, and prepared in all manner of dishes, including crab cakes, crab soup, and crab stuffing. Crab cakes are one of the most popular items on City Tavern's menu. At home, they are ideal for entertaining, because you can make them ahead. Our Herb Rémoulade makes a perfect sauce.

Crab Cakes Makes 12 to 15 cakes; Serves 4 to 6

2 pounds jumbo lump crab meat
½ cup fine dry bread crumbs
¼ cup Homemade Mayonnaise (see page 205)
2 eggs, lightly beaten
¼ green bell pepper, finely chopped
¼ red bell pepper, finely chopped
½ small onion, finely chopped
2 tablespoons fresh lemon juice (about 1 small lemon)
½ teaspoon hot pepper sauce
2 teaspoons salt
1 teaspoon freshly ground white pepper
4 tablespoons (½ stick) unsalted butter, for frying

Herb Rémoulade Makes 2 cups

1 small onion, chopped
1 whole kosher dill pickle, chopped
1 bunch fresh basil, stemmed and chopped (about ½ cup)
½ bunch fresh dill, stemmed and chopped (about 2 tablespoons)
½ bunch fresh parsley, stemmed (about 3 tablespoons)
1½ cups Homemade Mayonnaise (see page 205)
2 tablespoons fresh lemon juice (about 1 small lemon)
1 teaspoon small capers, drained
½ teaspoon Dijon mustard
¼ teaspoon hot pepper sauce
Salt and freshly ground black pepper

1. Prepare the Crab Cakes: Pick over the crab meat to discard the cartilage and pieces of shell.
2. Transfer crab meat to a medium mixing bowl. Add the bread crumbs, Homemade Mayonnaise, eggs, bell peppers, onion, lemon juice, pepper sauce, salt, and pepper. Mix well.
3. Shape mixture into twelve to fifteen 2-inch round cakes. Place the crab cakes on a large baking sheet. Cover and refrigerate for 2 hours to allow the crab cakes to firm.
4. Prepare the Herb Rémoulade: In a food processor bowl, purée the onion, pickle, and fresh herbs. Transfer to a medium mixing bowl. Add the mayonnaise, lemon juice, capers, mustard, and pepper sauce. Mix well. Season with salt and pepper to taste. Cover with plastic wrap and refrigerate until chilled (about 2 hours). Will keep in the refrigerator for up to 3 days.
5. When ready to serve the crab cakes, preheat oven to 350°F. In a large skillet melt the butter over medium heat.
6. Place the crab cakes in skillet with space between each and cook until golden brown on each side.
7. Remove the crab cakes from skillet and place on baking sheet.
8. Bake the crab cakes for 10 to 15 minutes until crisp.
9. Serve with Herb Rémoulade and garnish with lemon wedges and kale if desired.

Cornmeal Fried Oysters with Pickapeppa® Rémoulade

The rivers around Philadelphia teemed with oysters, making them a staple of the eighteenth-century diet. The earliest cookbooks, including Martha Washington's *Booke of Cookery*, were full of oyster recipes, from stuffings for fowl to easy starters like this one. Cornmeal, a plentiful and a common ingredient of the day, was used for skillet breads, stuffings, and breading seafood, including oysters.

Fried Oysters Serves 4 to 6
1½ cups yellow cornmeal
½ cup all-purpose flour
4 eggs, lightly beaten
24 extra-large Bluepoint oysters, shucked (see Chef's Note)
4 cups (1 quart) vegetable oil, for frying

Pickapeppa® Rémoulade Makes 2 cups sauce
¼ cup chopped kosher dill pickles
¼ cup chopped yellow onions
1¾ cups Homemade Mayonnaise (see page 205)
1 tablespoon Pickapeppa® sauce
1 teaspoon Dijon mustard
1 teaspoon finely chopped fresh dill
1 teaspoon fresh lemon juice

2 lemons, each cut into 4 or 6 wedges, for garnish

Oysters can be tricky to open; doing so safely requires a special glove, a special knife, and a practiced hand. I recommend buying oysters already shucked from your favorite fishmonger.

1. Prepare the Fried Oysters: Place the cornmeal, flour, and eggs in separate dishes. Dip each oyster, first into the flour, then the egg, then the cornmeal to evenly coat.
2. Place the coated oysters on a baking sheet and refrigerate until ready to fry.
3. Pour the oil into a deep-fat fryer or 4-quart heavy saucepan. Heat the oil over high heat to 350°F (if you drop a small amount of the cornmeal mixture into the oil and it sizzles, it's hot enough). To prevent the coated oysters from sticking together, carefully drop them into the heated oil one at a time.
4. Fry the oysters, a few at a time, for 2 minutes, until golden. Using a slotted spoon, remove the oysters from the oil and place on a baking sheet lined with paper towels to absorb any excess oil.
5. Prepare the Pickapeppa® Remoulade: In a food processor bowl, purée the pickles and onions.
6. Transfer the purée to a medium mixing bowl. Add the remaining ingredients. Mix well.
7. Cover with plastic wrap and refrigerate until chilled, about 1 hour. Will keep for up to 3 days.
8. To serve, arrange the oysters on individual plates and serve with the Pickapeppa Rémoulade.
9. Garnish with the lemon wedges.

Pickapeppa®, made from a variety of tropical fruits and spices from all over the world, is a commercially prepared West Indies condiment that is, even today, aged in oak barrels for one year. You can find it at most supermarkets and gourmet stores.

Chestnut Fritters

Throughout its history, City Tavern has featured spectacular chestnut dishes as part of its menu. Because the nuts are seasonal, we serve chestnut recipes, such as this perennial favorite, only from September to February. To enjoy these tender fritters year round, cook and peel the chestnuts in season, then freeze them for later.

Advance preparation required

Serves 8

1½ pound chestnuts (about 27), baked, peeled, and chopped (see Chef's Note, page 122)
8 tablespoons (1 stick) unsalted butter
4 shallots, peeled and chopped
2 pounds lean raw bacon, finely chopped
1 bunch fresh parsley, chopped (about 6 tablespoons)
1 teaspoon five-spice powder
¼ teaspoon chopped fresh coriander
Salt and freshly ground black pepper
16 slices lean raw bacon
3 tablespoons vegetable oil
1 bunch fresh chives, finely chopped (about 6 tablespoons), for serving
4 sprigs fresh watercress, for garnish

1. To bake the chestnuts, take 1½ pounds of fresh chestnuts. Penetrate the skin of each chestnut with a small paring knife.
2. Preheat the oven to 450°F. Bake chestnuts for 35 minutes.
3. When cooked, let the chestnuts cool. Peel them and chop finely.
4. To prepare the fritters: In a small skillet, place 1½ tablespoons of the butter and cook shallots over medium heat for 2 minutes, until golden brown.
5. In a large mixing bowl, mix together the cooked shallots, the 2 pounds chopped bacon, parsley, five-spice powder, coriander, and salt and pepper to taste.
6. Add chopped chestnuts.
7. Mix thoroughly until fine in food processor. Divide the mixture into 16 equal portions.
8. Place the bacon slices on a work surface. Place one portion of the shallot mixture in the center of each bacon slice and fold each end over the middle.
9. Flatten each fritter with the palm of your hand; place them on a baking sheet. Cover with plastic wrap and refrigerate for 10 to 20 minutes.
10. In a large sauté pan, melt the remaining 6½ tablespoons of butter and the oil over medium heat.
11. Place the fritters ¼ inch apart in the skillet and cook for 2 minutes on each side, until golden and crisp.
12. Place on ovenproof baking sheet. Preheat the oven to 375°F. Bake for 5 to 10 minutes.
13. To serve, sprinkle the fritters with the chives and a generous amount of black pepper. Garnish with the watercress.

Giant chestnut trees once filled
eastern forests and provided builders
with exquisite hardwood and everyone
with delicious nuts.

Mustard Eggs

This rich and lively cousin to deviled eggs is flavored with both shallots and chives. The eighteenth-century chef would have roasted the eggs in the hot ashes—but cooking them in boiling water will do just fine. For a special presentation, serve these eggs on a pool of tangy Mustard Sauce (see page 205).

Serves 6

6 extra-large eggs, hard-cooked (see Chef's Note)
4 medium shallots, peeled and chopped
2 tablespoons unsalted butter
3 tablespoons heavy cream
3 tablespoons chopped fresh chives
3 tablespoons chopped fresh tarragon
2 tablespoons Dijon mustard
Salt and freshly ground white pepper
¼ teaspoon Hungarian paprika

1. Preheat the oven to 350°F.
2. Shell and halve the hard-cooked eggs lengthwise.
3. Remove the yolks and reserve. Place the whites on a baking sheet lined with foil.
4. In a small skillet, cook the shallots in 1 tablespoon of the butter over medium heat for 2 minutes, until golden brown. Reserve.
5. In the small bowl of an electric mixer fitted with a paddle attachment (or a food processor bowl), combine the reserved egg yolks, cooked shallots, cream, chives, tarragon, and mustard into a paste. Season with salt and pepper to taste.
6. Fill a pastry bag with the mixture and pipe into the egg white halves.
7. Dot each egg white half with a piece of the remaining 1 tablespoon butter, sprinkle with paprika, and bake for 5 to 8 minutes, until browned on top.
8. Serve with Mustard Sauce, if desired.

Chef's Note

Hard-Cooking Eggs
To make no-fail hard-cooked eggs, place the eggs in a small saucepan and cover with boiling water. Bring back to a boil. Boil for 8 minutes. (In southern Germany we traditionally add 1 tablespoon white vinegar to the water. In case the eggs crack during cooking, the vinegar seals the egg. However, the vinegar is not necessary.) Remove from heat, drain, and place the eggs under cold running water. When cool, peel and discard the shells.

Smoked Pheasant en Croûte

In the early days the Pennsylvania woods were full of game, which was a staple in households and taverns alike. In doing my research, I found that pheasant was a popular choice for many recipes, although it has fallen out of vogue in recent years—a pity because it is richly flavorful. You can mail order smoked pheasant (see Resources, page 211) or simply substitute smoked turkey, which is available at most supermarkets.

Makes eighteen 3-inch turnovers; Serves 6

1 yellow onion, finely chopped
2 shallots, finely chopped
1 garlic clove, chopped
1 tablespoon unsalted butter
1 pound smoked, cooked pheasant (or turkey) meat,
    finely chopped
1 yellow squash, finely chopped
1 zucchini, finely chopped
½ cup dry white wine
1½ tablespoons chopped fresh parsley
1 sprig fresh thyme
Salt and freshly ground black pepper
½ cup Demi-glace (see page 202)
1 sheet of purchased puff pastry (see Chef's Note)
1 egg, lightly beaten
1 cup Madeira Wine Sauce (see page 203)

Commercially made puff pastry is available in the frozen foods section of most supermarkets.

1. In a medium saucepan, sauté the onion, shallots, and garlic in butter over medium heat for 3 to 4 minutes until translucent.
2. Stir in the pheasant, yellow squash, and zucchini.
3. Add the wine to deglaze the pan, loosening any browned bits on the bottom of the pan with a wooden spoon.
4. Add the parsley and thyme. Cook the mixture over medium heat about 5 minutes, until it becomes dry. Season to taste with salt and pepper.
5. Add the Demi-glace. Reduce the heat and simmer about 3 minutes, until it reduces and becomes thick.
6. Transfer the mixture to a medium bowl and reserve.
7. Preheat the oven to 350°F.
8. On a lightly floured surface, roll out the puff pastry sheet; cut the pastry into eighteen 3½-inch squares.
9. Brush the edges of the puff pastry squares with the beaten egg.
10. Divide the pheasant mixture into 18 equal portions. Place one portion in the center of each puff pastry square.
11. Fold each square over diagonally to form a triangle and press the edges firmly to seal.
12. Pierce the pastry with a fork so the steam can escape.
13. Place on a baking sheet and bake for 10 to 15 minutes, until golden brown. Serve with Madeira Wine Sauce.

Basil Shrimp

Shrimp was in abundance in the New World, and was often prepared grilled on skewers over an open fire. This recipe uses basil, an ingredient that would have been only available from the summer garden in the eighteenth century. As Culinary Ambassador of Philadelphia, I have had many occasions to break bread with Mayor Edward Rendell, a man who really loves to eat. Every time he pays a visit to City Tavern, I make him this appetizer—it's his favorite, and he can easily eat a dozen shrimp at one sitting.

Makes 16 shrimp; Serves 4

16 jumbo shrimp (thawed if frozen), peeled and deveined
16 fresh basil leaves (preferably purple)
16 slices apple-smoked bacon (see Resources, page 211) or regular bacon
16 flavorless wooden toothpicks
2 cups vegetable oil
12 ounces barbecue sauce
4 teaspoons grated horseradish
2 dashes hot pepper sauce

1. Preheat the oven to 375°F heat.
2. To butterfly the shrimp, make a deep slit along the back of each, but not all the way through. Rinse the shrimp; pat dry. Place one basil leaf inside the slit in each shrimp.
3. Wrap each shrimp in a slice of bacon and secure with a toothpick.
4. In a medium stockpot or saucepan, heat the oil over high heat to 350°F; when hot, carefully add the shrimp a few at a time.
5. Deep-fry for 2 to 3 minutes, until crisp.
6. Using a slotted spoon, remove the shrimp from the oil and place on a tray lined with paper towels to absorb any excess oil.
7. In a skillet, combine the barbecue sauce, horseradish, and pepper sauce.
8. Add the precooked shrimp to the sauce and heat, basting the shrimp for 5 minutes, until the shrimp is heated through.
9. Serve on a platter garnished with lemon wedges and extra basil leaves.

Duck Liver Pâté

The appreciation Americans have for this French delicacy reflects the strong influence the French had on our culinary development. To make pâté, Colonial City Tavern chefs relied on the wild ducks that were plentiful in the forests just outside Philadelphia. Originally, fat back would have been used, but because it may be difficult to find, I have substituted lean bacon, losing little flavor in the translation. Celery Root Salad (see page 48) makes a fine accompaniment for this dish.

Overnight preparation required

Serves 10 to 12

5 pounds boneless duck meat, skinned, fat trimmed, and cut into ¼-inch pieces
1 cup sweet Madeira
¾ cup brandy
1 tablespoon vegetable oil
1 tablespoon unsalted butter
1 pound lean bacon, finely chopped
1 pound boneless pork shoulder, fat trimmed and cut into ¼-inch pieces
2 bay leaves
1 pound fresh chicken livers
3 garlic cloves, chopped
4 sprigs fresh thyme, chopped (about 1 teaspoon)
4 egg whites
4 teaspoons salt
2 teaspoons freshly ground black pepper
1 pound lean bacon

1. Place the duck meat in a large mixing bowl. Add the Madeira and brandy. Cover; marinate in the refrigerator for 6 hours.
2. In a large skillet, heat the oil and butter over high heat.
3. Add the chopped bacon and, stirring continuously, sauté about 3 minutes, until the fat is cooked out.
4. Add the pork shoulder and the bay leaves and cook for 5 to 8 minutes, until the mixture is reduced and there is no liquid in the pan.
5. Add the chicken livers and sauté about 5 minutes, until mixture once again becomes dry.
6. Remove from the heat and add the garlic and thyme.
7. Remove the bay leaves. Stir in the egg whites. Transfer the mixture to a food processor bowl and process into a paste (the mixture should be smooth, but have some consistency).
8. Add the salt and pepper and mix well. Reserve.
9. Remove the duck meat from the marinade; discard the marinade. Sprinkle the duck meat with additional pepper.
10. Line the bottom and sides of a 9 x 4-inch loaf pan with the bacon slices, allowing at least 2 inches overhang, so you can fold the bacon over the top of the liver mixture. Place the duck meat on the bottom. Press the liver mixture on top of the duck meat.
11. Cover with foil and refrigerate at least 10 hours or overnight.
12. When ready to bake the mixture, preheat the oven to 375°F.
13. Place the foil-covered loaf pan into a larger, higher-sided ovenproof dish. Pour boiling water into the larger dish to come within ½ inch of the top of the loaf pan.
14. Bake about 1 hour and 40 minutes, until liquid rises to top.
15. Remove the loaf pan from the larger dish and let cool on a wire rack for 10 minutes.

16. Cut a piece of cardboard to fit the inside of the loaf pan and cover the cardboard with foil.

17. Place it on top of the pâté and weigh it down with a heavy weight (such as a large can of tomatoes). Refrigerate for at least 8 hours.

18. When ready to serve, remove the foil-lined cardboard. Invert the pâté onto an oblong serving plate and cut into ¼-inch-thick slices. Serve with Celery Root Salad (see page 48), if desired.

Salmon Carpaccio

In colonial times, Atlantic salmon was so plentiful that it was used as a fertilizer. Over the decades, Atlantic salmon has been fished out, so that most of the salmon used in dishes served in American restaurants is imported. This light and tasty salmon adaptation of a traditional Italian beef carpaccio makes a terrific opener for a festive summer supper.

Serves 8

2 pounds extremely fresh (sushi quality) raw salmon fillets
   (see Chef's Note)
½ cup extra-virgin olive oil
2 teaspoons green peppercorns, crushed, for serving
2 teaspoons coarsely ground black pepper, for serving
½ bunch finely chopped chives (about 3 tablespoons),
   for serving
1 tablespoon small capers, drained, for serving
1 medium red onion, finely chopped, for serving
¼ cup lemon juice (about 1 large lemon), for serving

To reduce the risk of food-borne illness, be sure to buy only the highest quality and freshest fish from a reputable supplier.

1. Rinse the salmon; pat dry with paper towels. Remove all the skin and bones from the salmon.

2. Cut diagonal slices, as thinly as possible.

3. Place the slices on a large serving plate or divide evenly among 8 individual plates.

4. Drizzle the olive oil over the salmon. Cover with plastic wrap and refrigerate for 1 hour.

5. To serve, sprinkle with the peppercorns, black pepper, chives, capers, onion, and lemon juice.

Minced Turkey

While "chili" per se didn't exist in the early colonies, there are many reference to dishes and stews made with minced meats and poultry. This hearty turkey appetizer relies on a spicy marinade for its full flavor. Be sure to grind the allspice just before making this dish, using a small coffee grinder or mini-chopper. (Pre-ground allspice does not do justice to the dish.)

Overnight preparation recommended

Makes 10 cups; Serves 8 to 10

½ pound dried red kidney beans
2 medium onions, peeled and diced
1½ cups soy sauce
½ cup olive oil
1 bunch scallions, chopped (about 1 cup)
4 tablespoons freshly ground allspice
4 sprigs fresh thyme, leaves pulled
½ Scotch bonnet pepper (see Chef's Note)
3 garlic cloves, chopped
4 pounds fresh turkey breast slices
2 quarts (8 cups) Chicken Stock (see page 199)
½ cup tomato paste (4 ounce can)
1 teaspoon salt
½ teaspoon freshly ground black pepper
2 medium tomatoes, peeled, seeded, and diced

Always wear rubber gloves when handling the fiery hot Scotch bonnet pepper, which is a close relative of the habañero *pepper.*

1. Presoak the beans (see Chef's Note, page 117). Drain and reserve.
2. In a food processor bowl, purée one of the onions, soy sauce, olive oil (reserving 1 tablespoon for Step 8), scallions, 2 tablespoons of the allspice, thyme, Scotch bonnet pepper, and garlic to make the marinade.
3. Place the turkey in a shallow dish; add the marinade. Cover the dish with plastic wrap and marinate in the refrigerator at least 8 hours or overnight.
4. In a small saucepan, cook the reserved beans in enough boiling, lightly salted water to cover over medium heat for 25 to 35 minutes, until the beans are tender. Drain and reserve.
5. Preheat the oven to 350°F.
6. Remove the turkey from the marinade, reserving the marinade. Place the turkey in a shallow baking pan.
7. Bake the turkey about 20 minutes, until the meat no longer appears pink. Remove from the oven and let cool for 10 minutes. Cut the turkey into ½-inch cubes and reserve.
8. In a large saucepan, sauté the remaining onion in the reserved 1 tablespoon oil over high heat for 2 to 3 minutes, until translucent.
9. Add the cooked beans, reserved turkey cubes, 2 tablespoons of the reserved marinade, Chicken Stock, tomato paste, and the remaining 2 tablespoons of allspice, salt, and pepper.
10. Bring to a boil. Reduce the heat to medium and cook for 30 minutes.
11. Stir in the tomatoes and cook for 5 minutes more.
12. Serve in a bowl.

Soups, Stews, and Chowders

The soups prepared at City Tavern in the late 1700s offer keen insight into the city's ethnic mix. Recipes ranged from the exotic Pepper Pot Soup, borrowed from the Spaniards and West Indians, to hearty German vegetable soups to the cream-based soups of the French. At City Tavern, as in many private homes, there was always a pot of soup simmering on the stove, a practice which continues at the Tavern today.

Pumpkin Bisque

When the colonists arrived in North America, they found the Indians cultivating pumpkins. The flavorful fruit was embraced by the settlers, who made it into everything from pie to soup. To give this creamy soup a more exotic flavor, serve it with minced boiled beef and garnish it with slivers of Scotch bonnet or habañero peppers and fresh thyme sprigs.

Serves 8

1 large pumpkin (about 6 pounds)
1 large onion, chopped
¼ Scotch bonnet pepper (see Chef's Note, page 28)
2 bay leaves
1 garlic clove, chopped
5 cups heavy cream
1 cup dry white wine or dry sherry
Salt and freshly ground black pepper
2 cups Herb Croutons (see page 120), for serving
2 tablespoons finely chopped fresh chives, for garnish

1. Cut the pumpkin into 8 wedges; remove and discard the seeds and membranes. Scoop out the pumpkin flesh and reserve. Discard the rind.
2. Cut the flesh into cubes and transfer to a large stockpot; add enough salted water to cover. Add the onion, Scotch bonnet pepper, bay leaves, and garlic. Bring to a boil over high heat.
3. Reduce the heat to medium and cook for 30 minutes, until the pumpkin is fork-tender. Remove from the heat. Remove and discard the bay leaves. Strain the pumpkin mixture through a fine wire sieve and discard the liquid.
4. Place the pumpkin mixture in a blender container or food processor bowl and purée until smooth.
5. Transfer the mixture to a medium saucepan. Stir in the cream and wine.
6. Simmer about 20 minutes, until creamy and heated through. Season to taste with salt and pepper.
7. To serve, divide the soup among soup bowls. Sprinkle with the Herb Croutons and chives.

Snapper Turtle Soup

Early on, fresh terrapin was the species of turtle most favored for this recipe, because it had the sweetest meat. Sherry or Madeira was added to the soup to enhance its flavor. Today, turtle meat is sold fresh at some seafood stores or it's available frozen or canned.

Serves 6 to 8

1 tablespoon unsalted butter
1 pound skinless and boned turtle meat, cubed
1 cup chopped carrots
1 cup chopped onion
1 cup chopped celery
2 medium shallots, chopped
2 garlic cloves, chopped
12 cups (3 quarts) Beef Stock (see page 198)
1½ cups dry sherry or Madeira
4 sprigs fresh thyme
1 bunch fresh parsley, chopped (about 6 tablespoons)
1 bay leaf
1 teaspoon ground cloves
¾ cup tomato paste
4 tablespoons unsalted butter
¼ cup all-purpose flour
Salt and freshly ground black pepper
3 hard-cooked eggs (see Chef's Note, page 23), yolks and whites separated and chopped, for garnish

1. In a 5-quart stockpot, melt the butter over medium heat and add the turtle meat. Cook, stirring frequently, for 3 minutes, until brown.
2. Add the carrots, onion, celery, shallots, and garlic. Sauté for 5 minutes, until the vegetables become soft.
3. Add the Beef Stock, 1 cup of the sherry, thyme, parsley, bay leaf, and cloves. Bring to a boil.
4. Reduce the heat and simmer for 1½ hours, until the turtle meat begins to fall apart.
5. Remove the mixture from the heat. Strain the mixture through a fine wire sieve or cheesecloth into a large bowl. Reserve the strained stock.
6. Remove and discard the bay leaf. Place the turtle meat and vegetables in a food processor bowl. Process until the mixture has a coarse consistency.
7. Return the strained stock and turtle-vegetable mixture to the stockpot. Bring to a boil.
8. Stir in the tomato paste.
9. In a separate medium saucepan, over low heat melt the butter, add flour, then mix well. Cook for 15 minutes.
10. Slowly stir the flour-butter mixture into the turtle-vegetable mixture until combined. Reduce the heat to medium and cook for 5 minutes, until heated through.
11. Stir in the remaining ½ cup sherry (or else pour it into a cruet and serve alongside the soup at the table). Season with salt and pepper to taste.
12. Serve immediately in a tureen or divide among individual soup bowls. Garnish with the chopped eggs.

Philadelphia's two main rivers, the Delaware and the Schuylkill, teemed with fish, including shad, salmon, perch, rockfish, catfish, as well as terrapins, the small, diamond-back turtles for which the city was known.

Corn Chowder

At the City Tavern, this hearty soup would have been served in a big tureen on the table—never in individual bowls—and then ladled out as part of the first plates course. It always would have been served with fresh baked bread or biscuits, the same way we serve it at the Tavern today.

Serves 8 to 10

1 cup chopped carrots
1 cup chopped celery
1 cup chopped onion
2 tablespoons unsalted butter
4 cups Vegetable Stock (see page 199)
1 tablespoon chopped shallots
1 tablespoon chopped fresh basil
1 teaspoon chopped fresh thyme
1 teaspoon sweet paprika
3 garlic cloves, chopped
3 large russet potatoes (about 1 pound), peeled and diced
10 ears fresh white corn, kernels cut from cobs
2 cups heavy cream
¼ cup cornstarch
¼ cup dry white wine
Chives or green onions, chopped, for garnish

1. In a medium stockpot, sauté the carrots, celery, and onion in the butter over medium heat for 5 minutes, until the onions are translucent.
2. Add the Vegetable Stock, shallots, basil, thyme, paprika, and garlic. Bring to a boil.
3. Stir in the potatoes and corn kernels; bring back to a boil.
4. Stir in the cream. Reduce the heat and simmer, stirring occasionally, for 10 to 15 minutes, until vegetables are tender and soup is heated.
5. In a small bowl, combine the cornstarch and wine; mix until velvety smooth. Add some of the boiling soup to the cornstarch mixture until thin. Gently stir mixture into the soup. Cook until bubbly. Serve hot with Herb Croutons (see page 120).

Chef's Notes

• *For an even more wonderful flavor, add 1 pound of chopped, cooked lobster, shrimp, or crab meat or 1½ pounds of chopped, cooked chicken breast to the chowder in Step 4.*

• *As with most cream-based soups, you can substitute half-and-half for heavy cream without giving up too much flavor or consistency. I don't recommend using whole or skim milk, but this is only a guideline. Experiment to find a balance between flavor and healthfulness to match your tastes.*

Corn was introduced to the colonists by Native Americans, who held it sacred, and used it as the foundation of their diet. Fresh maize or corn also was dried or parched so that it could be stored and used later in stews and other cooked dishes. Corn also could be pounded or ground to make a substitute for flour.

Oxtail Soup

The ox was an important animal to early Philadelphians, who used it as a beast of burden and to work the fields. Because meat of any kind was at a premium, nothing, including tough ox meat, was wasted. Even the tail of the ox was used, as in this recipe for hearty oxtail soup, an English classic usually flavored with Madeira. Because oxtail is quite bony, it's full of flavor. This cut of meat can be extremely tough, it is best prepared by long, slow braising or used in soups, such as this one. If you like, substitute red skinned potatoes for the lentils.

Overnight preparation recommended

Serves 6 to 8

½ cup dried lentils
3 pounds beef oxtails, cut into 1-inch pieces
1½ cups chopped onions
1 cup chopped carrots
1 cup chopped celery
1 tablespoon chopped garlic
2 tablespoons unsalted butter
¾ cup tomato paste
2 cups red burgundy wine
8 cups (2 quarts) Beef Stock (see page 198)
¼ cup chopped fresh parsley
1 teaspoon chopped fresh rosemary
1 bay leaf
4 tablespoons unsalted butter
¼ cup all-purpose flour
Salt and freshly ground black pepper

1. Pre-soak the lentils (see Chef's Note, page 117). Drain and reserve.
2. Preheat the oven to 400°F.
3. Place the oxtail pieces in a roasting pan and roast, stirring the meat frequently to prevent burning, about 35 minutes, until dark brown.
4. Remove the pan from the oven. Drain and discard any pan drippings. Let the meat cool for 15 minutes.
5. In a large stockpot, sauté the onions, carrots, celery and garlic in the butter over medium heat for 5 minutes, until the onions are translucent.
6. Add the reserved meat and the tomato paste.
7. Add the wine to deglaze the pan, loosening any browned bits on the bottom of the pan with a wooden spoon. Cook over high heat, stirring occasionally, about 10 minutes, until the mixture is reduced by half.
8. Add the Beef Stock, parsley, rosemary, and bay leaf. Bring to a boil over high heat.
9. Reduce the heat to medium and cook for 1½ hours.
10. Meanwhile, in a medium saucepan, cook the reserved lentils in boiling, lightly salted water for 10 to 15 minutes, until tender. Drain and add to the meat mixture.
11. Cook over low heat for 25 minutes until the meat falls off the bones. Remove and discard the bones.
12. In separate medium saucepan, over low heat melt butter, add flour, then mix well. Cook for 15 minutes.
13. Bring the soup to a boil over high heat. Slowly stir in the flour-butter mixture until combined. Reduce the heat to medium and cook for 5 minutes more, until the soup is heated through. Season with salt and pepper to taste. Serve hot.

Tripe Soup

Tripe, the honeycombed lining of a cow's stomach, has a long history of use in Spain, France, and Italy, and during the Tavern's first age, was a common ingredient. Tripe is usually used in soups and stews, where it is slow cooked to a buttery tenderness. Though we rarely feature it on today's Tavern menu, I personally love its delicate flavor.

Overnight preparation recommended

Serves 6

¾ cup dried cannellini beans
1 pound honeycomb beef tripe
1 cup chopped carrots
1 cup leeks cut into julienne strips
1 cup chopped celery
1 tablespoon chopped garlic
2 tablespoons unsalted butter
6 cups (1½ quarts) Beef Stock (see page 198)
1 cup red burgundy wine
1 bay leaf
¾ cup tomato paste
1 tablespoon chopped fresh parsley
1 large sprig fresh thyme, chopped (about 1 teaspoon)
¼ cup grated Parmesan cheese, for serving

Tripe is readily available in many supermarkets, especially those that cater to an ethnic clientele.

1. Pre-soak the beans (see Chef's Note, page 117). Drain.
2. In an 8-quart stockpot, cook the pre-soaked beans in enough lightly salted water to cover for 45 minutes, until tender. Drain and reserve.
3. In the same stockpot, cook the tripe in enough boiling, lightly salted water to cover about 30 minutes until tender. Strain the mixture though a fine wire sieve or cheesecloth and discard the liquid.
4. Let the tripe cool for 15 minutes and cut into ½-inch strips. Reserve.
5. In a 5-quart stockpot, sauté the carrots, leeks, celery, and garlic in butter over medium heat for 5 minutes, until soft.
6. Add the reserved tripe and beans. Sauté for 5 minutes more.
7. Add the Beef Stock, red wine, and bay leaf. Bring to a boil over high heat.
8. Reduce the heat. Add the tomato paste, parsley, and thyme, and simmer for 30 to 45 minutes, until the beans fall apart.
9. Serve in a soup tureen or divide among soup bowls. Sprinkle with the Parmesan cheese.

Madeira Onion Soup

Although the average cook in the eighteenth century would not have "wasted" good Madeira in food, the original Tavern chef used Madeira in recipes such as this one. The unique flavor of dry "Rainwater" Madeira contrasts perfectly with the sweetness of the onion and richness of the cheese. Still served today, this sweet and savory combination takes ordinary onion soup up a few flavor notches.

Serves 10

8 cups (2 quarts) Chicken Stock (see page 199)
4 pounds (about 16) yellow onions, thinly sliced
½ pound (2 sticks) unsalted butter
3 tablespoons all-purpose flour
1 loaf French bread, cut into ten ¼-inch slices
1 cup medium-dry Madeira (Rainwater style, preferably)
4 cups grated Swiss cheese
2 large eggs
Salt and freshly ground black pepper

If you prefer, you can substitute 1 quart dry white wine for half of the quantity of Chicken Stock (making a mixture of 1 quart white wine and 1 quart stock) and applejack for the Madeira. Adjust the amount of applejack to suit your own taste.

1. In a 3-quart stockpot, bring the Chicken Stock to a boil over high heat. Remove from the heat and reserve.
2. In a large skillet, cook the onions in 1 stick of the butter over medium heat about 15 minutes, until golden brown.
3. Sprinkle the flour over the onions and stir until a paste forms.
4. Slowly stir about 2 cups of the hot chicken stock into the onion mixture until the paste becomes a thin, smooth liquid. Transfer the onion mixture to the remaining stock in the stockpot.
5. Simmer for 30 minutes.
6. Preheat the oven to 400°F.
7. In a 12-inch skillet, cook the slices of bread, half at a time, in the remaining stick of butter over low heat for 5 minutes on each side, until crisp.
8. Pour ½ cup of the wine into a 3-quart ovenproof soup crock or casserole. Add the slices of bread and sprinkle with half of the cheese.
9. In a small bowl, beat the eggs and the remaining ½ cup wine until completely combined.
10. Pour the mixture into the onion mixture, stirring constantly.
11. Pour the onion mixture over the bread and cheese; sprinkle with the remaining cheese. Bake about 20 minutes, until golden brown.

Madeira, called for as an ingredient in many of the recipes included here, was the drink of the day during City Tavern's first incarnation. The island of Madeira, located about 100 miles off the coast of Casablanca, Morocco and 500 miles from Portugal, was a natural port of call when making an Atlantic crossing. The Madeira wine trade flourished with the rise of the English colonies in America. The frugal colonists preferred to send ships to tax-free Madeira for wine, rather than pay King George's high taxes on English port. Shipped as ballast, Madeira was so important to early American culture that it was used to toast both the Declaration of Independence and George Washington's inauguration. It is said that Washington drank a pint of Madeira at dinner daily.

Potato-Leek Soup

Marjoram, a Mediterranean herb considered by the ancient Greeks to be a symbol of happiness, has a wonderful but delicate flavor. Interestingly, this herb was commonly called for in eighteenth-century recipes yet rarely is used in today's recipes. For best results, always add the marjoram toward the end of the cooking time to preserve its subtle essence.

Serves 8

5 standard leeks (white part only), rinsed well and chopped (about 5½ cups)
3 tablespoons unsalted butter
6 cups (1½ quarts) Chicken Stock (see page 199)
6 medium red skinned potatoes (about 2 pounds), peeled and chopped
1 chopped medium yellow onion
½ cup (9 slices) chopped lean bacon
1 teaspoon dried marjoram
Salt and freshly ground black pepper
2 cups Herb Croutons (see page 120), for serving

1. In a large stockpot, sauté the leeks in butter over low heat for 10 minutes, until soft.
2. Add the Chicken Stock and potatoes and cook about 30 minutes, until the potatoes are fork-tender.
3. In a medium saucepan, sauté the onion and bacon over medium heat for 5 minutes, until the onion is golden brown. Drain off the bacon drippings. Add the onion mixture and the marjoram to the soup.
4. Season with salt and pepper to taste.
5. Serve in a soup tureen or divide among individual soup bowls. Sprinkle with the Herb Croutons.

Oyster Stew

Oysters were plentiful in the eighteenth century, which explains why oysters were popular in Philadelphia and ever present on the City Tavern menu. Philadelphians consumed so many oysters that the shells were used as street paving, for artificial wharves along the Delaware, and even as ballast for ships. We recommend that you avoid the task of removing oysters from their shells by buying shucked oysters, available in the seafood department of your supermarket or at seafood specialty stores.

Serves 4

2 cups whole milk
1 pint fresh select oysters (or 25 to 30 Bluepoint oysters), shucked
1½ tablespoons unsalted butter, at room temperature
Salt and freshly ground black pepper

1. In a small saucepan, bring the milk to a boil over medium heat and keep warm.
2. Place the oysters with liquid in a medium saucepan.
3. Cook over medium heat for 3 to 5 minutes. Keep an eye on the oysters; when the edges begin to curl, add the milk.
4. Add butter, and stir to combine. Season with salt and pepper to taste.

Chef's Note

Add 2 dashes hot pepper sauce or a pinch hot red pepper flakes for an extra bite.

Chicken–Tomato Soup

Stewing hens were typically used as a basis for soups and stews. Past their laying prime, these tough old birds needed a lot of slow cooking to coax flavor out of their stringy, tough meat. The housewife of the day could leave the pot to simmer unattended over the fire with flavorful results. Using chicken legs, as I recommend in this recipe, is a time-saver for today's home cook, with no sacrifice in flavor. This light soup takes advantage of summer's best—the fresh flavors of ripe plum (Roma) tomatoes, basil, and thyme.

Serves 8

6 cups (1½ quarts) Chicken Stock (see page 199)
1½ pounds skinless chicken legs
1 tablespoon salt
2 medium white onions, sliced
3 garlic cloves, chopped
2 tablespoons unsalted butter
12 large plum tomatoes, seeded and chopped (about 1 pound)
½ cup heavy cream
1 small bunch fresh basil, chopped (about ½ cup)
Salt and freshly ground black pepper

1. In a large stockpot, place the prepared stock, chicken legs, and salt and bring to a boil over high heat, skimming off any foam. Reduce the heat and simmer for 45 minutes.
2. Remove stockpot from heat and transfer the chicken to a cutting board. Remove the meat from the bones. Chop the meat and reserve.
3. In a medium skillet, sauté the onions and garlic in the butter over medium heat for 5 minutes, until translucent.
4. Add the tomatoes and cook over medium heat about 10 minutes, until all liquid is reduced.
5. Transfer the tomato mixture to a blender container or food processor bowl and purée until smooth. Transfer the puréed mixture to the stock and cook over medium heat about 20 minutes, until heated through.
6. Stir in the reserved chicken meat, cream, and basil. Cook about 5 minutes more, until completely hot.
7. Season with salt and pepper to taste.
8. Serve immediately in a soup tureen or divide among individual soup bowls.

Tomatoes were feared by some Northern Europeans and North Americans until the mid-1800s—the red fruit was thought to be poisonous. British settlers, however, called tomatoes love apples—they thought the red fruit an aphrodisiac that aroused human passion. Thomas Jefferson, always a free thinker, grew tomatoes at Monticello, serving them frequently at his table.

Cabbage and Turnip Soup

Many of the eighteenth-century recipes I researched for the City Tavern call for salt pork, which in colonial times was preserved in root cellars for the entire winter, to be used to give the flavor and benefit of animal fat when meat was a rare commodity. Salt pork was used to flavor everything from soups to stews to sauces. Because this "specialty meat" has long been out of favor with the modern palate, I found a fine substitute—bacon.

Serves 8

1 cup finely chopped lean salt pork or bacon (18 slices)
2 tablespoons unsalted butter
1 tablespoon vegetable oil
1 medium white onion, chopped
1 cabbage (about 3 pounds), trimmed and coarsely chopped
4 large carrots, quartered
3 large turnips, quartered
3 peppercorns, crushed
8 cups (2 quarts) Chicken Stock (see page 199)
½ cup heavy cream
2 egg yolks
Salt and freshly ground black pepper

1. In a large stockpot, sauté the salt pork in the butter and oil over medium heat for 3 minutes. Add the onion and sauté about 3 minutes more, until translucent.
2. Add the cabbage, carrots, turnips, and peppercorns.
3. Add the Chicken Stock and bring to a boil over high heat. Reduce the heat and simmer about 1½ hours, until the vegetables are soft and the turnips are dissolved.
4. Just before serving, whisk together the cream and egg yolks in a small bowl, until velvety smooth.
5. Stir the mixture into the hot soup. (Do not bring to a boil again.) Season with salt and pepper to taste.
6. Serve in a soup tureen or divide among individual soup bowls.

Split Pea and Potato Soup

Dried peas and beans were an important staple for the colonist, because they could be stored easily and would last indefinitely. They also traveled well, making them a common item for cooking on the wagon trails. The split pea is actually a field pea, a variety of yellow or green pea grown specifically for drying. If you like, enhance the flavor of this hearty soup by adding some finely chopped kielbasa or diced cooked pork sausage just before serving.

Overnight preparation recommended

Serves 10 to 12

1 pound dried split peas
6 medium round red skinned potatoes (about 2 pounds), peeled and cubed
½ pound (9 slices) lean bacon, finely chopped
4 tablespoons unsalted butter
1 large white onion, chopped
2 garlic cloves, chopped
12 cups (3 quarts) Chicken Stock (see page 199)
1 cup heavy cream
Salt and freshly ground black pepper
Fried Leek Garnish, optional

1. Pre-soak the split peas (see Chef's Note, page 117). Drain and reserve.
2. In a small saucepan, cook the potatoes in enough boiling, lightly salted water to cover for 5 to 10 minutes, until the potatoes are fork-tender. Drain and reserve.
3. In a large stockpot, sauté the bacon in butter over medium heat for 3 minutes.
4. Add the onion and garlic and sauté about 3 minutes more, until golden brown.
5. Add the reserved split peas and Chicken Stock. Bring to a boil over high heat.
6. Reduce the heat to medium and cook about 1½ hours, until the split peas have dissolved.
7. Press the split pea mixture through a fine sieve into a large bowl. Discard the bacon and return the mixture to the stockpot.
8. Add the cooked reserved potatoes and cream; season with salt and pepper to taste.
9. To serve, divide among individual soup bowls. Garnish with the reserved Fried Leek Garnish, if desired.

Fried Leek Garnish

1 medium leek, rinsed well to remove sand
1 cup vegetable oil, for frying

1. Cut the leek lengthwise into ½-inch long strips, julienne as fine as possible, and thoroughly pat dry between paper towels.
2. Pour the oil into a medium saucepan. Heat the oil over medium heat to 350°F.
3. Carefully add the leek and cook for several minutes, until golden brown. Be careful not to let the leek burn. Using a slotted spoon, remove the leek and place on a paper towel to absorb any excess oil. Reserve.

White Bean and Ham Soup

White beans, like all dried beans, lasted forever, were easy to store and provided an important source of nutrition during the winter months. Most eighteenth-century housewives wouldn't have used chicken stock as a base for this soup—meat was too dear. But the chefs at City Tavern, where cooking was elevated to the highest standards, certainly would have. When they're in season, plum tomatoes work the best because of their firm, meaty flesh.

Overnight preparation recommended

Serves 8 to 10

1 pound dried navy beans
10 cups (2½ quarts) Chicken Stock (see page 199)
2 medium yellow onions, chopped
3 garlic cloves, chopped
4 tablespoons unsalted butter
8 large plum tomatoes (1 pound), seeded and chopped
½ pound cooked ham, cut into ¼-inch cubes
1 teaspoon dried marjoram
Salt and freshly ground black pepper
2 bunches fresh parsley, finely chopped (about 12 tablespoons)

1. Pre-soak the beans (see Chef's Note, page 117). Drain.
2. Place the beans in a large stockpot, add the Chicken Stock, and bring to a boil over high heat.
3. Reduce the heat to low and cook about 1 hour, until beans are soft.
4. In a large skillet, sauté the onions and garlic in the butter over medium heat for 5 minutes, until light brown. Add the tomatoes, ham, and marjoram, and sauté for 3 to 5 minutes more, until the tomatoes begin to dissolve.
5. Add the tomato mixture to the beans in the stockpot. Simmer the soup about 10 minutes, until tomatoes are soft.
6. Season with salt and pepper to taste.
7. Just before serving, stir in the parsley.

Chef's Note

To add a smoky flavor to this thick soup, add smoked ham hocks to Step 2. If using a ham hock, cook until meat can be easily removed from the bone, cool, remove meat and dice, and return it to soup.

Clam Chowder

Clam chowder, originally named "la chaudiere" for the huge French copper fish cauldron in which it was cooked, originated in America in the Massachusetts colonies. The chowder was placed in the big stew pot and hung over the fire on an iron crane, where it could cook for hours.

Serves 8

30 large fresh cherrystone clams or 10 ounces cooked clams
   (See Chef's Note)
1½ cups dry white wine
½ pound (9 slices) lean bacon, finely chopped
4 medium yellow onions, finely chopped
6 medium round red skinned potatoes, peeled and chopped
2 medium green bell peppers, finely chopped
1 cup heavy cream
1 teaspoon hot pepper sauce
4 tablespoons unsalted butter
¼ cup all-purpose flour
Salt and freshly ground black pepper
1 bunch fresh chives, finely chopped (about 6 tablespoons), for garnish

If using cooked clams, which you can buy canned or fresh at supermarket fish counters, begin the recipe from Step 5. Add 1 dash Worcestershire sauce or 2 pinches hot red pepper flakes for added flavor.

1. To clean clams still in the shell, scrub them thoroughly, soak to remove sand, rinse, and drain well. Repeat soaking, rinsing, and draining twice.
2. Place claims in a stockpot.
3. In a small saucepan, heat the wine and pour over the clams. Cover the stockpot and cook the clams over high heat about 15 minutes, until the clams open. Discard any clam shells that do not open.
4. Remove open clams from the stockpot. Transfer the wine mixture to a medium bowl. Reserve.
5. Let the clams cool 10 minutes. With paring knife remove the clams from their shells and trim the clam combs.
6. Chop the clams into ¼-inch pieces and reserve.
7. In the stockpot, cook the bacon over medium heat for 5 minutes, until crisp.
8. Add the onions and sauté for 3 minutes.
9. Add the potatoes, green peppers, and reserved wine mixture. Cook over medium heat about 15 minutes, until potatoes are tender.
10. Stir in the reserved chopped clams, cream, and pepper sauce.
11. In separate medium saucepan over low heat melt the butter, add flour, then mix well. Cook for 15 minutes.
12. Stir the flour-butter mixture into the clam mixture until fully incorporated. Then heat again for 5 minutes. Season with salt and pepper to taste.
13. Garnish the soup with the chives.

Lentil Soup

Lentils were a common item in the eighteenth-century storehouse, where they were kept in burlap bags, along with other items kept in bulk, such as dried beans and rice. Early German settlers prepared lentils frequently—and to this day lentil soup is a common item on Amish and Pennsylvania Dutch menus. Adding a bit of chopped sausage, frankfurter, or virtually any kind of smoked cut of pork will boost the flavor of this stick-to-the-ribs soup. In my hometown in Germany, we added a shot of vinegar to the soup right before serving.

Overnight preparation recommended

Serves 8 to 10
½ cup dried lentils
2 medium yellow onions, chopped
2 large carrots, chopped
2 garlic cloves, chopped
¼ cup olive oil
10 cups (2½ quarts) Chicken Stock (see page 199)
1 bay leaf
1 sprig fresh thyme
Salt and freshly ground black pepper

1. Pre-soak the lentils (see Chef's Note, page 117). Drain and reserve.
2. In a large stockpot, sauté the onions, carrots, and garlic in the oil over medium heat, stirring frequently, about 4 minutes, until tender.
3. Add the reserved lentils, Chicken Stock, bay leaf, and thyme. Bring to a boil over high heat.
4. Reduce the heat to medium and cook about 1 hour, until the lentils have dissolved.
5. Season with salt and pepper to taste.
6. Serve in a soup tureen or divide among individual soup bowls.

Tomato–Dill Bisque

An absolutely beautiful addition to your table, this soup tastes like it's much more difficult to prepare than it is. Tomatoes were slow to gain popularity in the New World because many believed that this member of the nightshade family was poisonous. However, Thomas Jefferson, who was introduced to tomatoes in France where they were called "love apples," grew many varieties. He even perfected the art of drying them in the sun—a forerunner of the sun-dried tomatoes popular today.

Serves 6 to 8

1 small onion, finely chopped
1 garlic clove, chopped
1 tablespoon unsalted butter·
6 cups (1½ quarts) Vegetable Stock (see page 199) or Chicken Stock (see page 199)
1 cup dry white wine
¾ cup tomato paste
1 cup heavy cream
1 small bunch fresh dill, chopped (about 2 tablespoons)
4 tablespoons unsalted butter
¼ cup all-purpose flour
Salt and freshly ground black pepper

1. In a 4-quart stockpot, sauté the onion and garlic in the butter over medium heat for 5 minutes until golden brown.
2. Add the Vegetable Stock, white wine, and tomato paste. Bring to a boil over high heat.
3. Add the cream and bring back to a boil over high heat. Stir in the dill.
4. In a separate medium saucepan over low heat melt the butter, add flour, then mix well. Cook for 15 minutes.
5. Gradually stir the flour-butter mixture into tomato mixture until fully incorporated. Reduce the heat and simmer about 5 minutes, until thoroughly hot.
6. Season with salt and pepper to taste. Serve immediately in a soup tureen or divide among individual soup bowls.

Lobster Bisque

This rich, buttery bisque came to the New World from France, where lobsters—better known as *langouste*—were the spiny, clawless variety found in the temperate coastal waters of the Mediterranean. French immigrant chefs had no problem recreating the dish in Philadelphia—North Atlantic or Maine lobsters were considered commonplace and were readily available. Today, specialty supermarkets and seafood stores often will give away or charge next to nothing for lobster heads and body "scraps," which make exceptional stock for this rich bisque.

Serves 6 to 8
4 celery ribs, chopped
2 large carrots, chopped
1 medium white onion, chopped
1 tablespoon unsalted butter
5 pounds lobster shells (heads and bodies, without tails)
1 cup cognac
12 cups (3 quarts) water
2 tablespoons tomato paste
1 bay leaf
1 sprig fresh thyme
1 teaspoon black peppercorns
1 cup heavy cream
4 tablespoons unsalted butter
¼ cup all-purpose flour
Salt and freshly ground black pepper

Adjust the amount of cognac to suit your own taste. I also love to add a little Madeira just before serving; the mix of flavors is sensational.

1. In an 8-quart stockpot, sauté the celery, carrots, and onion in the butter over medium heat for 5 minutes, until tender.
2. Add the lobster shells and cognac.
3. Add the water, tomato paste, bay leaf, thyme, and peppercorns. Bring to a boil over high heat. Reduce the heat and simmer for 6 hours.
4. Strain the stock through a fine sieve or cheesecloth into a large bowl. Discard the shells and vegetables. Return the stock to the stockpot and add the cream.
5. In separate medium saucepan, over low hear melt the butter, add flour, then mix well. Cook for 15 minutes.
6. Bring the stock to a boil over high heat and gradually stir in the flour-butter mixture until fully incorporated. Heat thoroughly for 5 minutes. Season with salt and pepper to taste.
7. Serve immediately in a soup tureen or divide among individual soup bowls.

In the early 1880s, lobster's wholesale price was only 6 cents a pound.

West Indian Pepper Pot Soup

This recipe is the grandfather to the traditional Philadelphia Pepper Pot Soup—and to my taste, the superior recipe of the two. By far the most popular soup on our menu, our pepper pot soup is made from an authentic West Indian recipe that is more than 250 years old. Back then, English ships traveled through the islands transporting slaves as well as exotic foodstuffs, so that West Indian cookery found its way into the very fabric of Philadelphia life. I learned this recipe from Miss Betty, a great Jamaican lady of undetermined age, who prepared it on the banks of the Rio Grande River in Port Antonio.

Serves 10

¾ pound salt-cured pork shoulder, chopped (see Chef's Note)
¾ pound salt-cured beef shoulder, chopped (see Chef's Note)
2 tablespoons vegetable oil
1 medium white onion, chopped
4 garlic cloves, chopped
¼ Scotch bonnet pepper, seeded and chopped (see Chef's Note, page 28)
1 bunch scallions, chopped (about 1 cup)
1 pound taro root, peeled and cut into 2-inch by ¼-inch strips
4 quarts (1 gallon) Chicken Stock (see page 199)
2 bay leaves
1 teaspoon chopped fresh thyme
1 tablespoon freshly ground allspice (see Chef's Note)
1 tablespoon freshly ground black pepper
1 pound callaloo or collard greens, rinsed and chopped (see Chef's Note)
Salt

Chef's Notes

• To salt-cure pork and beef shoulder, choose meat that appears well-marbled. Then rub with coarse (kosher) salt and refrigerate for at least three days. Wash the salt off the meat before cooking as directed.

• The allspice must be freshly ground, or the flavor will be compromised.

The only substitution you can make in this recipe and still achieve the intended flavor is to use collard greens instead of callaloo, the leafy top of the taro root. You can find both the taro root and callaloo at most Asian and West Indian markets.

1. In a large stockpot, sauté the pork and beef in the oil over high heat for 10 minutes, until brown.
2. Add the onion, garlic, and Scotch bonnet pepper; sauté for 3 to 5 minutes, until the onion is translucent.
3. Add the scallions and sauté for 3 minutes.
4. Add the taro root and sauté for 3 to 5 minutes more, until translucent.
5. Add the Chicken Stock, bay leaves, thyme, allspice, and ground pepper. Bring to a boil over high heat. Reduce the heat to medium and cook about 30 minutes, until the meat and taro root are tender.
6. Stir in the callaloo. Reduce the heat and simmer about 5 minutes, until wilted.
7. Season with salt and pepper to taste. Serve in a tureen or divide among individual soup bowls. Serve with Thomas Jefferson's Sweet Potato Biscuits (see page 175), if desired.

The heat factor of peppers is measured by Scoville heat units. A jalapeño has 80,000 Scoville heat units while habañeros from Jamaica or the Yucatan Peninsula and Scotch bonnet peppers have been found to have 550,000 Scoville heat units.

Mushroom Bisque

The Pennsylvania woods are renowned for their many varieties of mushrooms. No doubt enterprising settlers would gather mushrooms and go into the city to peddle them door to door to restaurants and inns, where they would be incorporated into all kinds of dishes, including this French style soup. City Tavern, with its sophisticated menu that demanded a wide range of ingredients, was certainly a prime market for this emerging cottage industry of vendors hawking everything from mushrooms to herbs, vegetables, meats and fresh fish. A mix of fresh mushrooms is recommended in this recipe. I especially like the flavors of chanterelles and porcini for this silken soup. If you prefer a lighter flavor, you can substitute additional Vegetable Stock for part of the cream.

Serves 10 to 12

12 cups (2 pounds) assorted fresh mushrooms (portabella,
   porcini, or chanterelles), cleaned and chopped
2 tablespoons unsalted butter
16 cups (4 quarts) Vegetable Stock (see page 199)
1 bay leaf
2 large garlic cloves, minced
1 cup dry sherry
8 cups (2 quarts) heavy cream
Salt and freshly ground white pepper
Fresh parsley, chopped, for garnish

1. In Dutch oven, sauté the mushrooms in butter over medium heat for 5 minutes.
2. Remove from heat. Set aside to cool for 15 minutes.
3. Transfer mushrooms to food processor, and process until finely chopped. Set aside.
4. In a large stockpot, combine the Vegetable Stock, bay leaf, and garlic. Bring to a boil over high heat until the mixture is reduced by half, about 45 minutes. Add the sherry.
5. Add heavy cream, remove bay leaf, and reduce again by half, about 30 minutes.
6. Add the mushroom puree; bring to boil over high heat and then lower heat. Simmer for 10 minutes until heated through.
7. Season with salt and pepper to taste.
8. Serve immediately in a soup tureen or divide among individual soup plates. Garnish with the parsley.

Nearly half
the mushrooms
Americans eat come
from the state of
Pennsylvania.

Beef–Barley Soup

Barley was a favorite staple of the early colonists, who ground the seed for use as a cereal, in breads and cakes, and as "barley sugar." Barley also was served as we would rice, as an accompaniment to meats and fowl. We serve Herbed Barley (see page 118) as a side dish at the Tavern today, something you'll rarely see on a restaurant menu.

Serves 8 to 10

1 pound beef stew meat, cut into ¼-inch cubes
1 teaspoon unsalted butter
2 medium shallots, chopped
3 garlic cloves, chopped
1 cup chopped onion
1 cup chopped celery
1 cup chopped carrots
½ cup red burgundy wine
2 large tomatoes, seeded and chopped (about 1 cup)
½ cup dried regular pearl barley
1 bay leaf
1 sprig fresh thyme
1 small bunch fresh basil, chopped (about ½ cup)
12 cups (3 quarts) Beef Stock (see page 198)
1 tablespoon tomato paste
Salt and freshly ground black pepper
Fresh parsley, chopped, for garnish

For a tasty addition to this soup, add sliced mushrooms and/or snipped dried beef (such as Bunderfleisch air-dried beef) after Step 9.

1. In a large stockpot, cook the beef cubes in the butter over high heat for 10 minutes, until brown.
2. Add the shallots and garlic and sauté for 3 minutes.
3. Add the onion, celery, and carrots and sauté for 3 to 5 minutes, until the onions are translucent.
4. Add the red wine to deglaze the pan, loosening any browned bits on the bottom of the pan with a wooden spoon.
5. Add the tomatoes, barley, bay leaf, thyme, and basil.
6. Add the Beef Stock and bring to a boil over high heat.
7. Thoroughly stir in the tomato paste. Reduce the heat and simmer about 1 hour, until meat is tender.
8. Season with salt and pepper to taste.
9. Serve in a soup tureen or divide among individual soup bowls. Garnish with the chopped parsley.

Chicken Noodle Soup

This soup, the original comfort food in Germany, provided a final resting place for the colonial family's old stewing hen when she stopped laying eggs. These birds are larger and tougher than younger chickens, which makes them perfect for soup. Use about three cups of the chopped, cooked chicken in this soup and save the extra meat in any recipe that calls for cooked chicken, such as pot pie or chicken salad. Soup, along with a slab of bread, was a complete meal to most people in colonial days—only at the Tavern would this soup have been just one of many other starter dishes.

Serves 6 to 8

1 medium onion, chopped
1 tablespoon unsalted butter
3 celery ribs, chopped
2 large carrots, chopped
12 cups (3 quarts) Chicken Stock (see page 199)
1 sprig fresh thyme
1 pound chicken meat, cooked and chopped
½ pound Homemade Egg Noodles (see page 126), cooked and drained
Salt and freshly ground black pepper
Fresh parsley, chopped, for garnish

1. In a medium stockpot, sauté the onion in the butter over medium heat for 3 to 5 minutes, until translucent.
2. Add the celery and carrots and sauté for 3 to 5 minutes, until tender.
3. Add the Chicken Stock and thyme. Bring to a boil over high heat.
4. Reduce the heat and simmer about 30 minutes, until liquid is reduced by one-third.
5. Remove the sprig of thyme. Add the chicken meat and cooked noodles. Heat through.
6. Season with salt and pepper to taste.
7. Serve in a soup tureen or divide among individual soup bowls. Garnish with the chopped parsley.

Salads and Relishes

Salads in eighteenth-century Philadelphia weren't the tender green tosses of mesclun and baby greens we favor today. Instead, they were seasoned mixes of root vegetables, cabbage, kale, dried peas, and beans. Vegetables were available only seasonally, making beets, potatoes, carrots, and other crops that wintered well especially valuable. Almost everyone had root cellars—damp, underground storage areas where these precious items were kept. Salads were served as part of the first plates course, except among the British, who were in the habit of eating salads in the late afternoon, during tea. Because our mission is to offer the diner an interpretive and historic culinary experience, these salads and relishes are served seasonally in the Tavern today, just as they were in days gone by.

Celery Root Salad

Celery root was commonly grown in colonial times because, if properly picked and stored, it could last the whole winter. Although today it is the stalk that is the favored part of this vegetable, in the early days the root was used to flavor stocks, sauces, salads, and relishes. Celery root is still popular in Europe today. In fact in my hometown we made a delicious cooked celery root and carrot salad, flavored with onion and vinegar. If you've never tasted this root vegetable, you'll be pleasantly surprised at its distinctive, yet delicate, flavor.

Serves 4

1 large celery root
¼ cup lemon juice (about 1 large lemon), strained
¾ cup Homemade Mayonnaise (see page 205)
2 tablespoons Dijon mustard
1 tablespoon heavy cream
½ teaspoon curry powder
½ teaspoon Worcestershire sauce
Salt and freshly ground white pepper
1 butterhead (Boston or Bibb) lettuce, cored and rinsed, for serving
2 tablespoons chopped walnuts, for garnish

If you like a richer curry flavor, increase the curry powder to suit your taste.

1. Peel the celery root and cut into 2-inch-long strips (the finer, the better).
2. Place the strips in a medium bowl and coat thoroughly with the lemon juice.
3. Cover with plastic wrap and refrigerate for 45 minutes, until completely chilled.
4. In a small mixing bowl, blend together the Homemade Mayonnaise, mustard, cream, curry powder, and Worcestershire sauce. Add to the celery root.
5. Mix well and season with salt and pepper to taste.
6. To serve, arrange the lettuce leaves on salad plates. Divide the celery root mixture among the plates and garnish with the walnuts.

Warm Potato Salad

This salad is just one of the many versions of potato salad that German immigrants brought with them across the sea. I prefer red skinned potatoes or "boiling potatoes" because their exterior is firm and waxy, which ensures that the potato holds its shape in the salad. The combination of hard-cooked egg with bacon and chives is absolutely delicious. The mustard gives added bite.

Serves 6

6 medium red skinned potatoes
2 eggs, hard-cooked (see Chef's Note, page 23) and chopped
6 slices lean bacon, finely chopped
1 large yellow onion, finely chopped
1 egg, raw (see Chef's Note)
¼ cup cider vinegar
2 tablespoons Dijon mustard
Salt and freshly ground black pepper.
1 tablespoon chopped fresh chives, for serving

If you have concerns about eating or serving raw eggs, simply omit the egg from this recipe.

1. In a large saucepan, cook the potatoes in enough boiling, lightly salted water to cover for 20 to 25 minutes, until almost tender and a fork can barely pass through a potato.
2. Drain the potatoes. Cool slightly. Halve lengthwise, peel, and cut the potatoes into ¼-inch-thick slices.
3. Place the potatoes in a medium bowl. Add the chopped eggs. Reserve.
4. In a large skillet, cook the bacon over medium heat for 3 minutes, until crisp. Add the onion and sauté for 3 to 5 minutes, until the onion is translucent.
5. Drain off the fat, reserving it for the dressing.
6. Add the bacon mixture to the potato mixture; toss gently to combine.
7. For the dressing, in a small bowl, thoroughly beat the egg with a wire whisk.
8. Add the reserved bacon fat, vinegar, and mustard. Whisk to thoroughly combine.
9. Pour the dressing over the potato mixture. Toss to mix.
10. Season with salt and pepper to taste.
11. Sprinkle with the chives. Serve immediately while still warm.

In the eighteenth century, most restaurant patrons ate family-style, with serving dishes left on the table for guests to help themselves.

Spiced Pepper Slaw with Warm Bacon Dressing

Here's a German-inspired slaw with a traditional, tangy, full-flavored dressing. When colonial cooks made it in the winter, they omitted green peppers, which were only available in summer. Pepper relish may have been added as a substitute. This dressing is also great served simply with fresh spinach.

Serves 4

½ medium head green cabbage (about 4 cups), finely shredded
1 tablespoon salt
2 medium green bell peppers, finely chopped (about 1½ cups)
½ teaspoon hot red pepper flakes
1½ slices lean bacon, chopped
1 scallion, finely chopped (about 2 tablespoons)
2 tablespoons red wine vinegar
1 tablespoon chopped fresh parsley
1½ teaspoons whole-grain mustard
½ teaspoon cayenne
¼ teaspoon granulated sugar
¼ cup olive oil
Salt and freshly ground black pepper

1. Place the shredded cabbage in a large mixing bowl and sprinkle with the 1 tablespoon salt. Cover with plastic wrap and refrigerate about 1½ hours to remove excess water from cabbage.
2. Thoroughly rinse and drain the cabbage, pressing lightly to remove any additional water. Return it to the mixing bowl and stir in the green peppers and red pepper flakes.
3. In a small saucepan, cook the bacon over medium heat for 3 minutes, until crisp.
4. Remove the bacon from the pan and drain on paper towels. Reserve.
5. In the same skillet, cook the scallions in the bacon drippings for 1 minute, until lightly brown.
6. Add the vinegar to deglaze the pan, loosening any browned bits on the bottom of the pan with a wooden spoon. Remove from the heat.
7. In a medium mixing bowl, combine the parsley, mustard, cayenne, sugar, and the hot vinegar mixture.
8. Slowly add the olive oil, whisking constantly.
9. Add the warm dressing immediately to the cabbage mixture. Toss to mix.
10. Season with salt and pepper to taste. Sprinkle the reserved bacon on top of the salad before serving.

Mushroom Salad

Mushroom salad is of French origin and is still served in Paris brasseries to this day. Because the colonies were full of every sort of mushroom, this salad was probably served at the Tavern, where French-style cuisine often was emulated.

Serves 4

5½ cups sliced button mushrooms (1 pound)
¼ cup fresh lemon juice (about 1 large lemon), strained
1 medium onion, finely chopped
3 tablespoons rice wine vinegar
3 tablespoons extra-virgin olive oil
1 tablespoon Dijon mustard
Dash chili powder
Salt and freshly ground white pepper

1. In a medium mixing bowl, toss the mushrooms with the lemon juice.
2. In a small bowl, combine the onion, vinegar, oil, mustard, and chili powder.
3. Pour the onion mixture over the mushrooms. Gently toss to coat, being careful not to bruise the mushrooms.
4. Season with salt and pepper to taste.

As a serving suggestion, complement the salad by serving it over radicchio leaves and garnishing with finely chopped red bell pepper.

Dandelion Salad

Dandelions come into season late March into early April, depending on your geographic location. According to the *Dictionary of American Regional English*, Pennsylvanians colloquially called dandelion greens salad Dutch Salad. If you pick your own, choose young, tender wild dandelion leaves, because once the dandelions start to flower, the leaves are bitter and virtually inedible. Dandelion greens are available at many farmers markets, as well as any large supermarket with a comprehensive produce department.

Serves 8

2½ pounds fresh dandelion greens, rinsed
6 slices lean bacon, cut into thin strips
¼ cup balsamic vinegar
2 garlic cloves, chopped
Salt and freshly ground black pepper

1. Pat the dandelion greens dry with paper towels. Tear into bite-size pieces. Place the greens in a large mixing bowl.
2. In a medium saucepan, cook the bacon over medium heat for 3 minutes, until crisp. Drain off the fat into a ovenproof container and pour in a thin stream over the dandelion greens. Toss to mix.
3. Add the balsamic vinegar to the bacon in the saucepan, and pour over the dandelion greens.
4. Add the garlic and toss to mix.
5. Season with salt and pepper to taste.

If you pick your own dandelion greens, be sure to pick from an area that hasn't been sprayed with chemicals.

Apple and Walnut Salad

This salad makes the most of two tried-and-true ingredients: apples and walnuts, which were both indigenous to Pennsylvania. In colonial times, it was one of the few fresh salads that could be eaten in the winter. Even though the apples may have shriveled over time in the cellar, once the skins were removed, the flesh would be sweet and intact. Both tart and sweet apples will work; choose whichever type suits your taste.

Serves 4

4 large apples, peeled, cored, and thinly sliced
¼ cup fresh lemon juice (about 1 large lemon), strained
½ cup chopped walnuts
¼ cup Homemade Mayonnaise (see page 205)
2 tablespoons heavy cream
¼ teaspoon Worcestershire sauce
⅛ teaspoon curry powder
Salt and freshly ground white pepper
Fresh parsley, chopped, for garnish

1. In a medium mixing bowl, toss the apple slices with the lemon juice.
2. In a small mixing bowl, combine the walnuts, Homemade Mayonnaise, cream, Worcestershire sauce, and curry.
3. Pour the mayonnaise mixture over the apples and toss gently to coat. Season with salt and pepper to taste.
4. Cover and refrigerate for 1 hour, until well chilled.
5. Just before serving, garnish with the parsley.

Chef's Note

To turn this side dish into a wonderful main course, add diced chicken, pineapple chunks, and cooked long-grain rice. To intensify the curry flavor, add double the amount.

Potato Salad

Potatoes were one of the few vegetables that could be stored in the root cellar and eaten all year long. The celery rib in this recipe is an addition for the modern palate—celery was eaten only in its root form in Colonial days. Although similar to German potato salad, this unique recipe calls for yellow prepared mustard as well as dry mustard, which adds both zest and color to the dish.

Serves 12

8 medium red skinned potatoes (about 2½ pounds), cubed
2 hard-cooked eggs, finely chopped (see Chef's Note, page 23)
1 medium yellow onion, finely chopped
½ celery rib, chopped
½ cup olive oil
½ cup white vinegar
2 tablespoons prepared yellow mustard
⅛ teaspoon dry mustard
Salt and freshly ground black pepper
1 bunch fresh chives, chopped (about 6 tablespoons), for garnish

1. In medium saucepan, cook the potato in enough lightly salted boiling water to cover for 20 to 25 minutes or until fork-tender.
2. Drain potatoes, cool with cold water.
3. In a large mixing bowl, combine the potatoes, eggs, onion, and celery.
4. In a small bowl, combine the oil, vinegar, prepared mustard, and dry mustard. Pour the mustard mixture over the potato mixture. Toss gently to coat. Season with salt and pepper to taste.
5. Cover and refrigerate for 1 hour, until completely chilled.
6. Just before serving, garnish with the chives.

Cabbage Salad

Cabbage, which wintered well, was a staple for the early settlers. A terrific source of nutrients, especially with winter's limited menu, cabbage was eaten braised, in salads, and as sauerkraut. The addition of lean bacon, garlic, and olive oil dressing to this cabbage salad elevates it heads above the average slaw.

Serves 8

9 slices lean bacon, chopped
7 tablespoons olive oil
2 tablespoons unsalted butter
4 tablespoons white wine vinegar
1 medium green cabbage, shredded or sliced into
   narrow strips (about 8 cups)
1 tablespoon Dijon mustard
Salt and freshly ground black pepper
2 garlic cloves, finely chopped
1 small bunch fresh parsley, chopped

1. In a large skillet, sauté the bacon in 1 tablespoon of the olive oil and all the butter over medium heat for 3 minutes, until crisp.
2. Add 2 tablespoons of the vinegar, then the cabbage.
3. Increase the heat to high and cook for 3 minutes, until the cabbage begins to wilt. Remove from heat.
4. In a large bowl, combine the mustard, the remaining 2 tablespoons vinegar, and the remaining 6 tablespoons oil.
5. Pour the mustard mixture over the cabbage mixture. Toss to coat.
6. Season with salt and pepper to taste.
7. Just before serving, add the garlic and parsley. Toss to mix.

Lentil Salad

This sophisticated French salad would have been common only at a restaurant as upscale as City Tavern—the typical colonial housewife would have never made this dish. The Tavern chefs continuously incorporated French and European dishes into the menu, and strove to creatively use the ingredients that were at hand, such as dried beans and lentils.

Serves 8

Salad
4 cups dried French lentils (see Chef's Note)
2 carrots, julienned
1 medium yellow onion, chopped
2 large garlic cloves, chopped
1 bay leaf
3 sprigs fresh thyme
1 teaspoon salt
½ teaspoon freshly ground black pepper
9 slices lean bacon, chopped
½ bunch fresh parsley, chopped (about 3 tablespoons)

Dressing
1 bunch fresh chives, chopped (about 6 tablespoons)
1 red onion, finely chopped
½ cup olive oil
¼ cup red wine vinegar
2 tablespoons Dijon mustard
3 garlic cloves, chopped
1 teaspoon salt
½ teaspoon freshly ground black pepper

• Turn this salad into a main dish by stirring in some chopped roast pork or cooked sausage and diced, cooked potato. Serve on lettuce leaves.
• Because this recipe requires a shorter-than-average cooking time, we soak the lentils to ensure an al dente texture.

1. Prepare the Salad: Presoak the lentils for at least 4 hours (see Chef's Note, page 117). Drain.
2. In a large saucepan, combine the pre-soaked lentils, carrots, onion, garlic, bay leaf, thyme, salt, and pepper. Add enough water to cover.
3. Bring to a boil over high heat. Reduce the heat. Cover and simmer about 10 minutes, until the lentils are tender, but not overcooked. Check frequently for doneness during cooking.
4. Drain the lentil mixture in a colander.
5. Remove the sprigs of thyme and bay leaf. Cover and refrigerate the lentil mixture for 1 hour, until chilled.
6. In a small saucepan, cook the bacon over medium heat about 3 minutes, until crisp. Remove the bacon from the saucepan and drain on paper towels.
7. Prepare the Dressing: In a large bowl, combine the onion, oil, vinegar, chives, mustard, garlic, salt, and pepper.
8. Add the lentil mixture to the dressing and mix gently.
9. Season with salt and pepper to taste.
10. Let stand at room temperature about 30 minutes to allow the flavors to develop. Before serving, adjust seasoning to taste.

Cucumber and Cream Salad

In days gone by, this dish was only served in warm months when cucumbers were in season. We can only imagine how much cooks and diners alike anticipated the fresh, tender bounty of summer after a winter of eating dried and root vegetables. The chili powder adds a kick of spice to this truly refreshing salad.

Serves 4

1 large European seedless cucumber or 4 small cucumbers,
   peeled and thinly sliced (about 4 cups)
½ cup sour cream
1 medium red onion, finely chopped
1 tablespoon cider vinegar
⅛ teaspoon Hungarian paprika
Dash chili powder
Salt and freshly ground black pepper
Fresh chives, chopped, for garnish

1. In a medium mixing bowl, place the cucumber and sprinkle with salt. Cover with plastic wrap and refrigerate about 1 hour, until chilled and the liquid has drained from the cucumbers.
2. Thoroughly rinse with cold water and gently squeeze out all of the excess water.
3. In a small mixing bowl, stir together the sour cream, onion, vinegar, paprika, and chili powder until combined.
4. Add to the cucumber and mix well.
5. Season with salt and pepper to taste.
6. Garnish with the chives.

Green Bean Salad

Every gardener knows that green beans are among the easiest crop to grow—and that they can take over a garden in no time. Early settlers, who did without green vegetables for much of the year, must have welcomed this hardy crop with great eagerness, using green beans fresh, as in this recipe, dried, or pickled in precious preserves for winter

Serves 8

2½ pounds fresh haricot verts, trimmed
5½ cups sliced fresh button mushrooms (about 1 pound)
3 medium shallots, chopped
6 tablespoon walnut oil
3 tablespoons red wine vinegar
2 teaspoons Dijon mustard
Salt and freshly ground black pepper

If you can't get walnut oil, substitute olive oil. Also, balsamic vinegar can be used in place of red wine vinegar, if you like.

1. Bring a large saucepan of salted water to a boil over high heat. Add the beans and cook for 10 to 15 minutes, until just firm but tender.
2. Drain the beans and place them in a large bowl.
3. Add the mushrooms and shallots and mix gently.
4. In a small bowl, whisk together the oil, vinegar, and mustard until blended. Pour over the green bean mixture and toss gently to coat.
5. Season with salt and pepper to taste.
6. Serve at room temperature.

Beet Salad

At City Tavern today, this dish regularly is offered as a special. It is extremely popular, which is surprising considering that beets aren't a favorite American vegetable these days. But when you think about what was important to the colonial chef, beets passed with flying colors—they stored well over the winter and were extremely versatile in soups, salads, and relishes. Hard-cooked eggs are a delicious complement to this recipe.

Serves 6

2 pounds whole fresh beets, stems trimmed ½ inch above the beets
1 cup olive oil
½ cup finely diced onions
¼ cup rice wine vinegar
1 tablespoon chopped fresh parsley
1 tablespoon fresh lemon juice
½ teaspoon crushed red pepper flakes
Salt and freshly ground black pepper

For a slightly different, mustardy flavor, substitute 1 tablespoon Dijon mustard for the crushed red pepper in Step 3.

1. In a Dutch oven, cook the beets in enough boiling lightly salted water to cover for 25 to 30 minutes, until the beets are firm but tender. Drain and cool slightly.
2. With a small paring knife, remove the beet skins and cut the beets into 1-inch cubes. Reserve.
3. In a medium mixing bowl, combine the remaining ingredients.
4. Stir in the cubed beets. Cover and refrigerate about 2 hours, until marinated and thoroughly chilled. Adjust seasoning to taste.
5. Serve chilled.

Tomato and Onion Salad

Nothing tastes more refreshing than juicy, ripe tomatoes—even today we eagerly anticipate that first crop of summer. Thomas Jefferson raised tomatoes in his Virginia garden, where an heirloom variety still grows to this day.

Serves 4

3 extra-large tomatoes, sliced ¼-inch thick (about 1½ pounds)
2 medium red onions, sliced ¼-inch thick
½ cup extra-virgin olive oil
¼ cup balsamic vinegar
Salt and freshly ground black pepper
4 sprigs fresh basil, leaves pulled and thinly sliced

1. Alternate the tomato and onion slices on a plate.
2. In a small bowl, whisk together the oil and vinegar.
3. Season with salt and pepper to taste.
4. Drizzle the tomatoes and onions with the oil-vinegar mixture.
5. Garnish with fresh basil and serve.

For exceptional flavor, season the salad with a little fresh garlic and serve it with thinly sliced fresh mozzarella cheese.

Butterhead Lettuce with Raspberry Shrub Vinaigrette

When I did my research on what was grown during colonial times, butterhead lettuce, which includes Boston and Bibb, is the only lettuce I found. Its seeds were brought over from France and Germany, and its tender leaves were enjoyed in the late spring and early summer seasons.

Makes 2 cups vinaigrette; Serves 6

½ cup raspberry shrub (see Resources, page 211)
2 teaspoons balsamic vinegar
1 teaspoon granulated sugar
1 teaspoon Dijon mustard
1½ cups olive oil
Salt and freshly ground white pepper
3 heads butterhead (Boston or Bibb) lettuce or mixed greens, rinsed and torn

1. In a medium mixing bowl, whisk together the raspberry shrub, balsamic vinegar, sugar, and mustard.
2. Slowly add the olive oil, whisking constantly.
3. Season with salt and pepper to taste.
4. Cover and refrigerate for 10 minutes, until chilled.
5. When ready to serve, whisk the dressing. Pour over the lettuce or mixed greens and toss to coat.

Romaine Lettuce with
Red Burgundy Wine–Dijon Vinaigrette

Roquefort cheese, introduced to the New World by the French, goes perfectly with French Dijon mustard and tart wine vinegar. This red wine dressing brings out the best in the refreshingly pungent flavors of crisp romaine lettuce and Roquefort cheese.

Makes 2 cups vinaigrette; Serves 6

¼ cup red wine vinegar
¼ cup red burgundy wine
1 tablespoon Dijon mustard
1 teaspoon granulated sugar
1½ cups olive oil
1 cup crumbled Roquefort, for serving
Salt and freshly ground white pepper
2 heads romaine lettuce, rinsed and torn

1. In a medium mixing bowl, whisk together the vinegar, wine, mustard, and sugar.
2. Slowly add the olive oil, whisking constantly.
3. Cover and refrigerate about 1 hour, until chilled.
4. Season with salt and pepper to taste.
5. When ready to serve, whisk the dressing. Pour over the romaine lettuce and toss to coat. Add the cheese.

Cranberry Relish

Cranberry bogs greeted the settlers when they first arrived on the shores of the New World. In fact, cranberries—along with grapes and blueberries—are the few fruits native to North America. This colorful relish is a wonderful accompaniment to poultry or pork.

Makes 2 cups; Serves 8

3 cups fresh cranberries (about 12 ounces)
½ cup granulated sugar
½ cup water
2 tablespoons grated orange rind

1. In a stainless steel or enameled saucepan, combine the cranberries, sugar, water, and orange rind.
2. Bring to a simmer over medium-low heat.
3. Cook, stirring occasionally, about 5 minutes, until the cranberries burst.
4. Remove from the heat and let cool. Store in a tightly sealed plastic or glass container and refrigerate for up to 8 weeks.

Pineapple Relish

Pineapples were a symbol of hospitality in the eighteenth century and remains so today. It seems that when a ship's captain returned home from a West Indian voyage, he would place a pineapple on a stick in front of his door as a signal to friends and neighbors that he had returned and was welcoming visitors.

Makes 4 cups; Serves 6 to 8

1 large fresh pineapple, peeled and finely chopped
1 medium white onion, very finely chopped
¼ cup honey
¼ cup pineapple juice
¼ cup rice wine vinegar
¼ Scotch bonnet pepper, finely chopped (see Chef's Note, page 28)
¼ teaspoon ground allspice
Salt and freshly ground white pepper

1. In a medium mixing bowl, combine all of the ingredients.
2. Cover and refrigerate about 2 hours, until completely chilled.
3. Serve chilled as an accompaniment to meats, poultry, or fish.
4. Store in a tightly sealed plastic or glass container and refrigerate for up to 8 weeks.

Preparing a Pineapple
Cut the top and bottom off of the pineapple. Then, remove the outer skin with a chef's knife. Cut the pineapple in half lengthwise and then in half again. Cut out and discard the core. Dice the remaining fruit.

Mango and Papaya Relish

In the 1700s, ships typically pulled into the harbor loaded with tropical fruits that had to be used immediately. Sun drying, making jams and chutneys, and cooking them into relishes, such as this one, were the colonial cook's primary means of preserving fresh fruits and vegetables. Serve this tropical treat as an accompaniment to seafood or poultry.

Makes 6 cups; Serves 8 to 12

3 medium papayas, peeled and chopped
2 medium mangoes, peeled and chopped
1 medium red onion, chopped
½ cup honey
¼ cup rice wine vinegar
1 teaspoon chopped fresh cilantro leaves
½ teaspoon ground star anise

1. In a medium mixing bowl, combine all of the ingredients.
2. Cover with plastic wrap and refrigerate for about 2 hours, until thoroughly marinated.
3. Store in a tightly sealed plastic or glass container and refrigerate for up to 8 weeks.

Spicy Corn Relish

This combination of fresh herbs, green onions, and sweet white corn is an ideal side-dish to go with grilled meats and fish.

Makes 6 cups; Serves 12

10 ears fresh white corn, kernels cut from cobs
1 medium red bell pepper, finely chopped
1 medium green bell pepper, finely chopped
1 medium white onion, finely chopped
¼ cup rice wine vinegar
¼ cup olive oil
2 medium scallions, finely chopped (about 3 tablespoons)
1 garlic clove, finely chopped
½ bunch fresh chives, finely chopped (about 3 tablespoons)
½ bunch fresh cilantro, finely chopped (about ¼ cup)
1 teaspoon ground cumin
1 teaspoon hot red pepper flakes
1 sprig fresh thyme
Salt and freshly ground black pepper

1. Bring a large saucepan of lightly salted water to a boil over high heat. Add the corn and cook for 5 to 7 minutes, until tender. *Do not overcook.*
2. Drain the corn and place in a medium mixing bowl. Add remaining ingredients and mix well.
3. Cover and refrigerate about 30 minutes, until chilled. Store in a tightly sealed plastic or glass container and refrigerate for up to 8 weeks.

Onion and Raisin Relish

Sweet and savory flavors team up in this chunky German-style relish made with tiny pearl onions. It is wonderful served with roasted meats.

Makes 6 cups; Serves 12

1½ pounds pearl onions (preferably small ones)
5 cups dry white wine
1 cup raisins
1 cup olive oil
½ cup red wine vinegar
3 tablespoons tomato paste
½ bunch fresh savory
1 sprig fresh thyme or 1 teaspoon dried thyme
2 bay leaves
5 garlic cloves, finely chopped
1 teaspoon dried rubbed sage
½ teaspoon hot red pepper flakes
Salt and freshly ground black pepper

1. Boil the onions for 5 minutes, then drain and reserve. With a small paring knife, make a crisscross cut in the stem end of each onion.
2. In a large saucepan, combine the onions, wine, raisins, oil, vinegar, tomato paste, savory, thyme, bay leaves, garlic, sage, and pepper flakes. Bring to a boil over high heat.
3. Reduce the heat and simmer, stirring frequently, for 35 to 50 minutes, until the liquid is evaporated. Let cool.
4. Season with salt and pepper to taste.
5. Store in a tightly sealed plastic or glass container and refrigerate for up to 4 weeks.

In colonial times, relishes and other types of preserves would have been kept away from sunlight and stored in a cool, dry pantry.

Peach Chutney

Chutney was brought to America by the British, who had learned to make the spicy condiment from the East Indians. It was made with a variety of fruits as a way of preserving perishable fruit, such as peaches, past their normal seasonal prime. At the Tavern, we serve this chutney with roasted duckling, but the hint of sweetness it adds to savory dishes can enhance any type of roasted meat or fowl.

Makes 3 cups; Serves 6

1 medium red onion, halved lengthwise and sliced
1 tablespoon vegetable oil
4 medium fresh peaches, peeled and cut into wedges (about 4 pounds)
1 red bell pepper, chopped
½ cup honey
½ cup white wine vinegar
1 tablespoon light brown sugar
¼ teaspoon freshly grated nutmeg

1. In a large saucepan, sauté the onion in the oil over medium heat for 3 minutes, until translucent.
2. Stir in the peaches, bell pepper, honey, vinegar, brown sugar, and nutmeg.
3. Bring to a boil over high heat. Reduce the heat and simmer, stirring occasionally, for 8 to 10 minutes, until liquid is reduced. Let cool.
4. Store in a tightly sealed plastic or glass container and refrigerate for up to 8 weeks.

Chef's Note

To ensure that chutneys and relishes maintain a long shelf life, always use a clean utensil when serving, and store in the refrigerator.

A typical dinner at City Tavern would include two tureens of soup, one at each end of the table, at least two fish dishes (such as shad or trout), a shoulder of mutton, a ham, pork or beef, or chicken or turkey, all served with appropriate salads, sauces, and relishes. Wild game, such as hare or pheasant, would also be served. Desserts would always include cakes, tarts, and puddings, followed by fruits and nuts with decanters of Madeira.

Part 2: Second Plates

In the Tavern's heyday, diners enjoyed their main course as part of what was called the "Second Plates" course. This litany of main dishes, including organ meats, such as tripe, heart, and other variety meats, along with accompanying side dishes, sauces, and relishes, was served "family style." At large parties at the Tavern, it was not unusual for up to twenty dishes to be served at one sitting, depending on the budget and the formality of the occasion. These feasts would typically last from three to four hours. As bounteous as this sounds, remember that the meat portions were typically smaller than what diners eat today.

Main Dishes

True to eighteenth-century dining style, our main dishes don't feature many of the tender cuts of meat common today. Back then, the animals were grass fed—the original "free-range" meat, with the tough texture and strong flavor to prove it; this explains the early cooks' penchant for long marinating times and slow-cooking methods. Although we serve the highest quality meats at the tavern—a much better product than was available in colonial days—we still marinate all our meats for at least twenty-four hours before cooking. For convenience, most of these recipes call for shorter marinating times.

Pecan-Crusted, Honey-Glazed Roasted Ducklings

This dish combines some of the most plentiful ingredients native to the colonies in the eighteenth century—duck, honey, pecans, and fresh herbs. A regular menu item at City Tavern, it is one of our most popular dishes at both lunch and dinner. Peach Chutney (see page 64) is especially tasty served along side.

Serves 6

3 whole boned and halved domestic ducks
   (2 to 4 pounds each) (see Chef's Note)
¼ cup fresh orange juice, strained
1 teaspoon light brown sugar
1 teaspoon chopped fresh thyme
1 teaspoon chopped fresh parsley
1 cup honey
½ cup chopped pecans

Have your butcher bone the ducks removing the wing bones but leaving in the thigh bone, and keeping the breast intact with the thigh. Then ask to have the ducks cut in half.

1. Preheat the oven to 425°F.
2. Place the duck halves skin sides up, in a large shallow baking pan.
3. In a small bowl, combine the orange juice, brown sugar, thyme, and parsley; mix well.
4. Using a pastry brush, brush the mixture over the skin of the ducks.
5. Roast for 20 to 25 minutes, until golden brown. Remove from the oven. Reduce the oven temperature to 350°F.
6. Brush the honey over the skin of the ducks and sprinkle with the pecans.
7. Roast for 15 to 20 minutes more, until crispy.
8. If desired, serve with the Peach Chutney.

Chicken Madeira

Madeira is an excellent cooking wine, ideal for both sweet and savory dishes. I prefer the semi-dry Rainwater style for cooking purposes, because it is less sweet than most other Madeiras and has a flavor closer to a dry sherry than a sweet wine, it's sometimes even served as an aperitif.

Overnight preparation recommended

Serves 6

6 skinless, boneless chicken breast halves (about 8 ounces each)
2 cups Rainwater-style Madeira
½ cup vegetable oil
½ bunch fresh basil, chopped (about ¼ cup)
1½ tablespoons chopped fresh parsley
1 teaspoon chopped fresh rosemary
1 sprig fresh thyme
2 garlic cloves, chopped
2 medium shallots, chopped
Salt and freshly ground black pepper
1 tablespoon unsalted butter
1 cup sliced button mushrooms
2 cups Demi-glace (see page 202)

1. In a medium bowl, combine the chicken, 1 cup of the Madeira, oil, basil, parsley, rosemary, thyme, garlic, shallots, and a sprinkling of salt and pepper.
2. Cover with plastic wrap and marinate in the refrigerator at least 6 hours or overnight.
3. Remove the chicken from the marinade; discard the marinade. Pat the chicken dry with paper towels.
4. In a 12-inch skillet, cook the chicken in the butter over high heat for 3 minutes on each side, until brown.
5. Add the mushrooms and sauté about 2 minutes, until golden.
6. Add the remaining 1 cup of Madeira to deglaze the pan, loosening any browned bits on the bottom of the pan with a wooden spoon.
7. Cook for 3 minutes, until the wine is reduced by half.
8. Stir in the Demi-glace and bring to a boil over high heat. Reduce the heat and simmer for 8 to 10 minutes, until reduced and thickened.
9. If desired, serve with Turnip, Potato, and Parsnip Mash (see page 111) and Creamed Spinach (see page 106).

Most of our main dishes feature pork, turkey, duck, venison, or a variety of fish and seafood because that is what was typically served in the 1770s. Chicken was served only on special occasions since hens were reserved instead for laying eggs.

Chef's Note

The unique process that renders Madeira so flavorful involves heating and aging in oak casks, as well as the addition of brandy. Madeira ranges in flavor from dry, pale, and crisp, to full-bodied and very fruity. For cooking purposes, I prefer Rainwater Madeira, a soft, medium-dry Verdelho-style Madeira that has undergone a clarifying process to create a more golden color. According to legend, when shipments of Madeira were put out on the island's beaches for pick-up by boats, rain was absorbed through the barrels, diluting the alcohol and reducing its potency, hence the name.

Pan–Seared Venison Medallions with Bourbon–Mushroom Sauce

Venison, though commonly thought of as deer meat, actually applies broadly to the meat of other wild game, including elk and moose. In colonial days, all of these animals were plentiful in the untamed forests of Pennsylvania. Today, elk and moose are difficult to obtain and venison often is farm raised (see Resources, page 211). Veal medallions work equally well in place of the venison.

Overnight preparation recommended

Serves 4 to 6

1½ pounds venison tenderloin, fat trimmed and silver skin removed
2 cups red burgundy wine
3 medium shallots, chopped
2 garlic cloves, finely chopped
1 sprig fresh rosemary, leaves pulled
1 teaspoon dried rubbed sage
2 teaspoons unsalted butter
1 medium leek (white part only), well rinsed and cut into 2-inch lengths and finely julienned
1½ cups sliced button mushrooms
½ cup bourbon
2 cups Demi-glace (see page 202)
Salt and freshly ground black pepper

1. Slice the venison into ¼-inch-thick medallions (about 3 ounces each).
2. Place the venison in a medium shallow dish. Add the red wine, shallots, garlic, rosemary, and sage.
3. Cover with plastic wrap and marinate in the refrigerator 8 hours or overnight.
4. Remove the venison from the marinade; discard the marinade. Pat the venison dry with paper towels.
5. In a large skillet, cook the venison in the butter over high heat for 3 minutes on each side (for medium-rare), until brown. Remove the venison from the pan. Reserve and keep warm.
6. Add the leek to the pan and sauté about 2 minutes, until soft.
7. Add the mushrooms and sauté about 3 minutes, until soft.
8. Add the bourbon to deglaze the pan, loosening any browned bits on the bottom of the pan with a wooden spoon.
9. Stir in the Demi-glace. Reduce the heat and simmer for about 3 minutes, until Demi-glace comes to boil.
10. Season with salt and pepper to taste. Fan out the venison on the serving plate and top with the mushroom mixture. Any kind of mashed root vegetables makes a good accompaniment.

Pork Medallions with Oatmeal Stout

Pork was a favored meat in early America because pigs were easy to feed, raise, and transport. This entrée is a wonderful medley of flavors—the delicate sweetness of the pork works beautifully with the slightly bitter oatmeal stout, the piquant mustard greens and the delicately sweet fried sweet potatoes.

Overnight preparation recommended

Serves 6

4 pounds pork tenderloin, fat trimmed and silver skin removed
4 cups (32 ounces) oatmeal stout or other dark beer
1 teaspoon salt
1 teaspoon freshly ground black pepper
1 cup vegetable oil
4 large sweet potatoes (about 2 pounds), peeled and cut lengthwise into ⅛-inch-thick slices
2 tablespoons unsalted butter
4 bunches mustard greens (about 1½ pounds), rinsed
4 medium shallots, finely chopped
½ bunch fresh parsley, chopped (about 3 tablespoons)
1 sprig fresh thyme
2 cups Demi-glace (see page 202)

1. Slice the pork into ¼-inch-thick medallions (about 3 ounces each).
2. Place the pork in a large shallow dish. Add 3 cups of the oatmeal stout, the salt, and pepper. Cover with plastic wrap and marinate in the refrigerator for at least 4 hours or overnight.
3. Prepare the potatoes: Pour the oil into a deep-fat fryer or a heavy medium saucepan. Heat the oil over medium heat to 350°F. Carefully add the potatoes, several slices at a time into the heated oil, and cook for 4 minutes, until crispy. Using a slotted spoon or a French fry skimmer, remove the potatoes from the oil and place on paper towels to absorb any excess oil. Reserve and keep warm in a 300°F oven.
4. Remove the pork from the marinade; discard the marinade. Pat the pork dry with paper towels.
5. In a large skillet, cook the pork in the butter over high heat for 2 minutes on each side, until brown. Remove the pork from the skillet. Reserve and keep warm.
6. Reduce the heat to medium and add the mustard greens, shallots, parsley, and thyme. Sauté for 2 minutes, until wilted.
7. Add the remaining 1 cup oatmeal stout to deglaze the pan, loosening any browned bits on the bottom of the pan with a wooden spoon. Stir in the Demi-glace and cook over medium to high heat about 5 minutes, until the liquid is reduced by half.
8. To serve, arrange a bed of the mustard greens mixture in the center of each plate. Top with the pork medallions and the fried sweet potatoes.

Roasted Cornish Game Hen with Apricot Glaze

Cornish hens, a cross breed between White Rock and Cornish chickens, offer a delicate flavor to this easy to prepare dish. The eighteenth-century chef would have dried the apricots called for in this recipe—along with other seasonal fruits like pineapple, apple, and cherries—and store them for use during the winter.

Serves 4

Hens

4 Cornish game hens (1¼ to 1½ pounds each)
2 cloves garlic, chopped
2 tablespoons olive oil
1 tablespoon chopped fresh parsley
1 tablespoon chopped fresh basil
1 tablespoon chopped fresh rosemary
1 teaspoon ground black pepper
½ teaspoon salt

Apricot Glaze

½ cup dried apricots, chopped
½ cup dry sherry
½ yellow onion, sliced
1 tablespoon unsalted butter
1 teaspoon light brown sugar
1 teaspoon white vinegar
1 cup Chicken Stock (see page 199)
Salt and freshly ground black pepper

1. Prepare the Hens: Preheat the oven to 375°F.
2. Trim the excess fat from the hens and remove any inner organs.
3. Combine the garlic, oil, parsley, basil, rosemary, pepper, and salt in a small mixing bowl.
4. Place the hens, breast sides up, on a rack in a large, shallow baking pan. Rub the herb-oil mixture over the hens.
5. Roast for 1 to 1¼ hours, until golden brown and a meat thermometer inserted in a thigh muscle registers 185°F.
6. Prepare the Apricot Glaze: In a small bowl, soak the apricots in the sherry for 15 minutes.
7. In a medium saucepan, sauté the onion in the butter over medium heat about 5 minutes, until golden brown.
8. Add the apricot mixture and bring to a boil over high heat.
9. Stir in the brown sugar and vinegar until the sugar dissolves. Add the Chicken Stock.
10. Bring back to a boil and cook for 15 minutes, until the mixture is reduced by one third.
11. Season with salt and pepper to taste.
12. Serve the hens with the Apricot Glaze and, if desired, Rice Pilaf (see page 120) and Pumpkin Gratin (see page 107).

Rack of Lamb with Rosemary Au Jus

In colonial kitchens, this recipe would have been made with mutton (the meat of older sheep) because the young animals were raised to produce wool rather than for food. Today's diners would be put off by the strong flavor of mutton, hence, this adaptation.

Serves 4

Lamb
1 full rack of lamb without the back bone (about 2 pounds), frenched
 (see Chef's Note)
½ cup Dijon mustard
¾ cup coarsely chopped black walnuts

Jus
1 teaspoon chopped shallot
1 teaspoon unsalted butter
½ cup red burgundy wine
1½ cups Beef Stock (see page 198)
1 sprig fresh rosemary
Salt and freshly ground black pepper

Frenching is a process whereby the meat trimmings are removed from between the bones; any butcher should be familiar with the procedure.

1. Prepare the Lamb: Preheat the oven to 425°F.
2. Place the lamb in a shallow roasting pan. Roast for 20 minutes.
3. Remove the lamb from the oven. Reduce the oven temperature to 375°F.
4. With a brush, coat the lamb with the mustard. Sprinkle with the walnuts.
5. Roast the lamb about 10 minutes more, until a meat thermometer inserted in the center registers 140°F for medium-rare. Transfer the roast to a platter and allow to rest.
6. Prepare the Jus: In a medium saucepan, sauté the shallot in the butter over medium heat for 3 minutes, until translucent.
7. Add the red wine and cook for approximately 10 minutes, until the mixture is reduced by half.
8. Add the Beef Stock and rosemary and cook for 10 minutes, until the mixture is reduced by half again.
9. Season with salt and pepper to taste. If desired, remove the sprig of rosemary.
10. Cut the lamb into individual chops and serve with the Jus.

In the eighteenth century, dinner at City Tavern was usually served at the fashionable hour of 4 P.M. To maintain this tradition, today's City Tavern starts serving dinner at this hour.

Baked Veal Chop

English colonists were familiar with veal because in England, where pasture land was scarce, young calves were routinely slaughtered for meat. In America, grazing land was plentiful, and cows were prized for their dairy production, making eating veal a rarity usually reserved for holidays or special occasions. But at the upscale City Tavern, this treat could be enjoyed any time.

Serves 8

8 veal chops from the rack (10 to 12 ounces each), cut 1-inch thick
Salt and freshly ground black pepper
1 cup all-purpose flour
3 tablespoons vegetable oil
4 tablespoons unsalted butter
6 medium yellow onions, finely chopped
3 sprigs fresh thyme, leaves pulled
1 tablespoon chopped fresh cilantro
1 teaspoon salt
½ teaspoon freshly ground black pepper
1 cup grated Romano cheese
1 cup dry white wine
1 cup Chicken Stock (see page 199)
Fresh chives, chopped for garnish

1. Preheat the oven to 375°F.
2. Sprinkle the chops with salt and pepper. Place the flour in a medium shallow bowl. Dip each chop into the flour evenly to coat, shaking off any excess flour.
3. In a large skillet, cook half of the chops in the oil and 2 tablespoons of the butter over medium heat for 5 to 8 minutes on each side, until brown. Remove and reserve. Repeat with remaining chops.
4. Discard the butter from the skillet and add the remaining 2 tablespoons butter and the onions. Sauté for 3 minutes, until golden brown.
5. In a large baking dish, place half of the cooked onions. Place the veal chops on top of the onions. Add the thyme, cilantro, 1 teaspoon salt, and ½ teaspoon pepper.
6. Cover with the remaining onions and the Romano cheese.
7. Pour in the wine and Chicken Stock.
8. Bake about 20 minutes, until a meat thermometer inserted in the veal registers 140°F (for medium).
9. To serve, arrange the veal chops and onion mixture on a large platter and sprinkle with the chives.

Roasted Leg of Lamb

At the original City Tavern, large cuts of meat, such as leg of lamb, were reserved for bigger parties that were held for special occasions. This old time French recipe uses the juices of the lamb to flavor the potatoes during cooking. I adapted this recipe from one we served in my family's restaurant in Pforzheim.

Serves 8

4 to 7 pounds leg of lamb, boned, rolled, and tied
4 garlic cloves, cut into slivers
2 sprigs fresh thyme
8 tablespoons (1 stick) unsalted butter
5 large yellow onions, sliced
6 large russet potatoes (about 2 pounds), very thinly sliced
Salt and freshly ground black pepper
1 cup dry white wine
Fresh parsley, chopped, for garnish

1. Using a small paring knife, cut shallow slits in the lamb. Insert the garlic slivers into the slits.
2. Place the sprigs of thyme over the lamb, cover, and refrigerate for 4 to 8 hours, allowing the flavors to marry.
3. Preheat the oven to 450°F.
4. In a Dutch oven, cook the lamb on all sides in 4 tablespoons of the butter over high heat for 10 minutes, until brown.
5. Place the Dutch oven in the oven and roast for 30 minutes.
6. In a large skillet, sauté the onions in the remaining 4 tablespoons butter over medium heat for 5 minutes, until the onions are translucent.
7. Transfer the onions to a large baking dish. Add the potatoes and sprinkle with salt and pepper.
8. Place the lamb on top of the potato mixture and pour in the wine.
9. Roast about 30 minutes, until the wine has evaporated.
10. Reduce the oven temperature to 350°F and roast about 30 to 40 minutes more, until a meat thermometer inserted in the lamb registers 145° to 150°F (for medium-rare).
11. Remove the string from the lamb. To serve, cut the lamb into ¼-inch-thick slices. Arrange the potato mixture on a serving platter and top with the lamb slices.
12. Garnish with the chopped parsley.

Madeira Pork Roast

The average family in eighteenth-century Philadelphia rarely ate pork, or other meats—it was simply too expensive. But the Tavern always had meat on the menu, often with Madeira as an ingredient in an accompanying sauce or stew. Here, sweet Madeira pairs beautifully with pork, giving it a sweet and tangy flavor that intensifies during marinating. The cream finishes the sauce to a wonderful richness.

Overnight preparation recommended

Serves 8 to 10

6 to 8 pounds boneless pork top loin roast (two 4-pound loins which can be separate or tied)
2 cups sweet Madeira
7 medium yellow onions, sliced
8 garlic cloves, chopped
1 bay leaf
1 sprig fresh thyme
3 tablespoons Dijon mustard
Salt and freshly ground black pepper
2 cups red burgundy wine
7½ cups sliced mushrooms (about 1½ pounds)
2 cups Demi-glace (see page 202)
1 cup heavy cream
Scallions (green part only), chopped, for garnish

1. Place the roast in a large casserole dish. Add the Madeira, onions, garlic, bay leaf, and thyme.
2. Cover with plastic wrap and marinate in the refrigerator, turning the roast occasionally, at least 4 hours or overnight.
3. Preheat the oven to 375°F.
4. Remove the roast from the marinade and place in a large baking dish. Reserve the marinade.
5. Spread the roast with the mustard and sprinkle with salt and pepper.
6. Bake about 2 hours, until a meat thermometer inserted in the pork registers 155°F.
7. Pour the reserved marinade into a small saucepan and bring to a boil over high heat. Cook for 10 minutes, until reduced to about ¼ cup. Remove and discard the bay leaf. Remove from the heat and reserve.
8. Transfer the roast to a platter and cover with foil and let stand 15 minutes before carving (the meat's temperature will rise 5 degrees while standing). Discard any excess fat in the pan.
9. Add the red wine to deglaze the pan, loosening any browned bits on the bottom of the pan with a wooden spoon. Add the reduced marinade and cook for about 10 minutes, until the liquid is reduced by half.
10. Add the mushrooms, Demi-glace, and cream. Reduce the heat and simmer about 5 minutes, until the mushrooms are soft.
11. Season with salt and pepper to taste.
12. To serve, remove the string and slice the roast. Serve the sauce with meat and garnish with the scallions.

John Adams, while known for disapproving of culinary excess, was a man who enjoyed his Madeira. While attending one of many feasts associated with the first Continental Congress, he wrote "I drank Madeira at a great rate and found no inconvenience in it."

Beef and Morels

Morels would have arrived dried on ships from Europe—the same way we most frequently find them today. The morel is one of the best mushrooms, next to porcini, to preserve dried, a process which doesn't compromise the delicate mushroom's subtle, earthy flavor. This sophisticated dish shows off tender morels, with their delicate, earthy flavor, to perfection.

Overnight preparation recommended

Serves 6

3 pounds beef tenderloin, fat trimmed, sliced, and cut into 1-inch strips
2½ cups red burgundy wine
5 medium shallots, chopped
2 garlic cloves, chopped
1 tablespoon unsalted butter
¼ cup sour cream
¼ cup Dijon mustard
½ cup whole fresh morel mushrooms or ¼ cup dried morel mushrooms
½ bunch fresh parsley, chopped (about 3 tablespoons)
4 sprigs fresh thyme, leaves pulled
2 cups Demi-glace (see page 202)
Salt and freshly ground black pepper

1. Place the beef in a medium shallow dish. Add 1 cup of the wine, half of the shallots, and half of the garlic.
2. Cover with plastic wrap and marinate in the refrigerator, at least 4 hours or overnight.
3. Remove the beef from the marinade; discard the marinade. Pat the beef dry with paper towels. In a large skillet, sauté the remaining shallots and the remaining garlic in the butter over medium heat for 3 minutes, until golden brown.
4. Add one-fourth of the beef strips and sauté for 5 minutes, until brown. Repeat with remaining.
5. Add the remaining 1½ cups wine to deglaze the pan, loosening any browned bits on the bottom of the pan with a wooden spoon.
6. Stir in the sour cream and mustard. Stir in the morel mushrooms, parsley, and thyme. Reduce the heat and simmer for 2 to 3 minutes, until the cream and mustard are velvety.
7. Stir in the Demi-glace and simmer for 5 minutes, until Demi-glace comes to a boil.
8. Season with salt and pepper to taste.
9. If desired, serve with Homemade Egg Noodles (see page 126).

At City Tavern we marinate our meats overnight for culinary historic accuracy and flavor—a practice of necessity in the eighteenth century to flavor and tenderize lean, tough game and free-range beef.

Roast Turkey with Madeira Gravy

Turkey isn't reserved for Thanksgiving at the Tavern. Not a week goes by without our preparing three or four "Thanksgiving" feasts with all the trimmings. The secret to our delicious turkey is the marinating process. We place the herb mixture between the flesh and the skin, which intensifies the flavor.

Serves 8 to 10

1 whole turkey with giblets (12 to 14 pounds)
Salt and freshly ground black pepper
2 medium yellow onions, 1 of them quartered,
　the remaining onion coarsely chopped
¼ cup chopped fresh parsley
2 tablespoons chopped fresh thyme
2 tablespoons chopped fresh rosemary
2 medium shallots, finely chopped
1½ tablespoons olive oil
2 large carrots, chopped
2 celery ribs, chopped
3 cups Chicken Stock (see page 199)
¼ cup dry white wine
1 cup Madeira
1½ tablespoons cornstarch

Madeira's sweet and mellow flavor, not unlike sherry, beautifully enhances a turkey gravy—especially if you add Chestnut Stuffing (see page 122) to the mix.

1. Preheat the oven to 325°F. Set the oven rack to the bottom level.
2. In a large roasting pan, set a wire roasting rack sprayed with vegetable cooking spray.
3. Remove the giblets and neck and any visible fat from the turkey cavity and reserve for the giblet stock. Discard the liver.
4. Rinse the turkey inside and out with cold water and pat dry with paper towels.
5. Sprinkle the turkey cavity with salt and pepper.
6. Place the quartered onion in the cavity.
7. In a small bowl, combine the parsley, thyme, rosemary, shallots, and 1 tablespoon of the oil. Sprinkle with salt and a generous grinding of pepper.
8. With your fingers, separate the turkey skin from the breast meat, taking care not to tear the skin or pierce the meat.
9. Rub the herb mixture on the meat under the skin on each side of the breastbone.
10. If you aren't stuffing the turkey, tie the drumsticks together with kitchen string and twist the wing tips behind the back. Otherwise, see Step 14, Chestnut Stuffing, page 123.
11. Place the turkey, breast side up, in the prepared roasting pan.
12. Loosely cover the turkey with aluminum foil and roast for 2 hours.
13. While the turkey roasts, in a large saucepan, cook the coarsely chopped onion, the carrots, celery, and reserved giblets and neck in the remaining ½ tablespoon oil over medium heat, stirring frequently, about 15 minutes, until the giblets, onion, carrots, and celery are well browned.
14. Add the Chicken Stock and bring to a boil over high heat.
15. Reduce the heat to low, partially cover the pan, and simmer for 30 minutes.
16. Strain the giblet stock through a fine sieve into a medium bowl (you should have about 2 cups). Discard the giblets and vegetables. Cover and refrigerate the stock up to 6 hours, until ready to use.
17. Remove the foil from the turkey and roast about 1 or 1¾ hours more, or until a meat thermometer inserted in a thigh muscle registers 185°F. Baste with ½ cup of the Madeira wine every 15 minutes.

18. Transfer the turkey to a carving board.
19. Loosely cover the turkey with aluminum foil and let rest for 15 to 20 minutes before carving.
20. While the turkey rests, pour the drippings from the roasting pan through a fine sieve into a small bowl. Place the bowl in the freezer about 20 minutes to solidify the fat.
21. Meanwhile, set the roasting pan back on the stovetop over medium heat. Add the rest of the Madeira to deglaze the pan, scraping up any browned bits on the bottom of the pan with a wooden spoon. Cook about 1 minute, until it comes to boil. Strain the liquid through the fine sieve into a medium saucepan.
22. Skim the fat from the chilled pan and discard. Add the drippings to the saucepan. Add the reserved giblet stock. Bring to a simmer over medium heat.
23. In a small bowl, dissolve the cornstarch in 2 tablespoons cold water. Slowly add to the simmering mixture, whisking until the gravy thickens slightly.
24. Season with salt and pepper to taste.
25. Remove the string from the turkey and carve (see directions below).
26. Serve the turkey with the warm Madeira gravy.

CARVING A TURKEY

ONCE YOU LEARN A FEW BASIC CUTS, YOU'LL GET THE CARVING RIGHT, EVERY TIME.

1. Using a carving knife and fork, cut between the lower part of the breast and the thigh, pushing down until the leg joint separates.

2. Wiggle each leg to find the joint between the thigh and the drumstick and slice downward through the joint. Slice the meat off the bones.

3. Bend each wing to find the joint, then cut straight downward to remove the wing.

4. Make a long cut along one side of the breastbone. Carve the meat from the breast, working toward the first cut in smooth, even slices.

Salmon Corn Cakes

Seafood was abundant in the early colonies. These savory fish cakes, which use every last morsel of the fish, appealed to the colonists sense of frugality. They are more flavorful and more full textured than traditional crab cakes because they're made with fresh corn and bell pepper. I recommend serving them with Pickapeppa Rémoulade (see page 21). Prepared in smaller portions, they make an ideal appetizer.

Serves 4 for main course; 8 to 10 for appetizers

2 ears fresh white corn, kernels cut from cobs
6 cups Court Bouillon (see page 200)
1½ pounds fresh salmon fillets or trimmings, skinned and boned, ¾-inch thick
1 small yellow onion, finely chopped
1 large red bell pepper, finely chopped
1 large green bell pepper, finely chopped
2 eggs
¼ cup dry fine bread crumbs
¼ cup fresh lemon juice (about 1 large lemon)
½ bunch fresh dill, finely chopped (about 1 tablespoon)
Dash Worcestershire sauce
Dash hot pepper sauce
4 tablespoons unsalted butter

1. In a small saucepan, cook the corn kernels in enough boiling salted water to cover for 5 to 8 minutes, until tender. Do not overcook.
2. Drain and let cool.
3. In a medium saucepan, bring the Court Bouillon to a boil over high heat.
4. Add the salmon. Reduce the heat and simmer for 5 to 8 minutes, until the salmon is cooked and appears thoroughly light pink, not dark or translucent.
5. Drain the salmon. Transfer to a medium mixing bowl and let cool.
6. Break up the salmon into ¼-inch pieces. Add the cooked corn, the onion, red and green bell peppers, eggs, bread crumbs, lemon juice, half of the chopped dill, Worcestershire sauce, and pepper sauce. Mix well.
7. Preheat the oven to 350°F.
8. Using your hands, form the salmon mixture into 8 patties and place them on a baking sheet.
9. Refrigerate for 30 minutes.
10. In a large skillet, cook half of the salmon patties in the butter over medium heat for 2 minutes on each side, until brown.
11. Place the patties back on the baking sheet and bake about 10 minutes until golden brown.
12. To serve, place the salmon cakes on individual plates and garnish with the remaining dill.

Brook Trout with Black Walnuts

One of the fish most commonly enjoyed by the colonists, mild-tasting brook trout provides the perfect foil for the distinctive flavor of black walnuts used in this dish. With this great-tasting and quick recipe, you'll have dinner on the table in less than thirty minutes.

Serves 4

4 whole fresh trout (8 to 10 ounces each), heads, tails, and fins removed
1 cup all-purpose flour
½ cup vegetable oil
2 medium shallots, finely chopped
2 tablespoons unsalted butter
½ cup dry white wine
½ cup fresh lemon juice (about 2 large lemons)
¼ pound (1 stick) unsalted butter, cut into ½-inch pats
Salt and freshly ground black pepper
Fresh parsley, chopped, for garnish
¾ cup chopped black walnuts, for garnish

1. Preheat the oven to 350°F.
2. Place each trout on its back, cavity facing up, and remove the excess bones. Rinse the fish; pat dry.
3. Place the flour in a medium shallow bowl. Dip both sides of the trout into the flour.
4. In a large skillet, cook the trout in the oil over high heat for 2 minutes on each side, until golden brown.
5. Transfer the trout to a baking sheet. Bake for 3 to 4 minutes, until crisp.
6. Transfer to a serving platter. Keep warm.
7. In the same skillet, sauté the shallots in the 2 tablespoons butter over medium heat for 3 minutes, until golden brown.
8. Add the wine to deglaze the pan, loosening any browned bits on the bottom of the pan with a wooden spoon.
9. Add the lemon juice and bring to a boil over high heat. Add the butter pats one at a time, whisking with a wire whisk, until all of the butter is incorporated into the sauce.
10. Season with salt and pepper to taste.
11. To serve, spoon the sauce over the trout. Garnish with the parsley and walnuts.

Roasted Rib Eye on Yorkshire Pancakes with Creamed Horseradish Sauce

Before we serve this British specialty to our guests, the rib eye must be marinated for no less than two days, imbuing it with great flavor. In colonial days, the roast would have been served with Yorkshire pudding, but ours is served on Yorkshire Pancakes, which I prefer to the traditional pudding. In many restaurants, when you order Yorkshire pudding, you are served a popover that is virtually flavorless. Our pancakes are prepared the same way the English have been doing it for centuries, with one exception: we omit the kidney fat traditionally used for flavor. For an authentic touch, serve the roast with Creamed Horseradish Sauce.

Overnight preparation required

Serves 12

Roast
chopped fresh parsley
2 tablespoons chopped fresh thyme
2 tablespoons chopped fresh rosemary
2 medium shallots, finely chopped
1½ tablespoons olive oil
1 beef rib eye roast (4 to 6 pounds)
Fresh watercress, for garnish

Creamed Horseradish Sauce Makes 1 cup sauce
¾ cup sour cream
¼ cup grated fresh horseradish
1 teaspoon chopped fresh parsley
1 teaspoon fresh lemon juice, strained
½ teaspoon sweet paprika
Salt and freshly ground white pepper

Yorkshire Pancakes Makes 6 large pancakes
2 cups all-purpose flour
1½ cups whole milk
1 cup Beef Stock (see page 198)
4 eggs
2 teaspoons chopped fresh parsley
2 teaspoons chopped fresh rosemary
1 teaspoon ground nutmeg
1 teaspoon chopped shallot
1 teaspoon chopped garlic
¼ pound (1 stick) unsalted butter
Salt and freshly ground black pepper

1. The day before serving, marinate the Roast: prepare the Herb Rub by thoroughly combining the parsley, thyme, rosemary, shallots, and olive oil in a small mixing bowl. Rub the mixture over the beef. Place the meat in a deep dish and refrigerate overnight.
2. Preheat the oven to 500°F.
3. Place a rack in a roasting pan and transfer the beef, fat side up, to the rack. Roast for 15 minutes.
4. Reduce the oven temperature to 350°F.

5. Roast about 1½ to 2 hours more until a meat thermometer inserted in the center registers 140°F for rare (160°F for medium).
6. Prepare the Creamed Horseradish Sauce: In a small mixing bowl, combine the sour cream, horseradish, parsley, lemon juice, and paprika.
7. Thoroughly whisk together. Season with salt and pepper to taste.
8. Cover with plastic wrap and refrigerate for at least 1 hour.
9. Prepare the Yorkshire Pancakes: in a medium mixing bowl, combine the flour, milk, Beef Stock, eggs, parsley, rosemary, nutmeg, shallots, and garlic.
10. Whisk until there are no lumps.
11. For each pancake, in a 7-inch nonstick skillet, add a small amount of the butter to coat the pan and ladle ½ cup of the batter into the skillet.
12. Cook for 3 minutes on each side, until brown. Transfer the pancakes to a plate and keep warm.
13. Remove the beef from the oven and let rest for 15 minutes. Cut the beef into 1½-inch-thick slices.
14. Cut each pancake in half.
15. To serve, place the beef slices on the pancake halves.
16. Serve with the Creamed Horseradish Sauce. Garnish with the watercress.

From 1790 to 1800, after the Revolution, Philadelphia glittered as the new nation's capital, the center of wealth, intellect, and power for America. Balls, parties, and social affairs—many attended by high-ranking visitors from Europe and aristocratic refugees of the revolution in France and the French West Indies— transformed the city into a cosmopolitan scene, with drinking and dining elevated to the loftiest heights.

Baked Swordfish and Sorrel

Because it has been overfished in many waters, numerous restaurants and consumers are boycotting swordfish. I am including this recipe, however, because swordfish was plentiful in colonial days and City Tavern would have been the place to enjoy a sophisticated dish like this one. If you can't find (or don't want to use) swordfish, red snapper or grouper makes an ideal substitute. Sorrel, which can refer to any of several varieties of perennial herbs belonging to the buckwheat family, has grown wild for centuries in North America. Looking very much like spinach, fresh sorrel is at its peak in the spring. Be sure to choose young, mild sorrel for the cream sauce—although you can substitute spinach if you like.

Serves 8

8 fresh swordfish steaks (8 to 10 ounces each), 1 inch thick
2 bay leaves
1 tablespoon unsalted butter
Salt and freshly ground white pepper
½ cup dry sherry
1 cup heavy cream
1 cup shredded fresh sorrel

1. Preheat the oven to 375°F.
2. Place the fish in a large baking dish and place the bay leaves on top of the fish.
3. Dot the fish with the butter.
4. Bake about 10 minutes, until a white film, like the texture of cooked egg white, appears on top. Remove from the oven. Remove and discard the bay leaves and sprinkle the fish with salt and pepper. Keep warm.
5. Pour the sherry into a medium saucepan, and heat over high heat until the sherry comes to a boil.
6. Add the cream and cook over medium heat, stirring frequently, about 5 minutes, until the sauce thickens and coats the back of a spoon.
7. Stir in the sorrel and bring to a boil over medium heat. Remove from the heat.
8. To serve, spoon the sauce over the fish.

Salmon with Fresh Mint and Tomatoes

In colonial days—before pollution and over-fishing decimated the East Coast catch—salmon traveled all the way up the Delaware River to Philadelphia. This easy access to salmon explains why it was prepared in so many ways at the original City Tavern. This elegant dish is baked in parchment paper and is perfect for a refreshing summer supper. I like to plate it with the Fennel Purée (see page 105) and Herbed Barley (see page 118), which can be served chilled or warm.

Serves 8

3 cups Court Bouillon (see page 200)
8 skinless salmon fillets (8 to 10 ounces each)
8 large ripe tomatoes (about 2½ pounds), thickly sliced
2 cups loosely packed fresh mint leaves
¼ teaspoon chopped fresh cilantro
Salt and freshly ground black pepper
Fresh chives, finely chopped
1½ cups Sherry Cream Sauce (see page 203)

1. Preheat the oven to 350°F. Cut parchment paper into eight 10-inch squares.
2. In a large skillet, bring the Court Bouillon to a boil over high heat. Reduce the heat to low. Add the salmon and cook about 5 minutes, until firm to the touch.
3. Remove the salmon from the skillet. Let cool and reserve.
4. Place the parchment paper squares on a greased baking sheet.
5. On each square, place 3 tomato slices, a few mint leaves, and a cooked salmon fillet.
6. Sprinkle with the cilantro and salt and pepper to taste. Add the remaining tomato slices and mint leaves.
7. Fold each square over diagonally to form a triangle, leaving as much space inside as possible.
8. Bake about 15 minutes, until the paper is brown.
9. Cut open the pouches and sprinkle the salmon with cilantro.
10. Remove salmon. Pour Sherry Cream Sauce over and garnish with cilantro.

Ale–Braised Mallard Duck Sausage

Although the early American cooks made their own sausage, most of us don't have the time or energy to do the same. Instead, I've found a wonderful source for mail ordering duck sausages (see Resources, page 211). You can substitute kielbasa or any garlic-flavored pork sausage (except Italian-style) for the duck sausage. I serve this distinctive ale-seasoned sausage dish with Potato Dumplings (see page 127) and Pennsylvania Dutch-Style Sauerkraut (see page 109).

Serves 4

8 cooked purchased mallard duck sausages (about 2 pounds)
2 large yellow onions, thinly sliced
2 medium shallots, chopped
2 garlic cloves, chopped
2 tablespoons unsalted butter
4 cups dark ale
2 teaspoons Dijon mustard
1 cup Demi-glace (see page 202)
Salt and freshly ground black pepper

1. Preheat the oven to 350°F.
2. With a small paring knife, make shallow, diagonal cuts in the sausage.
3. Place the sausage in a shallow baking pan and bake about 5 minutes, until brown. Remove from the oven and reserve.
4. In a large skillet, cook the onions, shallots, and garlic in the butter over high heat for 3 minutes, until golden.
5. Add the precooked duck sausage.
6. Add the ale to deglaze the pan, loosening any browned bits on the bottom of the pan with a wooden spoon. Cook over medium heat about 10 minutes, until the ale is reduced so it just coats the bottom of the pan.
7. Transfer the sausage to a serving platter and keep warm.
8. Increase the heat to high and stir the Demi-glace and mustard into the onion mixture. Cook about 5 to 8 minutes, until the mixture is reduced by half. Season with salt and pepper to taste.
9. Spoon the onion mixture over the sausage and serve, if desired, with the Potato Dumplings and Sauerkraut.

Stews, Ragoûts, and Savory Pies

Stews, ragoûts, and hearty pies were dishes that crossed cultural and economic borders in colonial days. Teamed with a slab of homemade bread, stick-to-your-ribs "spoonfood"—a term which colonists used to describe such hearty stews and casseroles—made a meal fit for a peasant or a president. Because City Tavern was the finest establishment of the era, the stews, ragoûts, and pies it offered were a step up in sophistication from the versions made at humbler inns or in home kitchens.

Pork Ragoût

Pork was a popular meat in early American days—as it is today—and not one scrap of the animal was ever wasted. Ragoût is traditionally prepared with a bone-in shoulder, but using a boneless one makes preparation and serving easier for today's busy cook.

Serves 8

5 pounds boneless pork shoulder, cut into 2-inch cubes
3 tablespoons olive oil
2 tablespoons unsalted butter
5 large white onions, chopped
9 slices lean bacon, chopped
3 garlic cloves, finely chopped
3 cups red burgundy wine
1 teaspoon dried rubbed sage
1 teaspoon Hungarian paprika
2 sprigs fresh thyme
2 bay leaves
1 tablespoon arrowroot or 2¼ teaspoons cornstarch (see Chef's Note)
Salt and freshly ground black pepper
Fresh chives, finely chopped, for garnish

1. In a medium stockpot, cook the pork cubes in the oil and butter over high heat, stirring frequently, about 5 minutes, until brown. Reduce the heat to medium.
2. Add the onions, bacon, and garlic and sauté, stirring frequently, about 10 minutes more, until the juices are reduced.
3. Remove the pork mixture from the pan and drain.
4. Add 2¾ cups of the wine to deglaze the pan, loosening any browned bits on the bottom of the pan with a wooden spoon.
5. Add the pork mixture, sage, paprika, thyme, and bay leaves.
6. Bring to a boil over high heat. Reduce the heat to low, cover, and simmer about 1 hour, until thickened. Remove and discard the bay leaves.
7. In a small mixing bowl, whisk together the remaining ¼ cup wine and the arrowroot until velvety smooth. Slowly stir the mixture into the ragoût.
8. Simmer about 5 minutes more, until the ragoût thickens.
9. Season with salt and pepper to taste.
10. Serve in a deep platter or large serving bowl. Garnish with the chives.

Chef's Notes

• *This ragoût is even more flavorful when made with mushrooms, such as chanterelles or cèpes. Simply sauté the mushrooms and add them to the stew prior to stirring in the arrowroot mixture.*

• *Arrowroot, a thickener commonly used by colonial cooks, is a delicate starch obtained from the West Indian plant of the same name. Cornstarch makes an ideal substitute. Note: 2¼ teaspoons of cornstarch is equivalent to 1 tablespoon of arrowroot.*

Lamb Stew

In the eighteenth century, this stew would have been made with goat or mutton, because young lambs were rarely sacrificed. As with all dishes, be sure to use only fresh garlic. To my taste, jarred chopped garlic lacks the flavor of the real thing. If desired, serve this thyme-accented stew with Herbed Barley (see page 118) or Homemade Egg Noodles (see page 126).

Overnight preparation recommended

Serves 8

5 pounds boneless lamb shoulder, cut into 2-inch cubes
1 large carrot, thinly sliced
1 large onion, chopped
3 garlic cloves, chopped
3 bay leaves
1 large sprig fresh thyme
⅛ teaspoon cayenne
4 cups (32 ounces) red burgundy wine
4 tablespoons unsalted butter
2 medium white onions, chopped
3 garlic cloves, chopped
Salt and freshly ground black pepper
Fresh parsley, chopped, for garnish

This stew also is delicious curried— add about 1 teaspoon curry powder to the marinade and then another teaspoon when you boil the marinade.

1. To marinate the lamb, in a large bowl or casserole dish, combine the lamb cubes, carrot, onion, garlic, bay leaves, thyme, and cayenne.
2. Pour the wine over the mixture. Cover with plastic wrap and marinate in the refrigerator, stirring occasionally, at least 6 hours or overnight.
3. To prepare the stew, remove the lamb cubes from the marinade, reserving the marinade. Pat the lamb dry with paper towels.
4. In a large Dutch oven, sauté the lamb in the butter over high heat for 8 to 10 minutes, until the lamb is brown and juices are reduced.
5. Reduce the heat to medium and add the onions and garlic. Cook, stirring frequently, about 10 minutes, until the onions are translucent.
6. Add the reserved marinade and bring the mixture to a boil over high heat. Reduce the heat to low. Cover and cook, stirring frequently, for 1½ to 2 hours, until the lamb no longer appears pink.
7. Before serving, discard the bay leaves and sprig of thyme. Season with salt and pepper to taste.
8. Serve in a large serving bowl or deep platter. Garnish with the chopped parsley.

Tavern Cassoulet

This traditional French dish—minus the fresh tomato—could have been prepared at the original City Tavern any time of year, with many variations of ingredients. Today, we frequently offer this dish as a special, and it always disappears.

Overnight preparation recommended

Serves 4

1 pound dried navy beans
½ cup vegetable oil
1 pound boneless pork shoulder, fat trimmed and cut into 1-inch cubes
12 ounces uncooked garlic sausage in 2-inch links
4 duck legs (about 2 pounds)
1 medium onion, diced
2 cups (16 ounces) red burgundy wine
16 cups (4 quarts) Beef Stock (see page 198)
2 plum tomatoes, seeded and chopped
1 teaspoon tomato paste
2 sprigs fresh thyme, chopped (about 1 tablespoon)
1 bay leaf
2 garlic cloves, chopped
Salt and freshly ground black pepper
Fresh parsley, chopped, for garnish
2 tablespoons dry bread crumbs, for garnish

1. Pre-soak the beans (see Chef's Note, page 117). Drain and place in a small bowl. Reserve.
2. Preheat the oven to 425°F.
3. Heat a large ovenproof skillet over high heat. Add the oil.
4. Add the pork, sausage, and duck legs and cook for 3 minutes on each side, until uniformly browned.
5. Carefully remove and discard the excess fat; remove the skillet from the heat. Remove the meat from the pan.
6. In the same skillet, sauté the onion over high heat for 5 minutes, until translucent.
7. Add the wine to deglaze the pan, loosening any browned bits on the bottom of the skillet with a wooden spoon. Bring to a boil over high heat.
8. Add the reserved beans, Beef Stock, tomatoes, tomato paste, thyme, bay leaf, and garlic and bring back to a boil. Add the cooked, reserved meats to the skillet.
9. Cover the skillet and bake for 40 to 50 minutes, until all of the liquid is absorbed by the mixture. Remove and discard bay leaf. Season with salt and pepper to taste.
10. To serve, transfer the cassoulet to a serving platter. Garnish with the chopped parsley and bread crumbs.

Braised Turkey

The famous French gastronome Anthelme Brillat-Savarin (1755–1826) said in his book, *Art of Dining*, that turkey is one of the greatest culinary gifts that the Old World received from the colonies. And this simple, but tasty, turkey recipe proves the point. It is a marriage of European technique and New World ingredients. For ease of preparation, I recommend having your butcher cut the turkey into pieces for you—the backbone is strong and difficult to cut through. Or, you could simply use turkey thighs, which are readily available at the grocery store. This dish is excellent served with Smashed Red Potatoes (see page 112) and Brussels Sprouts (see page 104).

Serves 8

1 whole turkey (12 to 14 pounds), cut into 16 pieces
3 tablespoons vegetable oil
3 tablespoons unsalted butter
6 medium white onions, chopped
4 slices lean bacon, chopped
3 garlic cloves, chopped
2 tablespoons all-purpose flour
2 to 3 bottles (750 ml each) red burgundy wine (see Chef's Note)
2 tablespoons salt
1½ tablespoons freshly ground black pepper
2 bay leaves
1 large sprig fresh thyme
1 teaspoon dried rubbed sage
Salt and freshly ground black pepper
3 tablespoons chopped fresh tarragon, for garnish

Chef's Note

The amount of wine you'll use will vary, depending on how the turkey is cut (see Step 4).

1. Preheat the oven to 350°F.
2. In an 8-quart roasting pan, cook the turkey pieces on all sides in the oil and butter over high heat for 5 minutes, until golden brown.
3. Add the onions, bacon, and garlic and cook, stirring frequently, about 5 minutes, or until golden brown.
4. Reduce the heat to medium. Sprinkle the turkey with flour and add enough wine to cover the turkey pieces. Bring to a boil over high heat. Stir frequently to prevent sticking.
5. Add the 2 tablespoons salt, 1½ tablespoons pepper, bay leaves, thyme, and sage.
6. Cover the pan and bake about 1½ hours, until the meat no longer appears pink and a thermometer inserted in the center of the turkey registers at least 185°F.
7. Remove the turkey from the pan and arrange on a serving platter. Cover with foil and keep warm.
8. Discard the bay leaves and sprig of thyme. Strain the sauce though a fine wire sieve or cheesecloth into a large saucepan and boil over high heat for about 5 minutes, until the sauce is reduced by half. Season with salt and pepper to taste.
9. To serve, pour the sauce over the turkey pieces and garnish with the tarragon.

Veal Fricassée (Stew)

This slow-cooked French-inspired white stew, which is a slight variation of the one found in *Martha Washington's Booke of Cookery*, renders veal shoulder completely tender. This recipe also works well with chicken or turkey thighs. Serve it with Rice Pilaf (see page 120) or Homemade Egg Noodles (see page 126).

Serves 8

5 pounds boneless veal shoulder, cut into 2-inch cubes
8 cups (32 ounces) Chardonnay or other dry white wine
8 cups (2 quarts) water
4 large carrots, cut into cubes
4 leeks (white part only), well rinsed and chopped
2 celery ribs, chopped
2 large yellow onions, chopped
1 garlic clove, chopped
1 Bouquet Garni (see page 201)
3 tablespoons salt
1½ teaspoons freshly ground white pepper
1 cup all-purpose flour
6 tablespoons unsalted butter, at room temperature
½ cup heavy cream
4 egg yolks, lightly beaten
¼ cup fresh lemon juice (about 2 large lemons), strained
Salt and freshly ground black pepper
¼ cup small capers, drained
Fresh parsley, chopped, for garnish

1. Place the veal cubes into a medium stockpot and add wine and water.
2. Bring to a boil over high heat, skimming off and discarding any foam that rises to the surface. Add the carrots, leeks, celery, onions, garlic, Bouquet Garni, 3 tablespoons salt, and 1½ teaspoons pepper. Bring back to a boil over high heat.
3. Reduce the heat and let simmer for 1 hour.
4. Strain the stock through a fine wire sieve or cheesecloth into a large bowl. Remove the veal and reserve. Discard the vegetables and Bouquet Garni. Return the stock to the stockpot. Bring to a boil over high heat and cook for about 15 minutes, until reduced by half.
5. In a small bowl, mix the flour and butter into a paste.
6. Slowly whisk the paste into the stock.
7. Reduce the heat and simmer, stirring continuously, for 15 minutes more, until velvety.
8. Strain the stock again and return to the stockpot. Add the reserved veal. Do not boil.
9. In a small bowl, whisk together the heavy cream and egg yolks.
10. Slowly fold the egg yolk mixture into the stew. Simmer over low heat for 3 minutes, until heated through. (Do not allow to boil; this may cause the egg yolks to separate.)
11. Stir in the lemon juice and season with salt and pepper to taste.
12. To serve, garnish with the capers and chopped parsley.

Chicken Ragoût

This dish is similar to coq au vin, a traditional recipe that came across the ocean with the French innkeepers and chefs who settled in the New World. Although we make this entrée with chicken, the recipe will work with most game birds. It is ideal for entertaining because is can be prepared well in advance. If you like, serve it with Sweet and Sour Red Cabbage (see page 108) and Herbed Spaetzle (see page 125).

Serves 6

6 cups (48 ounces) red burgundy wine
24 small pearl onions, peeled
6 tablespoons unsalted butter
1 teaspoon granulated sugar
Salt
9 slices lean bacon, chopped
8 tablespoons olive oil
5½ cups button mushrooms (about 1 pound), quartered
2 cups all-purpose flour
2 tablespoons salt
1 teaspoon freshly ground black pepper
3 fryer chickens (2½ pounds each), cut into 8 pieces
2 large onions, finely chopped
2 garlic cloves, finely chopped
3 large carrots, chopped
2 bay leaves
2 sprigs fresh thyme
Fresh parsley, chopped, for garnish

The neatest and most efficient way I've found to flour chicken pieces is to put the flour and seasonings into a clean paper bag, add the chicken pieces one at a time, and shake to coat the chicken evenly.

1. Pour the wine into a large saucepan. Bring to a boil over high heat and cook about 15 minutes, until the mixture is reduced by 2 cups, leaving 4 cups remaining. Remove from the heat and reserve.
2. Place the pearl onions in a small saucepan. Add 2 tablespoons of the butter, sugar, salt, and enough water to cover the mixture. Bring to a boil over high heat. Reduce the heat and simmer about 10 minutes, until the pearl onions are tender.
3. Remove the onion mixture from the heat, drain, and reserve.
4. In a large skillet, sauté the bacon in 2 tablespoons of the oil over high heat for 2 minutes, until crisp.
5. Remove the bacon from the skillet and reserve (do not drain the bacon drippings from the skillet).
6. In the same skillet, sauté the mushrooms in the reserved bacon drippings for 5 minutes, until brown. Transfer the mushrooms to a platter and reserve.
7. In a large paper bag, mix the flour, 2 tablespoons salt, and pepper (see Chef's Note). Evenly coat the chicken with the flour mixture, shaking off excess mixture.
8. In the same skillet, cook the floured chicken pieces on all sides in the remaining 4 tablespoons of the butter and 6 tablespoons of the oil over medium heat for 5 minutes, until brown.
9. Add the chopped onions and garlic and cook, stirring frequently, about 20 minutes, until the juices are reduced.

10. Pour the 4 cups of reduced wine over the chicken.

11. Add the carrots, bay leaves, and thyme. Bring to a boil over high heat. Reduce the heat, cover, and simmer about 25 minutes, until the chicken no longer looks pink.

12. Add the reserved pearl onions, bacon, and mushrooms and simmer for 5 to 10 minutes more, until all of the ingredients are heated through.

13. Remove and discard the bay leaves and the sprigs of thyme. Season with salt and pepper to taste.

14. Serve in a large serving bowl or on a platter. Garnish with the chopped parsley.

Braised Rabbit Legs

The eighteenth-century Pennsylvania woods were rich with all kinds of small game, including wild rabbits. I can imagine a skillful hunter carrying a day's kill of rabbits and game birds, tied to a stick, to peddle to the City Tavern chef, who was almost always in the market to buy. If you're not familiar with rabbit, what they say is true—it really does taste like chicken—a cross between dark and white meat with a slightly more delicate flavor. Rabbit embraces the flavor of a sauce, which is why marinating is so important.

Overnight preparation recommended

Serves 8

5 pounds domestic rabbit legs, skinned
3 cups red burgundy wine
½ cup vegetable oil
4 tablespoons unsalted butter
4 celery ribs, chopped
2 carrots, chopped
1 large onion, chopped
3 garlic cloves, chopped
6 cups Demi-glace (see page 202)
½ bunch fresh parsley (about 3 tablespoons), chopped
1 bay leaf
1 sprig fresh thyme, leaves pulled and chopped
2 medium zucchini, chopped
2 medium yellow squash, chopped
½ small head red cabbage (about 1 cup), shredded
1 cup button mushrooms (4 ounces), sliced
2 large plum tomatoes, seeded and chopped
Salt and freshly ground black pepper

The legs are the only meaty cut of the rabbit. Rabbit legs are available at any specialty butcher shop or by mail order (see Resources, page 211).

1. Cut each rabbit leg in half at the joint.
2. Place the rabbit pieces in a medium bowl and add 2 cups of the wine. Cover with plastic wrap and marinate in the refrigerator, at least 4 hours or overnight.
3. Remove the rabbit from the wine; discard the wine. Pat the rabbit dry with paper towels.
4. In a large skillet, cook the rabbit on all sides in the oil and 2 tablespoons of the butter over high heat for 3 minutes, until brown. Reduce the heat to medium.
5. Add the celery, carrots, onions, and garlic and sauté for 5 to 8 minutes, until the vegetables are tender.
6. Add the remaining 1 cup wine and the bay leaf.
7. Add the Demi-glace, parsley, and chopped thyme.
8. Bring to a boil over high heat. Reduce the heat and simmer about 20 minutes, until the rabbit is tender and no longer appears pink. Remove from the heat and set aside.
9. In another large skillet, sauté the zucchini, yellow squash, and red cabbage in the remaining 2 tablespoons butter over medium heat for 5 minutes, until tender.
10. Stir in the mushrooms and tomatoes and cook for 5 minutes, until the mushrooms are soft.
11. Add the rabbit mixture to the vegetables and mix well. Simmer for 5 to 10 minutes, until all of the ingredients are heated through. Season with salt and pepper to taste.
12. Serve on a large platter.

Tavern Lobster Pie

Up until the end of the nineteenth century, lobster was so plentiful that it was typically used for fish bait. At the Tavern we call this irresistible pie "lazy man's lobster," because all our customers have to do is enjoy it.

Serves 6

Lobster Sauce
2 tablespoons shallots, peeled and thinly sliced
1 teaspoon butter
1 cup dry sherry
1 tablespoon tomato paste
4 cups (1 quart) Lobster Stock (see page 200)
1 cup heavy cream
4 tablespoons unsalted butter
¼ cup all-purpose flour
1 tablespoon chopped fresh parsley, for serving
Salt and freshly ground white pepper

3 pounds Quick Puff Pastry (see page 207) or purchased puff pastry
1 egg, lightly beaten with 1 teaspoon water

Lobster Filling
6 pounds lobster tail meat, split in half
18 jumbo shrimp (about 1¼ pounds), peeled and deveined
1 cup sliced button mushrooms
1 tablespoon unsalted butter
½ cup dry sherry
Salt and freshly ground black pepper

1. Prepare the Lobster Sauce: In a 4-quart saucepan, sauté the shallots in the 1 teaspoon butter until brown.
2. Add the sherry and bring to a boil. Continue cooking until the liquid is reduced by half.
3. Stir in the Lobster Stock, bring back to a boil.
4. Stir in the heavy cream, bring back to a boil. Reduce the heat to let simmer.
5. In a separate small saucepan, melt the 4 tablespoons butter, the tomato paste, and slowly stir in the flour until a smooth paste. Cook over medium heat until the roux mixture bubbles. Remove from the heat and slowly whisk into the sherry-stock mixture.
6. Return to the heat and cook over medium until the sauce starts to thicken, about 2 minutes. Add the parsley and season to taste with salt and pepper. Reserve.
7. Prepare the Lobster Filling: Preheat the oven to 450°F.
8. In a large skillet, sauté the lobster meat, shrimp, and mushrooms in the butter over medium heat for 5 minutes, until the mushrooms are soft and the lobster and shrimp are white.
9. Add the sherry to deglaze the pan, loosening any browned bits on the bottom of the pan with a wooden spoon.
10. Divide the Lobster Filling among six 14- to 16-ounce au gratin or casserole dishes. Divide the reserved Lobster Sauce among the six dishes. (The sauce should cover the filling.)
11. On a lightly floured surface, roll out the Quick Puff Pastry to ⅛-inch thickness. Cut out 6 circles allowing 1-inch overhang and place on top of the au gratin dishes. Crimp pastry to edge of dishes, prick the dough with fork to allow steam to escape, and brush with the egg-water wash.
12. Bake for 12 minutes, until the edges of the pastry are brown and the centers are golden brown.

Ham and Veal Pie

Meat pies, such as this one, were common on sixteenth- and seventeenth-century tables. If the average colonial housewife were to make this dish, she most likely would have doubled the amount of ham, and omitted the veal—which was a rare commodity in those days. Savory pies were popular because they could be prepared ahead and they offered the cook yet another way to use leftover meat. This recipe works as well cold as it does straight from the oven. Serve it with Apple Walnut Salad (see page 52).

Overnight preparation recommended

Serves 8

1 pound country-style ham, chopped
1 pound boneless veal shoulder roast, chopped
4 medium white onions, sliced
1 cup dry white wine
½ cup brandy
4 garlic cloves, chopped
3 sprigs fresh thyme
2 bay leaves
12 ounces Pâte Brisée (see page 206)
2 bunches fresh parsley, finely chopped (about ¾ cup)
1 tablespoon salt
1½ teaspoon freshly ground black pepper
1 egg yolk, lightly beaten with 1 tablespoon water

1. In a shallow, medium bowl, combine the ham, veal, onions, wine, brandy, garlic, thyme, and bay leaves. Cover and marinate in the refrigerator at least 6 hours, or overnight.
2. Preheat the oven to 400°F.
3. Divide the prepared Pâte Brisée Dough in half. On a lightly floured surface, roll out half of the dough as thinly as possible (⅛-inch thick) and drape over the bottom and side of a buttered 9-inch pie pan.
4. Strain the ham mixture through a fine wire sieve or cheesecloth draining the marinade into another container. Transfer the meat and onions to a medium bowl and reserve. Discard the bay leaves. Reserve the marinade.
5. Coarsely chop the meat and onions in a food processor or by hand. Return the chopped meat and onions into the bowl.
6. Add the parsley, salt, and pepper to the meat and onions and mix well. Place heaping spoonfuls, about ¼ inch apart, in the dough-lined pie pan.
7. Roll out the remaining dough and cover the top of the pie. Crimp the edges of the pastry with moistened fingers.
8. With kitchen scissors or a knife, cut a 2-inch hole in the center of the top pastry.
9. To make a "chimney," roll a 6 x 2-inch piece of parchment paper into a cylinder about 2 inches in diameter. Insert the chimney into the hole at least ¼-inch deep.
10. In a medium skillet, bring the reserved marinade to a boil over high heat and cook until it's reduced to about ¼ cup. Reserve.
11. Brush the top and edges of the pastry with the egg yolk mixture and bake about 12 minutes, until golden brown.

Chef's Note

If you want to serve this meat pie cold, to enjoy for a summer supper or take to a picnic, do not remove the chimney after the pie has been cooked. Instead, add one packet of unflavored gelatin to a ¼ cup of cooled reserved wine mixture and stir to dissolve. While the pie is still warm—but not hot—pour the gelatin-wine mixture into the chimney. Refrigerate for 2 hours before cutting.

12. Reduce the oven temperature to 300°F and bake about 20 minutes, until the meat mixture reaches 190°F.

13. Remove the pie from the oven and pour the reserved reduced wine into the pie through the chimney.

14. Return the pie to the oven and bake about 10 minutes more, until the wine mixture has been absorbed.

15. To serve, remove the chimney and let the pie cool on a wire cooling rack for 10 to 15 minutes, until it's warm but not hot.

The main difference between dining at City Tavern today, and dining there in the 1770s, is that women and children are now allowed to dine in public. In the eighteenth century, the very idea of a woman eating in public was scandalous. Although women did attend the balls held in the Long Room, the second largest ballroom in the nation (the largest was in Independence Hall, just blocks away), they were confined to the two or three upstairs guest rooms, should they ever want to eat.

Goose and Turnips

Long ago, wild geese were plentiful in the Colonies and were prized for their hearty flavor and copious layer of fat. Today, they are farm-raised and are not as popular as chicken because they are so fatty. If you want to try this recipe with a goose, ask your butcher to cut it into 16 pieces. Duck, chicken, or turkey thighs also can be substituted, although the flavor won't be quite the same. This dish is excellent served with Potato Dumplings (see page 127).

Serves 8

1 domestic goose (8 to 10 pounds), cut into 16 pieces
3 large white onions, sliced
9 slices lean bacon, chopped
3 garlic cloves, chopped
2 tablespoons unsalted butter
1 tablespoon vegetable oil
2 tablespoons all-purpose flour
8 cups (2 quarts) Chicken Stock (see page 199)
1 cup dry white wine
2 bunches scallions, green and white parts chopped separately,
    greens reserved for garnish
1 bunch fresh parsley, chopped (about 6 tablespoons)
2 bay leaves
10 small turnips (about 2 pounds), peeled and quartered (see Chef's Note)
Salt and freshly ground black pepper

All varieties of turnips do not cook at the same rate, test them often with a fork to avoid overcooking.

1. Trim all excess fat from the goose pieces.
2. In a small skillet, sauté the onions, bacon, and garlic in the butter and oil over medium heat about 3 minutes, until golden brown. Reserve.
3. In a large Dutch oven, cook the goose pieces on all sides in the oil over medium heat for 10 minutes, until brown. Sprinkle the flour over the goose and cook for 3 to 5 minutes more, until the juices are thickened.
4. Add the cooked bacon mixture, Chicken Stock, wine, chopped scallion whites, parsley, and bay leaves. Bring to a boil over high heat.
5. Reduce the heat, cover, and simmer for 40 minutes.
6. Add the turnips and simmer, covered, about 20 minutes more, until the vegetables are fork-tender. Season with salt and pepper to taste. Remove and discard the bay leaves.
7. To serve, place the goose pieces on a large platter and arrange the turnip mixture around the goose. Garnish with the reserved chopped scallion greens.

Traditional Beef Stew

Even grass-fed beef, which tended to be lean and tough, turned buttery tender when stewed for hours over the colonial hearth. The sky's the limit with this basic beef stew recipe! You can vary it by adding mushrooms, pearl onions, spring vegetables—whatever is in season. A sharp Hungarian paprika or a teaspoon of hot red pepper flakes added at Step 7 gives punch to this dish. To make the stew truly authentic, I recommend adding freshly ground allspice. A small coffee grinder grinds the spice nicely.

Overnight preparation required

Serves 8 to 10

5 pounds boneless beef chuck, cut into 2-inch cubes
6 cups (48 ounces) red burgundy wine
5 medium yellow onions (1 quartered; 4 chopped)
3 tablespoons olive oil
2 bay leaves
1 teaspoon crushed black peppercorns
1 sprig fresh thyme
9 slices lean bacon, cut into small cubes
3 garlic cloves, chopped
2 tablespoons all-purpose flour
3 large carrots, sliced
20 pearl onions, peeled
1 tablespoon sweet paprika
1 teaspoon freshly ground allspice
2½ cups button mushrooms (about 8 ounces)
2 tablespoons unsalted butter
Salt and freshly ground black pepper
Fresh parsley, chopped, for garnish

1. In a medium bowl, combine the beef cubes, wine, the 1 quartered onion, 1 tablespoon olive oil, bay leaves, peppercorns, and thyme. Cover with plastic wrap and marinate in the refrigerator overnight.
2. Remove the beef cubes from the marinade, reserving the marinade. Pat the meat dry with paper towels. Strain the reserved marinade through a fine sieve or cheesecloth into a large bowl and reserve.
3. In a Dutch oven, sauté the bacon in remaining 2 tablespoons olive oil over high heat for 3 minutes, until crisp.
4. Remove the bacon from the pan and reserve.
5. Add the beef cubes and cook about 10 minutes, until brown. Add the 4 chopped onions and garlic, and sauté for 3 minutes, until the onions are golden. Stir the flour into the beef and onions. Set aside.
6. In a large saucepan, bring the reserved marinade to a boil over high heat. Pour 3 cups of the marinade over the meat in the pan. Bring to a boil over high heat. Reduce the heat to medium and cook, stirring frequently, about 30 minutes, until the sauce thickens.
7. Add the reserved bacon, the carrots, pearl onions, paprika, allspice, and the remaining 3 cups marinade. Cook over high heat for 3 minutes.
8. Reduce the heat to low, cover, and cook about 1 hour, until meat is done.
9. In a large skillet, sauté the mushrooms in the butter over medium heat for 5 minutes, until browned.
10. Add the browned mushrooms to the stew and simmer for 5 minutes more.
11. Season with salt and pepper to taste.
12. To serve, place in a large serving bowl or platter and garnish with the chopped parsley.

Tavern Turkey Stew with Fried Oysters

A favorite on City Tavern's luncheon menu, this dish is inspired by one in *Martha Washington's Booke of Cookery*. It pairs oysters with poultry, a common practice in the eighteenth century. The difference between preparing this dish today and back then is that we prefer our vegetables slightly crisp, while in colonial days, vegetables typically were cooked into mush.

Overnight preparation recommended

Serves 4 to 6

3 pounds skinless boneless turkey thighs, cut into 2-inch cubes
4 medium shallots, chopped
4 garlic cloves, chopped
½ bunch fresh basil, chopped (about ¼ cup)
½ bunch fresh parsley, chopped (about 3 tablespoons)
1 sprig fresh thyme, chopped (about 1 tablespoon)
¾ cup olive oil
1 leek (white part only), well rinsed and cut into 2-inch strips, for garnish
½ cup all-purpose flour
3 medium yellow onions, diced
4 celery ribs, diced
3 large carrots, diced
½ cup dry sherry
4 cups (1 quart) Chicken Stock (see page 199)
1 bay leaf
2 cups Demi-glace (see page 202)
2 cups shredded red cabbage
2 medium zucchini, halved lengthwise and sliced
2 medium yellow squash, halved lengthwise and sliced
½ pound (2 sticks) unsalted butter
½ cup chopped tomato
Salt and freshly ground black pepper

Homemade Egg Noodles (see page 126), for serving

Cornmeal Fried Oysters (see page 21), for serving

1. In a large mixing bowl, combine the turkey cubes, shallots, garlic, basil, parsley, thyme, and 2 tablespoons of the oil. Cover with plastic wrap and marinate in the refrigerator, stirring occasionally, at least 6 hours or overnight.
2. Pour ¼ cup of the oil into a large saucepan. Heat the oil over high heat to 350°F. Add the leek and cook for 1 minute, until golden brown, being careful not to let the hot oil splatter. Using a slotted spoon, remove the leek from the oil and place on a paper towel to absorb any excess oil. Reserve.
3. Remove the turkey cubes from the marinade, discarding the marinade. Pat the turkey dry with paper towels and place in a medium mixing bowl.
4. Sprinkle the ½ flour over the turkey cubes and toss to coat thoroughly.
5. In a large skillet, cook the turkey in 2 tablespoons of the oil over high heat for 5 minutes, until brown.
6. Add the onions, celery, and carrots, and sauté for 5 to 8 minutes, until the vegetables are crisp-tender.

7. Add the sherry to deglaze the pan, loosening any browned bits on the bottom of the pan with a wooden spoon. Reduce the heat to medium and cook, until the liquid is reduced by half, about 30 minutes. Add the Chicken Stock and bring to a boil over high heat.

8. Add the bay leaf. Reduce the heat and simmer, until liquid is reduced by half. Add the Demi-glace and bring to a boil over high heat. Remove from the heat.

9. In another large skillet, sauté the red cabbage, zucchini, and yellow squash in the butter and remaining oil over medium heat for 5 minutes, until the vegetables are soft.

10. Add the tomato and sauté for 2 minutes more, until the tomato is soft.

11. Gently stir the vegetable mixture into the turkey mixture.

12. Serve the stew over the Homemade Egg Noodles and garnish with the Cornmeal Fried Oysters and the reserved Fried Leeks.

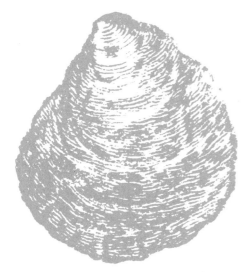

The modern-day City Tavern offers features we take for granted today, but which would be unheard of in the 1700s—indoor plumbing, walk-in refrigerators, and central heating and air-conditioning. Today, fireplaces aren't lit because of fire codes, and electric "candles" illuminate the sconces, for the same reason.

Tavern Turkey Potpie

Turkey was a prized bird in the colonies. Wild turkeys "of incredible Bigness" weighing up to forty pounds, were mentioned by naturalist and writer Robert Beverley in his writings of 1705. Our customers like this old-fashioned turkey dish as much for its eye-catching presentation—it is served in a pewter casserole dish and topped with puffed pastry—as for its rich, comforting flavor. We serve it Pennsylvania Dutch style, with a side order of Homemade Egg Noodles (see page 126) and topped with Demi-glace (see page 202).

Overnight preparation recommended

Serves 8

½ cup vegetable oil
3 sprigs fresh thyme, chopped (about 1 tablespoon)
½ bunch fresh parsley, chopped (about 3 tablespoons)
1 medium shallot, chopped
4 garlic cloves, chopped
1 whole turkey (8 to 10 pounds)
1 large white onion, diced
4 celery ribs, diced
2 large carrots, diced
1 cup dry white wine
4 cups (1 quart) Chicken Stock (see page 199)
1 cup shelled fresh peas
1 cup sliced button mushrooms
1 cup chopped red skinned potatoes
2 cups heavy cream
Salt and freshly ground black pepper
¼ pound (1 stick) unsalted butter, softened
½ cup all-purpose flour
3 pounds Quick Puff Pastry (see page 207) or purchased puff pastry
1 egg, lightly beaten with 1 teaspoon water

If you can't marinate the turkey overnight, I recommend a minimum of 4 hours for the best flavor.

1. In a small bowl, mix together the oil and 1½ teaspoons each of the thyme, parsley, shallot, and garlic. Reserve the remaining herbs for later use.
2. Rub the oil-seasoning mixture all over the turkey. Place the turkey on a tray, cover with plastic wrap, and refrigerate overnight (see Chef's Note).
3. Preheat the oven to 450°F.
4. Place the turkey on a rack in a large roasting pan.
5. Reduce the oven to 350°F and roast the turkey for about 2½ hours or until a meat thermometer inserted into the thigh reads 185°F.
6. Remove the turkey from the oven and let cool thoroughly. Remove the skin and the meat from the bones.
7. Cut the turkey meat into 1-inch pieces and reserve. Discard the skin and bones.
8. Preheat the oven to 350°F. Discard the pan drippings in the roasting pan and place the pan on the stove top.
9. Add the onion, celery, and carrots and sauté over medium heat for 3 minutes, until tender.
10. Add the wine to deglaze the pan, loosening any browned bits on the bottom of the pan with a wooden spoon.
11. Add the Chicken Stock, peas, mushrooms, and potatoes. Bring to a boil over high heat.

12. Add the heavy cream and the reserved thyme, parsley, shallot, and garlic. Season with salt and pepper to taste.
13. Bring to a boil over high heat and add turkey meat.
14. Bring back to a boil. Reduce the heat and simmer about 5 minutes, until ingredients are fully cooked.
15. In a small bowl, combine the butter and flour into a paste.
16. Slowly stir butter-flour mixture into the turkey mixture until it is combined and the mixture is thickened.
17. Ladle the turkey mixture into a large ovenproof dish or eight 14- to 16-ounce individual casserole dishes. Cover with the Quick Puff Pastry, allowing a 1-inch overhang. Crimp pastry to the edge of the bowl.
18. Using a fork, gently prick the pastry to allow steam to escape, being careful not to break the dough.
19. Gently brush the egg mixture over the surface of the puff pastry.
20. Bake for 12 to 15 minutes, until the pastry edges are brown.

Tavern Beef and Pork Pie

Making meat pies was actually a safety measure in colonial times. Since refrigeration was nonexistent back then, cooking leftover meat a second time in a pie eliminated any bacteria which might have developed since the first roasting. At the City Tavern, we serve this satisfying pie for lunch on a bed of Sweet and Sour Cabbage (see page 108), drizzled with Demi-glace, and garnished with chopped parsley. You also can serve it with Cabbage Salad (see page 54).

Overnight preparation required (for roasting meat)

Makes 8 large or 24 small triangles; Serves 8

1½ pounds cooked boneless beef chuck roast, cut into ½-inch cubes
   (see opposite page)
1½ pounds cooked boneless pork shoulder roast, cut into ½-inch cubes
   (see opposite page)
1 cup chopped yellow onions
4 garlic cloves, chopped
1 tablespoon unsalted butter
1 cup red burgundy wine
1 cup chopped button mushrooms
1 small bunch fresh basil, chopped (about ¼ cup)
½ small bunch fresh parsley, chopped (about 3 tablespoons)
1 sprig fresh thyme
2 teaspoons salt
1 teaspoon freshly ground black pepper
1 cup Demi-glace (see page 202)
3 pounds Quick Puff Pastry (see page 207) or purchased puff pastry
1 egg, lightly beaten with 1 tablespoon water

This recipe can be easily adapted into a tasty appetizer, by making individual pastry triangles—perfect finger food for a party.

1. In a large skillet, sauté the precooked beef and pork cubes, onions, and garlic in the butter over high heat for 5 minutes, until the onions are golden brown.
2. Add the red wine to deglaze the pan, loosening any browned bits on the bottom of the pan with a wooden spoon. Add the mushrooms, basil, parsley, thyme, salt, and pepper and cook until the liquid has evaporated
3. Stir in the Demi-glace and cook about 5 minutes more, until all liquid has evaporated again.
4. Remove from the heat. Spread the mixture out onto a baking sheet and let it cool for 10 minutes. Refrigerate the mixture about 1 hour to cool completely.
5. Preheat the oven to 450°F.
6. On a lightly floured surface, roll out the Quick Puff Pastry to ⅛-inch thickness. Cut out six 6- to 8-inch squares and brush the edges with the egg mixture.
7. Place 1 cup of the meat mixture in the center of each square. Fold each square over diagonally to form a triangle and press the edges firmly to seal. Using a fork, gently prick the center of each triangle to allow steam to escape. Lightly brush the edges again with the egg mixture.
8. Arrange the triangles 2 inches apart on a greased baking sheet.
9. Bake for 8 to 10 minutes, until golden brown.

Roasting Pork Shoulder and Beef Chuck

Makes 3 pounds of cooked meat

¼ cup vegetable oil
2 teaspoons salt
1 teaspoon freshly ground black pepper
2¼ pounds boneless pork shoulder roast
2¼ pounds boneless beef chuck roast

1. Preheat the oven to 350°F.
2. In a small bowl, mix together the oil, salt, and pepper. Rub the oil mixture over the meats.
3. Roast the pork shoulder about 1 hour; roast the beef chuck about 1½ hours, until a meat thermometer registers 170°F for each meat.
4. Remove the meats from the oven and let cool for 20 minutes. Cover and refrigerate up to one day or until ready to use.

Side Dishes

Hearty side dishes were served in copious numbers at City Tavern feasts—it wasn't uncommon to have as many as ten served in one meal, including vegetables, barley, and stuffing. Although meat was on the Tavern menu daily, it was very precious and served in small portions, so the sides made up a significant portion of the meal. In fact, the average cook in colonial times considered vegetables and starches as main dishes and only rarely flavored them with meat, fowl, or fish.

Brussels Sprouts

Said to have been cultivated as far back as the thirteenth century in Belgium, these hardy members of the cabbage family were a favorite of Thomas Jefferson, who grew them in his garden. Brussels sprouts were popular with colonial cooks because they wintered well, a fact I know from experience. As a child, my grandfather would send me out in the winter to pick a bowl of Brussels sprouts, I remember shaking the ice and snow from the stalks, and plucking perfectly preserved sprouts into my bowl. In fact, the Amish in Lancaster County, Pennsylvania still harvest sprouts the same way today.

Serves 6

1½ pounds fresh Brussels sprouts, trimmed
2 slices lean bacon, finely chopped
1 medium yellow onion, finely chopped
1 teaspoon olive oil
¾ cup Chicken Stock (see page 199)
1 teaspoon fennel seeds, lightly crushed in a mortar and pestle (or with the bottom of a pan)
Salt and freshly ground black pepper

1. With a small paring knife, cut a small cross ⅛-inch deep into the stem end of each Brussels sprout.
2. Bring a large saucepan of salted water to a boil over high heat.
3. Add the Brussels sprouts and cook for 6 to 8 minutes (depending on size), until just tender.
4. Drain. Add enough cold water to cover the Brussels sprouts. Let stand about 5 minutes, until cool. Drain again.
5. In a large skillet, cook the bacon over medium heat, stirring occasionally, about 5 minutes, until crisp and brown.
6. Remove from the skillet and drain on a paper towels.
7. Wipe out the skillet with paper towels.
8. Add the onions and cook in the oil over medium heat, stirring occasionally, about 5 minutes until soft.
9. Stir in the Chicken Stock, fennel seeds, Brussels sprouts, and bacon, and cook over medium heat, stirring frequently, about 3 minutes, until most of the liquid is evaporated.
10. Season with salt and pepper to taste. Serve hot.

Fennel Purée

I consider fennel one of the most underrated vegetables in America. Long appreciated in Italy and France for its delicate anise flavor and toothsome texture, it was among the many crops in Thomas Jefferson's garden.

Serves 8

5 large fresh fennel bulbs, leaves chopped and reserved for garnish
2 medium round red skinned potatoes (about 4 ounces), peeled and sliced
3 tablespoons heavy cream
Salt and freshly ground black pepper
½ cup grated Parmesan cheese, for serving
1 tablespoon sweet paprika, for serving

1. Cut off the bases, tops, and any bruised or tough outer layers of the fennel.
2. Cut each fennel bulb into 6 pieces and remove the core.
3. In a large saucepan, cook the fennel and potatoes in enough boiling, lightly salted water to cover for 15 to 20 minutes, until the vegetables are fork-tender.
4. Drain the vegetables. Cool slightly.
5. Transfer the vegetables to a blender container or food processor bowl and purée until smooth.
6. Add the cream and process until combined. Season with salt and pepper to taste.
7. Transfer to a serving bowl.
8. Sprinkle with the Parmesan cheese and paprika. Garnish with 1 tablespoon of the chopped fennel leaves. Serve hot.

Because freezers and refrigeration didn't exist in colonial America, root cellars—a storage system very familiar to me—were common. When I did my chef's apprenticeship in Germany, we still depended on root cellars for storage. Because it was the apprentice's job to store the foodstuffs in the cellars, I learned exactly how to place every fruit and vegetable to make it last as long as possible. I developed an eye for stocking the root cellar bins, and could look at a beet or an apple and detect even the smallest weak spot—which could endanger the entire bin's worth of goods.

Creamed Green Beans

Green beans, brought to Europe in the sixteenth century by returning Portuguese and Spanish explorers, are native to Mexico and Central America. Europeans, in turn, brought the beans back across the Atlantic to North America. This dish goes with fish, stew, roasts, and poultry.

Serves 8

3 pounds fresh tender green beans, such as haricot verts
2 medium onions, finely chopped
2 garlic cloves, chopped
2 tablespoons unsalted butter
1 cup Sauce Béchamel (see page 204)
½ cup heavy cream
⅛ teaspoon cayenne
Salt and freshly ground white pepper
Fresh parsley, chopped, for garnish

1. Bring a large saucepan of lightly salted water to a boil over high heat.
2. Add the beans and cook for 5 to 8 minutes, until crisp-tender. Drain and reserve.
3. In a medium saucepan, sauté the onions and garlic over medium heat for 3 minutes, until translucent.
4. Slowly stir in the Sauce Béchamel, cream, and cayenne.
5. Gently stir in the green beans and allow to heat through for about 3 minutes, until they turn bright green.
6. Season with salt and pepper to taste. Transfer to serving bowl. Garnish with the chopped parsley. Serve immediately.

Creamed Spinach

This rich version of a traditional British favorite is a perfect companion for any fish, shellfish, meat, or poultry dish.

Serves 4

1 pound fresh spinach, well rinsed and stems removed
1 teaspoon salt
1 cup Sauce Béchamel (see page 204)
½ cup heavy cream
¼ teaspoon freshly grated nutmeg
2 tablespoons unsalted butter
Salt and freshly ground black pepper

1. Place spinach in a large saucepan. Add the salt, and cook over low heat for about 5 minutes, stirring occasionally, until wilted. Let cool for 3 to 5 minutes.
2. Drain and squeeze out the excess water from the spinach with your hands or several paper towels. Transfer the spinach to a cutting board and finely chop and reserve.
3. In a medium saucepan, combine the Sauce Béchamel, cream, and nutmeg.
4. Cook the mixture over medium heat, stirring occasionally, about 3 minutes, until thoroughly heated. Stir in the chopped spinach and the butter.
5. Season with salt and pepper to taste.

Pumpkin Gratin

Although edible gourds were used in soups as early as the sixteenth century, it was Native Americans who introduced the colonists to pumpkin. I like the slightly spicy flavor the cinnamon and nutmeg impart to this colorful recipe. Although seasonal, this dish is a delicious taste treat during the peak pumpkin season.

Serves 8

1 small pumpkin (about 3 pounds), seeded,
   peeled, and cut into large pieces
9 slices lean bacon, cut into pieces
4 medium onions, chopped
4 eggs, lightly beaten
¼ teaspoon freshly grated nutmeg
⅛ teaspoon ground cinnamon
Salt and freshly ground black pepper
1 cup grated Parmesan cheese
2 tablespoons unsalted butter, at room temperature

1. Preheat the oven to 350°F.
2. Bring a Dutch oven of salted water to a boil over high heat. Add the pumpkin pieces and cook about 20 minutes, until fork-tender. Drain.
3. In a medium skillet, cook the bacon over medium heat, stirring occasionally, about 5 minutes, until crisp and brown. Remove from the skillet and drain on paper towels. Reserve.
4. In the same skillet with the bacon drippings, sauté the onions over medium heat about 5 minutes, until golden brown. Reserve.
5. Place the pumpkin pieces on a baking sheet and bake for 3 to 5 minutes, until dry.
6. Increase the oven temperature to 375°F.
7. Place the pumpkin in a food processor bowl and purée until smooth. (Or press through a sieve or food mill.)
8. Transfer to a large bowl. Stir in the eggs, reserved onions, reserved bacon, nutmeg, and cinnamon. Sprinkle with salt and pepper.
9. Pour the mixture into a 2-quart au gratin dish or medium baking dish. Sprinkle with the Parmesan cheese and dot with the butter and bake for 20 to 30 minutes, until golden brown.

Sweet and Sour Red Cabbage

Cabbage, both red and green, has been a staple of the European diet for centuries. This Alsatian dish, which shows up on many Eastern European tables with slight variations, is excellent as an accompaniment for venison, sausage, and pork. Early German settlers would have cooked the cabbage down to a mushy consistency. Today, my version of this dish is prepared slightly al dente.

Serves 8

1 medium shallot, chopped
1 garlic clove, chopped
2 tablespoons unsalted butter
2½ to 3 pounds red cabbage, shredded (about 10 cups)
½ cup red burgundy wine
1¼ cups balsamic vinegar
½ cup granulated sugar
Salt and freshly ground black pepper

1. In a 12-inch skillet, sauté the shallots and garlic in the butter over medium heat for 1 minute, until golden brown.
2. Add the shredded cabbage.
3. Add the wine to deglaze the pan, loosening any browned bits on the bottom of the pan with a wooden spoon.
4. Stir in the vinegar and sugar. Season with salt and pepper to taste.
5. Increase the heat to high and bring to a boil, stirring constantly to prevent the sugar from burning.
6. Reduce the heat and simmer about 10 minutes, until the liquid is reduced by three-fourths.

Pennsylvania Dutch–Style Sauerkraut

Although sauerkraut is the German word for sour cabbage, this dish is actually Chinese in origin, where it was served fermented in rice wine. It eventually found its way to Europe, where the Germans and Alsatians adopted it as their own, later bringing it to the New World. In Pennsylvania, with its large number of German settlers, sauerkraut was a popular side dish.

Serves 6

9 slices lean bacon
3 tablespoons unsalted butter
2 medium onions, chopped
1 garlic clove, chopped
4 cups (32 ounces) refrigerated or canned sauerkraut (see Chef's Note),
   rinsed and drained
1½ cups Chicken Stock (see page 199)
1 cup sweet white wine
½ teaspoon caraway seeds
2 large apples, peeled, cored, and thinly sliced
1 large red skinned potato (about 3 ounces), peeled and grated
Salt and freshly ground white pepper

1. In a large saucepan, cook the bacon in the butter over medium heat for 3 minutes, until crisp.
2. Add the onions and garlic and sauté about 5 minutes, until golden brown.
3. Stir in the drained sauerkraut, Chicken Stock, wine, and caraway seeds.
4. Bring to a boil over high heat. Reduce the heat to medium and cook about 30 minutes, until the stock is reduced by three-fourths.
5. Stir in the apples and potato and cook about 30 minutes more, until the apples and potato are dissolved. Season with salt and pepper to taste.

I prefer refrigerated-style sauerkraut because it tends to be cooked less than the canned variety. Use any of the different types of commercially prepared sauerkraut available, but be sure to rinse it several times to remove the salt. Then, drain it thoroughly in a colander.

Sweet Potatoes and Apples

Although called a potato, the sweet potato is actually a root vegetable in the morning glory family. Sweet potatoes go exceptionally well with pork and turkey.

Serves 8

6 medium sweet potatoes (about 3 pounds)
4 medium Granny Smith apples, peeled, cored, and sliced
1 cup packed light brown sugar
4 tablespoons unsalted butter
1 teaspoon ground mace
Salt and freshly ground black pepper

1. Preheat the oven to 325°F.
2. In a Dutch oven, cook the sweet potatoes in enough boiling water to cover for 15 to 20 minutes, until just fork-tender. *Do not overcook.* Drain.
3. Peel and cut the potatoes into ¼-inch-thick slices.
4. Place half of the potato slices in the bottom of a buttered large baking dish.
5. Top with half of the apple slices.
6. Sprinkle with half of the sugar, butter, and mace. Season to taste with salt and pepper.
7. Repeat with alternate layers of the remaining potato slices, apple slices, sugar, butter, and mace.
8. Bake about 1 hour, until the top is brown and the liquid has evaporated.

Candied Sweet Potatoes

Thanksgiving wouldn't be complete without this dish—although it's delicious any time of year. The addition of chopped lemon and orange makes it extra special.

Serves 6 to 8

6 medium sweet potatoes (about 3 pounds),
    peeled and cut into julienne strips
1¼ cups water
1 cup packed light brown sugar
1 large orange, peeled and chopped
1 large lemon, peeled and chopped
2 tablespoons unsalted butter
¼ teaspoon salt

1. Preheat the oven to 350°F.
2. Arrange the sweet potatoes in a large baking dish.
3. In a medium mixing bowl, combine the water, sugar, orange, lemon, butter, and salt. Pour over the sweet potatoes.
4. Cover with aluminum foil and bake for 30 minutes.
5. Uncover and bake, basting frequently, about 30 minutes more, until the potatoes are tender and golden brown.

Turnip, Potato, and Parsnip Mash

Turnips and parsnips were brought to America as early as the 1600s by Europeans. Colonial cooks used these, which stored well in a root cellar, to add variety to winter meals. Especially when young, both root vegetables have a pleasantly sweet flavor and are excellent when mixed with potatoes.

Serves 6 to 8

½ pound white turnips, peeled and cut into 1-inch cubes
½ pound russet potatoes, peeled and cut into 1-inch cubes
½ pound parsnips, peeled and cut into 1-inch cubes
6 cups Chicken Stock (see page 199)
1 small onion, finely chopped
4 tablespoons unsalted butter
¼ cup heavy cream
1 small bunch fresh parsley, chopped (about ¼ cup)
½ teaspoon freshly grated nutmeg
Salt and freshly ground black pepper

1. In a large saucepan, combine the turnips, potatoes, parsnips, and Chicken Stock and bring to a boil over high heat.
2. Reduce the heat and simmer for 15 to 20 minutes, until fork-tender.
3. Drain the vegetables and return to the saucepan.
4. In a small saucepan, sauté the onion in 1 tablespoon of the butter over medium heat for 3 minutes, until golden brown. Transfer to the vegetables.
5. Add the cream, the remaining 3 tablespoons butter, parsley, and nutmeg and mash with a potato masher until smooth.
6. Season with salt and pepper to taste. Serve hot.

Smashed Red Potatoes

Mashed potatoes don't get any simpler than this—but the addition of shallots gives them a subtle onion flavor.

Serves 8

2 pounds red skinned potatoes, halved (quartered if large)
½ cup sour cream
¼ cup finely chopped shallots
1 bunch fresh parsley, chopped (about ¼ cup)
3 tablespoons whole milk
1 tablespoon olive oil
Salt and freshly ground black pepper

1. Bring a large saucepan of salted water to a boil over high heat. Add the potatoes and cook for 10 to 15 minutes, until fork-tender.
2. In a small bowl, combine the sour cream, shallots, parsley, milk, and oil. Stir until smooth and reserve.
3. Drain the potatoes and "smash" with a potato masher or the back of a large spoon. *Do not completely mash the potatoes.*
4. Stir in the sour cream mixture and season with salt and pepper to taste. Serve hot.

The Tavern staff is dressed exactly as their counterparts were two centuries ago, as servants to the upper class. A colonial observer could tell the class of a servant by the material of his buttons, with wood buttons indicating the lowest strata, working up to bone and ivory buttons. City Tavern staff close their breeches with metal buttons, indicating that the original servants were placed somewhere in the middle of the servant class social ladder.

Potato, Mushroom, and Onion Casserole

This typically European dish would have fit perfectly into the colonial menu, prepared with, or without mushrooms, depending on the season. This is an ideal side dish for entertaining because you can make it ahead of time. If you like flavorful exotic mushrooms, such as porcini or chanterelles, substitute them for their milder white cousin.

Serves 8

6 cups sliced button mushrooms (about 1½ pounds)
7 tablespoons unsalted butter
2 tablespoons vegetable oil
2 large onions, sliced
2 garlic cloves, chopped
8 medium round red skinned potatoes (about 1½ pounds), peeled and very thinly sliced
Salt and freshly ground white pepper
2 bunches fresh parsley, finely chopped (about ½ cup)
1 cup heavy cream

1. Preheat the oven to 375°F.
2. In a large skillet, sauté the mushrooms in 4 tablespoons of the butter and the oil over high heat for 5 minutes, until light brown and tender. Remove from the skillet. Reserve.
3. In the same skillet, sauté the onions and garlic for 3 minutes, until golden brown. Reserve.
4. Pat the sliced potatoes dry with paper towels. Place half of the potato slices in the bottom of a large baking dish.
5. Sprinkle with salt and pepper. Add the parsley, the reserved mushroom and onion mixtures, and the remaining potato slices. Sprinkle again with salt and pepper.
6. Dot the potatoes with the remaining 3 tablespoons butter.
7. Bake for 15 minutes.
8. Pour the cream evenly over the potato mixture and bake about 10 minutes more, until the potatoes are fork-tender and the mixture is bubbly. Serve hot.

Crisp Potato Cake

In colonial days, this dish would have been prepared in a cast iron skillet and cooked over hot coals.

Makes 1 large cake; Serves 8

10 large round red skinned potatoes (about 2½ pounds),
   peeled and cut into ½-inch-thick slices
½ cup vegetable oil
5 tablespoons unsalted butter
2 cups grated Swiss cheese (about 8 ounces)
¼ teaspoon dried marjoram
¼ teaspoon grated nutmeg
Salt and freshly ground black pepper
1 bunch fresh chives, chopped, for serving

For a richer flavor increase the amount of cheese and add a cup of heavy cream to the mixture in Step 5.

1. Preheat the oven to 350°F.
2. Pat the potato slices dry with paper towels.
3. In a large skillet, sauté one-third of the potato slices in one-third of the oil and 3 tablespoons of the butter over medium heat for 15 minutes, until lightly brown. Scrape the bottom of the pan from time to time with a spatula.
4. Transfer the potatoes to a well-buttered large baking dish or cast iron skillet. Add one-third of the cheese and half of the marjoram and nutmeg. Sprinkle with salt and pepper.
5. Add another one-third of the oil to the skillet and sauté another one-third of the potatoes about 15 minutes. Transfer to the baking dish. Add another one-third of the cheese and remaining marjoram and nutmeg. Sprinkle with salt and pepper.
6. Repeat with the remaining oil and potatoes. Cover the dish with foil and bake for 35 minutes, or until cooked and golden brown.
7. Carefully flip the baking dish upside down onto the serving platter. Lift off the baking dish. Dot the top of the potato cake with the remaining butter, sprinkle with fresh chives.

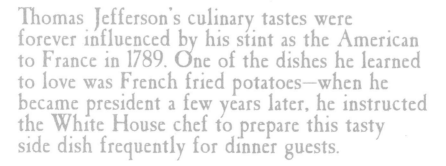

Thomas Jefferson's culinary tastes were forever influenced by his stint as the American to France in 1789. One of the dishes he learned to love was French fried potatoes—when he became president a few years later, he instructed the White House chef to prepare this tasty side dish frequently for dinner guests.

Molasses Baked Beans

Baked beans actually had their roots as a Native American dish—beans mixed with maple sugar and bear fat and cooked in "bean holes" which were lined with hot rocks. The colonists substituted molasses or sugar for the maple syrup and bacon or ham for the bear fat. They simmered their beans for hours in pots over the fire, instead of in underground bean holes—but the savory results were the same.

Overnight preparation recommended

Serves 8

1 pound dried navy beans
9 slices lean bacon, chopped
¼ cup packed dark brown sugar
½ cup molasses
1½ teaspoons dry mustard
½ cup Chicken Stock (see page 199), optional
Salt and freshly ground black pepper

1. Pre-soak the beans (see Chef's Note, page 117). Drain.
2. Preheat oven to 300°F.
3. In a large saucepan, cover the pre-soaked beans with water and bring to a boil over high heat. Reduce the heat to medium and cook, covered, for 30 minutes.
4. Drain the beans. Stir in the bacon, sugar, molasses, and mustard.
5. Transfer the bean mixture to a medium bean pot or casserole dish and bake, covered, about 7 hours, until tender.
6. Check the consistency several times during baking. If the beans become overly dry, add the Chicken Stock.
7. Season with salt and pepper to taste.

The Pilgrims started the tradition of Boston baked beans to adhere to the rules of their religion. They were not allowed to do any work on the Sabbath, so they started cooking their beans the night before.

White Beans and Shallots Purée

Dried beans, rich in protein, calcium, phosphorus, and iron, were a staple in the colonial larder. This onion-and-garlic-flavored dish is an excellent accompaniment to leg of lamb.

Overnight preparation required

Serves 8 to 10

2 pounds dried white beans, such as great Northern
1 tablespoon salt
1 teaspoon freshly ground black pepper
1 Bouquet Garni (see page 201)
4 medium red skinned potatoes, peeled and coarsely chopped
2 medium onions, chopped
3 garlic cloves, chopped
6 tablespoons unsalted butter, at room temperature
¼ cup heavy cream
Salt and freshly ground black pepper
5 medium shallots, finely chopped

1. Pre-soak the beans (see Chef's Note, opposite page). Drain.
2. In a Dutch oven, cover the beans with water; add the 1 tablespoon salt and pepper.
3. Bring to a boil over high heat. Reduce the heat to medium and add the Bouquet Garni. Cover and cook for 1½ hours, until the beans are tender. Stir the potatoes into the beans and cook for an additional 30 minutes.
4. In a medium saucepan, sauté the onions and garlic in 1 tablespoon of the butter over medium heat for 3 minutes, until golden brown. Stir into the beans.
5. Remove the Bouquet Garni. Drain the beans in a colander.
6. Transfer the bean mixture to a food processor bowl and purée until smooth. Stir in the cream and 4 tablespoons of the butter; season with salt and pepper to taste. Transfer to a casserole dish. Keep warm.
7. In a small saucepan, sauté the shallots in the remaining 1 tablespoon butter over medium heat for 2 minutes, until golden brown.
8. To serve, spoon the shallots over the bean mixture.

Red Beans and Wine

This hearty dish has its roots in Burgundy, France. It can be adapted in countless ways, with the addition of such ingredients as shallots, bacon, and potatoes. Creative eighteenth-century cooks, faced with the prospect of preparing beans all winter long, no doubt developed an extensive repertoire. This side dish is a perfect accompaniment to meats and poultry.

Serves 8

1½ pounds dried red beans or red kidney beans
1 Bouquet Garni (see page 201)
1 tablespoon salt
1 teaspoon freshly ground black pepper
4 slices lean bacon
2 medium onions, chopped
1 garlic clove, chopped
2 large carrots, finely chopped
4 cups red burgundy wine
1 teaspoon dried rubbed sage
Salt and freshly ground black pepper

1. Pre-soak the beans (see Chef's Note). Drain.
2. In a large saucepan, cover the beans with water. Add the Bouquet Garni, 1 tablespoon salt, and 1 teaspoon pepper.
3. Bring to a boil over high heat. Reduce the heat and simmer for 1½ to 2 hours, until the beans are tender.
4. Remove the Bouquet Garni. Drain the beans in a colander and reserve.
5. In the same saucepan, cook the bacon over high heat for 3 minutes. Remove the bacon and reserve.
6. Sauté the onions and garlic in the bacon drippings over medium heat for 3 minutes, until golden brown.
7. Add the carrots and sauté for 5 to 10 minutes, until soft.
8. Add the reserved beans and bacon, wine, and sage.
9. Bring to a boil over high heat. Reduce the heat to medium and, stirring frequently, cook about 10 minutes, until the wine is absorbed by the beans.
10. Season with salt and pepper to taste.

Soaking Dried Beans
To soak dried beans or lentils, place the beans in a colander and rinse them thoroughly with water to clean beans. Place the drained beans in a large bowl and cover with water. Let stand at room temperature for at least 8 hours or overnight. Drain and thoroughly rinse the beans before cooking as directed.

Herbed Barley

Barley, one of the oldest cultivated grains, has long been prized both for its nutritional value and its healthfulness. A staple crop in colonial times, barely was filling and hearty enough to act as a main course for the average family. This simple recipe can be adapted with any fresh herb of your choice.

Serves 4

6 cups water
2 cups regular pearl barley
1 teaspoon salt
1 medium shallot, finely chopped
1 garlic clove, chopped
2 tablespoons unsalted butter
1½ tablespoons chopped fresh parsley
⅛ teaspoon curry powder
Salt and freshly ground black pepper

1. In a large saucepan, combine the water, barley, and 1 teaspoon salt and bring to a boil over high heat. Cook about 25 minutes, until al dente. Drain the barley in a colander and reserve.
2. In the same saucepan, sauté the shallot and garlic in the butter over medium heat for 2 minutes, until golden. Stir in the reserved barley, parsley, and curry. Season with salt and pepper to taste.
3. Transfer to a serving dish and serve hot.

Starch played a dominant role in the colonial diet, whether in the form of potatoes, German spaetzle or egg noodles, grains such as barley and rice, or freshly baked bread. Meat was an expensive commodity, not consumed by the average family except on special occasions. What the City Tavern served as hearty side dishes were main dishes to the common folk.

Wild Rice Stuffing

Native to North America, wild rice looks like rice, and is used in the same way, but it's actually a water grass. It was a familiar food to the eighteenth-century colonists. Julian Niemcewicz, a Polish visitor to America, writes in his book, *Under Their Vine and Fig Tree, 1797–1799*, about an encounter he had with wild rice, at a dinner with Thomas Jefferson and a Dr. Scandella in Philadelphia: "The Dr. showed us a bag of Wilde Rize . . . grains which grow wild in marshy places in all of America up to the Hudson Bay. Cattle are extremely fond of it. It even provides good nourishment for people." Today, guests at the Tavern enjoy the nutty goodness of wild rice in recipes such as this poultry stuffing.

Makes 6 cups; Serves 6

1 small yellow onion, finely chopped
3 celery ribs, finely chopped
4 tablespoons unsalted butter
3½ cups Chicken Stock (see page 199)
2 cups wild rice
1 cup dry white wine
½ bunch fresh parsley, chopped (about 3 tablespoons)
1 bay leaf
1 sprig fresh thyme
1 tablespoon salt
1 teaspoon freshly ground black pepper
½ cup fine dry bread crumbs
2 eggs, lightly beaten

1. In a medium saucepan, sauté the onion and celery in the butter over medium heat for 5 minutes, until tender.
2. Add the Chicken Stock, wild rice, wine, parsley, bay leaf, thyme, salt, and pepper.
3. Bring to a boil over high heat. Reduce the heat, cover, and simmer about 40 minutes, until most of the stock is absorbed. Set aside to cool.
4. Remove and discard the bay leaf and the sprig of thyme. Stir in the bread crumbs and eggs.
5. Use to stuff any type of poultry or transfer to a greased medium baking dish and bake in a 375°F oven about 30 minutes, until heated through.

Rice Pilaf

This recipe has its roots with the Spaniards and Portuguese, who used vegetables and seasonings in their water to infuse flavor into their rice.

Serves 6 to 8
1 medium onion, finely diced
2 ribs celery, finely diced
1 carrot, peeled and diced
4 button mushrooms, sliced
2 tablespoon unsalted butter
2 cups long-grain white rice
4 cups (1 quart) Chicken Stock (see page 199)
1 bay leaf
1 tablespoon chopped fresh parsely

1. Preheat oven to 400°F.
2. In large sauté pan cook onion, celery, carrot, and mushrooms in 1 tablespoon of the butter for 3 to 5 minutes, until the onions are translucent.
3. In a deep ovenproof dish, combine the the sautéed vegetables, the remaining 1 tablespoon butter, Chicken Stock, rice, and bay leaf.
4. Cover with aluminum foil or a lid and bake for 40 minutes.

Herb Croutons

The typical colonial cook was very frugal—even stale bread was used for something, such as these garlicky croutons. They take no time to prepare and the flavor is so much better than store-bought.

Makes 2 cups; Serves 8
2 medium shallots, chopped
3 garlic cloves, chopped
4 tablespoons unsalted butter
¼ cup olive oil
1 small bunch fresh basil, chopped (about ½ cup)
½ bunch fresh parsley, chopped (about 3 tablespoons)
1 sprig fresh thyme, leaves pulled
1 tablespoon grated Parmesan cheese
12 slices white bread (crusts optional), cut into ½-inch cubes

1. Preheat the oven to 300°F.
2. In a small saucepan, sauté the shallots and garlic in the butter over medium heat for 2 minutes, until golden.
3. Transfer to a large mixing bowl. Add the oil, basil, parsley, thyme leaves, and cheese and blend well. Add bread cubes to mixture and toss until well-coated.
4. Spread the bread cubes, in a single layer, in a shallow baking pan and bake for 10 to 15 minutes, until golden brown and crisp and dry. Croutons can be stored, uncovered, for up to 1 week.

Colonial Oyster Stuffing

In the colonial tradition of teaming oysters with poultry, we serve this superb stuffing with chicken or turkey.

Makes 8 cups; Serves 8

1 loaf firm white bread (about 1 pound), crust trimmed and cut into ½-inch cubes
4 medium onions, chopped
2 tablespoons olive oil
2 celery ribs, chopped
5 garlic cloves, chopped
1 tablespoon salt
1 teaspoon freshly ground black pepper
2 sprigs fresh thyme, leaves pulled
Dash dried rubbed sage
Dash chopped fresh oregano
½ cup dry white wine
1½ pounds fresh oysters, shucked
1 cup heavy cream
½ cup chopped fresh parsley
¾ cup Chicken Stock (see page 199)

1. Preheat the oven to 325°F. Spread the bread cubes, in a single layer, in a shallow baking pan.
2. Bake for 20 to 30 minutes, until crisp, dry, and golden. Transfer to a large bowl.
3. In a large skillet, sauté the onions in the oil over low to medium heat for 10 to 15 minutes, until golden.
4. Add the celery, garlic, salt, pepper, thyme, sage, and oregano and sauté for 5 minutes, until the celery is soft.
5. Add the wine and cook about 5 minutes, until the liquid is evaporated. Add the vegetable mixture to the bread cubes in the bowl. Mix well.
6. Add the oysters, cream, and parsley to the bread cube mixture. Mix well.
7. Add enough of the Chicken Stock to moisten the mixture, but be careful not to make it soggy.
8. Transfer the mixture to a lightly greased 3-quart baking dish and cover with aluminum foil.
9. Bake for 30 minutes. Uncover and bake about 10 minutes more, until crisp. Serve hot.

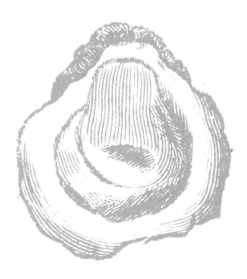

Chestnut Stuffing

In *Martha Washington's Booke of Cookery*, there is mention of wild turkeys being as large as forty pounds. Stuffing a bird that size would take some volume, which is why stuffings made of bread, rice, or cornmeal and embellished with nuts, vegetables, and other savories were common choices. This scaled-down Tavern recipe is perfect for today's more moderate-sized bird. If you prefer to skip the stuffing step, you can easily bake the chestnut mixture in a dish.

Makes 8 to 10 cups; Serves 8

1 pound fresh unshelled chestnuts (18 medium chestnuts)
1 loaf firm white bread (about 1 pound), crust trimmed and cut into ½-inch cubes
2 onions, chopped
1 tablespoon olive oil
2 celery ribs, chopped
3 garlic cloves, chopped
1 tablespoon fresh thyme leaves
1 tablespoon salt
1 tablespoon freshly ground black pepper
½ cup dry white wine
4 cups sliced mushrooms (about 12 ounces)
½ cup chopped fresh parsley
½ cup dried currants
¾ cup Chicken Stock (see page 199)

Buying Chestnuts
When buying fresh chestnuts, select heavy, plump, and hard chestnuts with shiny brown skins. Once you've peeled the chestnuts, be sure to cut away any dark or moldy spots you may find because they can affect the flavor of the stuffing. Vacuum-packed canned chestnuts are a great alternative to fresh, but water-packed canned chestnuts are unacceptable.

1. Prepare the chestnuts: With the point of a small paring knife, make a crisscross cut through the shell in the flat side of each chestnut shell.
2. Drop the chestnuts, 4 or 5 at a time, into a large saucepan of boiling water and cook until the chestnuts break.
3. Drain the chestnuts in a colander and allow them to cool slightly (if the chestnuts cool too much, they won't easily peel). Peel and discard the shells. Using a paper towel, rub off the thin layer of inner brown skins.
4. Return the peeled chestnuts to the saucepan and add enough water to cover. Bring to a boil over high heat. Reduce the heat and simmer for 30 to 45 minutes, until tender.
5. Drain and rinse with cold water. When cool enough to handle, cut each chestnut into quarters and reserve.
6. Preheat the oven to 350°F. Spread the bread cubes, in a single layer, in a shallow baking pan and bake for 15 to 25 minutes, until crisp, dry, and golden.
7. Transfer the bread cubes to a large bowl.
8. In a large skillet, sauté the onions in ½ tablespoon of the oil over medium-low heat for 10 to 15 minutes, until golden.
9. Add the celery, garlic, thyme, salt, and pepper and sauté for 5 minutes, until the celery is soft.
10. Add the wine and cook about 5 minutes, until the liquid is evaporated. Add the vegetable mixture to the bread cubes in the bowl.

11. In the same skillet, sauté the mushrooms in the remaining ½ tablespoon oil over high heat, until browned and the liquid is evaporated. Add to the bread cubes.
12. Add the quartered chestnuts, parsley, and currants. Mix well.
13. Add enough of the Chicken Stock to moisten the mixture, but be careful not to make it soggy.
14. If you wish to use the Chestnut Stuffing to stuff a turkey, allow the mixture to cool at this point. Meanwhile, rinse the cavity of the turkey with cold running water, drain, and then sprinkle salt and pepper into the clean cavity. Place the cooled stuffing into the turkey with your hand, loosely packing the mixture until it reaches the cavity opening. Transfer the turkey to a roasting pan and roast until a meat thermometer inserted in a thigh muscle registers 185°C. Otherwise, if you are not stuffing a turkey, transfer the mixture to a lightly greased 3-quart baking dish and cover with aluminum foil. You can refrigerate the stuffing for up to 24 hours before baking, but if you do, you'll need to increase the baking time.
15. Bake for 45 minutes. Uncover and bake about 15 minutes more, until crisp. Serve hot.

Employees of the Tavern are required by the National Park Service to be trained in the historic high points of the era. They must be well versed in the locations and significance of everything from the Liberty Bell to Independence Hall to the Betsy Ross House, which are all located within walking distance from City Tavern.

Spaetzle with Bread Crumbs

Spaetzle, which literally means "little sparrow," is comprised of irregularly shaped noodles or dumplings Germany is as important to that country's cuisine as pasta is to Italy's. The Pennsylvania Germans brought this tasty recipe with them to America. I started making spaetzle by hand in my family's restaurant when I was five years old. In Southern Germany, it is served plain or, as in this recipe, with bread crumbs.

Serves 4

1 cup all-purpose flour
2 large eggs
½ teaspoon salt
½ cup cold water
2 tablespoons unsalted butter
2 tablespoons dry bread crumbs
1 teaspoon chopped fresh parsley

1. In the bowl of an electric mixer, mix the flour, eggs, and salt on medium until combined.
2. Slowly beat in the water until the mixture is smooth. Beat about 5 minutes more, until the mixture becomes elastic.
3. In a large saucepan, bring 2 quarts of lightly salted water to a boil over high heat. Place the dough in a potato ricer or a colander with larger holes and press the dough through the ricer or colander into the boiling water with a wooden spoon. Cook for 5 to 10 minutes, until spaetzle are tender but firm; stir occasionally.
4. Using a sieve with a handle, remove the spaetzle and immediately place in an ice bath to cool quickly. Drain well.
5. In a large skillet, sauté the spaetzle in 1 tablespoon of the butter over medium heat for 3 minutes, until golden brown and heated through.
6. In a small saucepan, sauté the bread crumbs in the remaining 1 tablespoon butter for 1 minute, until slightly brown.
7. Transfer the spaetzle to a serving bowl. Sprinkle with the browned bread crumbs and the parsley. Serve immediately.

Herbed Spaetzle

This spaetzle, a variation of the traditional German recipe, is an ideal way to use fresh seasonal herbs. Herbed spaetzle is delicious served with stews or any dish with a sauce.

Serves 4

1 cup all-purpose flour
2 large eggs
1 teaspoon chopped fresh parsley
½ teaspoon salt
½ teaspoon chopped fresh thyme
½ teaspoon chopped fresh rosemary
½ cup cold water
2 tablespoons unsalted butter

1. In the bowl of an electric mixer, mix the flour, eggs, parsley, salt, thyme, and rosemary on medium until combined.
2. Slowly beat in the water until the mixture is smooth. Beat about 5 minutes more, until the mixture becomes elastic.
3. In a large saucepan, bring 2 quarts of lightly salted water to a boil over high heat. Place the dough in a potato ricer or a colander with large holes and press the dough through the ricer or colander into the boiling water with a wooden spoon. Cook for 5 to 10 minutes, until spaetzle are tender but firm; stir occasionally.
4. Using a sieve with a handle, remove the spaetzle and immediately place in an ice bath to cool quickly. Drain well.
5. In a large skillet, sauté the spaetzle in the butter over medium heat for 2 minutes, until golden brown and heated through. Serve immediately.

Homemade Egg Noodles

Noodles are another example of the German contribution to early American cuisine. In Lancaster County today, you'll still find cooks preparing these big fat egg noodles by hand everyday, just as their colonial ancestors did. The Tavern serves these noodles with all kinds of main dishes, including Tavern Turkey Pot Pie (see page 100) and Braised Rabbit Legs (see page 92). Unlike the early cooks, we prepare them al dente, rather than soft and tender.

Serves 4

1 cup all-purpose flour
1 egg, lightly beaten
1 egg yolk, lightly beaten
1 teaspoon vegetable oil
1 teaspoon salt
1 teaspoon unsalted butter

You can use a pasta machine for this recipe, if desired.

1. Place the flour in a mixing bowl.
2. Add the egg, egg yolk, oil, and salt.
3. Knead thoroughly with hands until it begins to form a stiff ball of dough. (This can also be done in the bowl of an electric mixer using a paddle.)
4. Wrap in plastic wrap and let sit for 1 hour at room temperature.
5. Roll dough into a ball and flatten it until ¼-inch thick. With a rolling pin, roll the dough out until ⅛-inch thick or as thin as possible.
6. Cut the dough into ½-inch wide by 2-inch long strips.
7. In a medium saucepan filled with 2 quarts water, add ½ teaspoon salt and bring to a boil over high heat.
8. Cook for 2 minutes or until al dente.
9. Strain and let cool. Add the butter to the noodles and toss until melted.

Potato Dumplings

Every culinary culture, European and otherwise, has some kind of dumpling in its recipe repertoire. This dumpling (much like the German-style dumpling my family served in our restaurant) is an updated version of the original dumpling recipes brought to America by the wave of German immigrants that first came here in the 1600s.

Makes 24 dumplings; Serves 8

15 slices three-day-old white sandwich bread, crusts trimmed
1 cup whole milk
7 large red skinned potatoes, peeled and grated (about 2 cups)
2 medium yellow onions, grated
1 bunch fresh parsley, chopped (about 6 tablespoons)
1 tablespoon salt
¼ teaspoon freshly ground white pepper
1 pinch freshly grated nutmeg
1 pinch dried marjoram
3 large eggs, beaten well
All-purpose flour, for coating

1. In a large mixing bowl, soak the bread in the milk 2 to 3 minutes, until soggy.
2. Using your hands, squeeze out and discard the milk.
3. Place the bread in a large mixing bowl. Stir in the potatoes, onions, parsley, salt, pepper, nutmeg, and marjoram.
4. Add the eggs to the mixture and mix well.
5. Shape the mixture into about twenty-four 1½-inch round dumplings.
6. Dip the dumplings into the flour to coat generously.
7. Bring a large saucepan of lightly salted water to a boil over high heat.
8. With a slotted spoon, gently add the dumplings to the water. Bring back to a boil.
9. Reduce the heat to medium. Cover and cook about 15 minutes, until the dumplings expand and float to surface.
10. Serve with any kind of stew.

Part 3: Desserts

Some things never change. Dessert played as important a role on the colonial table as it does on ours today. A handsomely arranged dessert table bearing sweets such as pies, pastries, puddings, and sweetmeats was considered the truly stylish conclusion of a long evening of music and dancing. In its earlier days, the Tavern would have served the fanciest of confections, while most home cooks at the time would have prepared simple cakes that were more like sweetened bread, studded with fruit and nuts. In this chapter you'll find original recipes for homemade specialties, such as fruit cobblers and rice pudding, as well as an updated recipe for chocolate cake that traces back to the first First Lady. It seems that Martha Washington had quite the sweet tooth, and was partial to chocolate.

Cakes and Pastries

When researching the cakes and pastries originally served at the Tavern, I couldn't help but notice the strong French influence. And it is no wonder—many colonists, including Thomas Jefferson were avid proponents of French baking techniques. (He even had French chefs in his personal residence in Monticello and in the White House while he was president.) Interestingly, the recipes I uncovered were generally much sweeter than we are used to eating today. I've adapted the amount of sugar to suit contemporary tastes.

Sour Cream Coffee Cake

Coffee houses were popular in the colonies before they caught on in Europe. In the City Tavern Coffee Room, cakes were served as an accompaniment to what was a relatively newfangled drink, coffee. This coffee cake, topped with streusel, is ideal for last-minute entertaining—it is easy and quick to prepare.

Makes one 9-inch cake; Serves 10 to 12

Crumb Topping
½ cup granulated sugar
½ cup chopped walnuts
2 tablespoons all-purpose flour
2 tablespoons unsalted butter, melted
1 teaspoon ground cinnamon

Cake
1 cup granulated sugar
¼ pound (1 stick) unsalted butter
2 cups all-purpose flour, sifted
1½ teaspoons baking powder
½ teaspoon baking soda
½ teaspoon salt
2 large eggs
1 teaspoon vanilla extract
8 ounces (1 cup) sour cream

1. Preheat the oven to 350°F. Lightly coat one 9 x 2½-inch round cake pan with vegetable cooking spray and dust lightly with flour.
2. Prepare the Crumb Topping: In a small bowl, combine the ½ cup sugar, nuts, 2 tablespoons flour, 2 tablespoons melted butter, and cinnamon. Set aside.
3. Prepare the cake: In the bowl of an electric mixer, cream the 1 cup sugar and the ¼ pound butter on medium until light and fluffy, scraping side of bowl often.
4. In a separate bowl, sift together the 2 cups flour, baking powder, baking soda, and salt.
5. Add the eggs and vanilla slowly and beat well, scraping down the side of the bowl often.
6. With the electric mixer on low, slowly add the dry ingredients, alternating with the sour cream.
7. Pour the batter into the prepared pan. Sprinkle the Crumb Topping on the top of the batter. Bake for 45 to 50 minutes, until golden brown and a toothpick inserted in the center comes out clean.
8. Cool cake in pan on wire rack for 10 minutes. Remove from pan. Cut into slices and serve.

Pound Cake

Throughout our research, we found that pound cake was the most common choice of colonial cooks for an easy dessert. Its name is derived from the total weight of the traditional ingredients—one quarter pound each of flour, butter, sugar, and eggs. Its first appearance in print was in 1747, according to *Webster's Ninth*, and its popularity continues to this day. This simple, moist cake is the ideal building block for a sumptuous dessert. It pairs wonderfully with fresh fruit, Chantilly Cream (see page 208), or Crème Anglaise (see page 209).

Makes two 9-inch round cakes; Serves 12

4 cups granulated sugar
½ pound (2 sticks) unsalted butter, at room temperature
12 large eggs
1 tablespoon vanilla extract
8 ounces (1 cup) sour cream
5⅓ cups all-purpose flour, sifted
1 teaspoon baking powder
1 teaspoon baking soda
½ teaspoon salt

1. Preheat the oven to 325°F. Lightly coat two 9 x 2½-inch round cake pans with vegetable cooking spray.
2. In the bowl of an electric mixer, cream the sugar and butter together on medium to high until light and fluffy, scraping side of the bowl often.
3. Add the eggs and vanilla slowly and beat well.
4. Add the sour cream and beat well.
5. In a separate bowl, sift together the flour, baking powder, baking soda, and salt.
6. With the electric mixer on low, slowly add the dry ingredients.
7. Divide the batter between the two prepared pans. Bake about 1 hour, until golden brown and cakes pull away from the sides of the pans.
8. Cool cakes in pans on wire racks for 10 minutes. Remove cakes from pans and completely cool before serving.
9. To store for later use, wrap the cakes well in plastic wrap and freeze for up to 4 weeks.

Gingerbread

Gingerbread, a quick cake that incorporates exotic spices originally brought from the West Indies, was extremely popular in the eighteenth century. During the American Revolution, both continental and British troops ate gingerbread. It was also a treat enjoyed by both Benjamin Franklin, who wrote about purchasing it on his way to Philadelphia when he was seventeen, and George Washington, whose mother Mary served it to her son and his friend the Marquis de Lafayette in Fredericksburg, Virginia, in 1784. This recipe is delicious when topped with Chantilly Cream (see page 208).

Makes one 10-inch cake; Serves 10

1 pound (2½ cups) brown sugar
3 large eggs
1⅓ cups bread flour
1 tablespoon baking powder
½ teaspoon baking soda
2 tablespoons ground cinnamon
1 teaspoon ground ginger
1 teaspoon ground cardamom
½ teaspoon ground cloves
½ teaspoon salt
6 ounces (1½ sticks) unsalted butter, melted
¾ cup half and half

1. Preheat oven to 350°F. Lightly coat one 10-inch round pan with vegetable cooking spray and dust with flour.
2. In the bowl of an electric mixer (or food processor), whip the sugar and eggs until light and foamy.
3. In another bowl, sift the dry ingredients together and add to the sugar and egg mixture in two increments.
4. In a separate bowl, combine the butter and the half and half and add to the batter slowly, scraping down the side of the bowl.
5. Pour the batter into the prepared pan. Bake for 45 minutes, or until golden brown.
6. Cool the bread in the pan on a wire rack for 10 minutes. Remove from pan and completely cool before serving.
7. Serve with Chantilly Cream, if desired.

Martha Washington's Chocolate Mousse Cake

A slightly sweeter version of this chocolate cake was a favorite of Martha Washington's. Chocolate was first mentioned in cookery recipes as early as 1675. But its use in baking and as a hot drink goes back much further—some authorities say Columbus actually brought cocoa beans to Spain, where hot, sweetened chocolate was first served. Before long, the drink spread in popularity all throughout Europe. Thomas Jefferson, who undoubtedly first tasted chocolate in France, believed that drinking chocolate was healthier than drinking coffee or tea. Here, chocolate is transformed into a classic French dessert.

Makes two 9-inch cakes; Serves 10 to 12

Chocolate Cake
2 cups granulated sugar
½ pound (2 sticks) unsalted butter
4 large eggs
5 cups cake flour, sifted
¼ cup unsweetened Dutch-processed cocoa powder, sifted
2 tablespoons plus 2 teaspoons baking soda
½ teaspoon salt
1 cup whole milk

Chocolate Mousse   Makes 3 cups
4 ounces (4 squares) semisweet chocolate
4 large eggs, separated (see Chef's Note)
½ cup heavy cream

Chocolate Ganache
1 pint (2 cups) heavy cream
24 ounces (4 cups) semisweet chocolate chips

Candied flowers or chopped nuts, for garnish (optional)

This recipe calls for eggs that are only partially cooked, which may present a health concern for the young, the elderly, or those whose immune systems are compromised.

1. Prepare the Chocolate Cake: Preheat the oven to 350°F. Lightly spray two 9-inch round cake pans with vegetable cooking spray and line the bottoms with parchment paper circles.
2. In the bowl of an electric mixer, cream the sugar and butter on medium to high until light and fluffy, scraping side of bowl often.
3. Add eggs slowly, scraping the side of the bowl often.
4. In a separate bowl, sift together the flour, cocoa powder, baking soda, and salt. Add to the butter-sugar mixture, alternating with the milk.
5. Divide the batter between the two prepared pans. Bake for 30 to 35 minutes, until firm to the touch or until a toothpick inserted in the middle comes out clean.
6. Cool cakes in pans on wire racks for 10 minutes. Remove cakes from pans and completely cool.
7. Prepare the Chocolate Mousse: Place water in the bottom pan of a double boiler so that the top of the water is ½ inch below the upper pan. Place the chocolate squares in the upper pan. Then place the double boiler over low heat. Stir the chocolate constantly until it is melted. The water in the bottom of the double boiler should not come to boiling while the chocolate is melting.
8. Remove the melted chocolate from heat. Add the egg yolks and beat well. Set aside to cool.
9. In a chilled bowl of an electric mixer with chilled beaters, beat the ½ cup heavy cream on low to medium until soft peaks form. Cover with plastic wrap and refrigerate, until chilled.

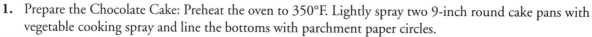

10. In a separate, clean, and dry bowl of an electric mixer, whip the egg whites on medium until soft peaks form. Reserve.

11. Gently fold the chilled whipped cream into the chocolate mixture until the cream is just combined into the mixture. Do not over fold. Gently fold the reserved whites into the chocolate until just combined. Cover the mixture with plastic wrap and refrigerate for at least 1 hour before using.

12. Prepare the Chocolate Ganache: In a heavy 1-quart saucepan, bring the 2 cups heavy cream just to a boil, stirring frequently. Remove the saucepan from heat.

13. In a large bowl, place the chocolate chips. Pour the hot cream over the chocolate and let set for 1 minute.

14. Whisk to thoroughly combine ingredients and allow to cool. When the mixture is room temperature, cover with plastic wrap and refrigerate until 1 hour before ready to use.

15. Assemble the cake: When the cake has cooled completely, using a serrated knife, carefully cut each cake in half horizontally to make a total of 4 layers, 2 per cake.

16. To assemble, place first cake layer on a large serving plate. Alternate the cake layers and mousse filling, spreading the mousse evenly onto each cake layer.

17. Frost the outside of the cake with the Chocolate Ganache. Refrigerate the cake until ready to serve. Garnish with candied flowers or chopped nuts.

Yule Log

The traditional holiday or yule log is French in origin and traveled to the New World in the memories and recipe boxes of French immigrants. Although the experienced baker might decorate this classic rolled dessert with edible holiday trimmings made from meringue and marzipan, this dessert doesn't need a lot of extra effort to delight your guests.

Makes one jelly roll; Serves 8 to 10

Chocolate Filling

9 ounces (1½ cups) semisweet chocolate chips
1 cup whole milk
4 egg yolks
½ pound (2 sticks) unsalted butter
1 cup confectioners' sugar, sifted

Chocolate Sponge Cake

4 large eggs
½ cup granulated sugar
¾ cup all-purpose flour, sifted
¼ cup unsweetened Dutch-processed cocoa powder, sifted

1. Prepare the Chocolate Filling: Place water in the bottom pan of a double boiler so that the top of the water is ½ inch below the upper pan. Place the chocolate squares in the upper pan. Then place the double boiler over low heat. Stir the chocolate constantly until it is melted. The water in the bottom of the double boiler should not come to boiling while the chocolate is melting. Transfer to a bowl and set aside.
2. Wash and dry the upper pan of the double boiler. Add the milk and yolks and heat until warm.
3. Add the melted chocolate, stir until combined.
4. Transfer to a bowl. Cover with plastic wrap and refrigerate for 30 minutes.
5. In the bowl of an electric mixer, cream the butter and confectioners' sugar on medium to high until light and fluffy, scraping down the side of the bowl often.
6. Add the cooled chocolate-milk mixture and mix until combined. Refrigerate.
7. Prepare the Chocolate Sponge Cake: Preheat the oven to 400°F. Lightly spray a jelly-roll pan with vegetable cooking spray and line the bottom with parchment paper.
8. In the bowl of an electric mixer, beat the eggs and sugar on high for 5 minutes, until pale yellow and thick.
9. Gently fold in the flour and cocoa.
10. Pour the batter into the prepared pan. Bake for 12 to 15 minutes, until golden and cake springs back when lightly touched and pulls away from sides of pan.
11. While cake still is warm, immediately turn the cake out onto a towel sprinkled with confectioners' sugar.
12. Carefully peel off the parchment paper. With the towel under the cake, gently roll up long side of the cake into a jelly roll shape so that the towel is both rolled up inside and covers the outside of the cake. Let cake completely cool.
13. To assemble the cake, unroll the cake. Spread with ⅓ of the Chocolate Filling, reserving the rest for coating the outside. Roll the cake back up into a log shape, with the seam side down. To make the roll look like a log, cut a 1½-inch diagonal piece from each end of the roll. Form "branches" by placing these wedge-shaped pieces of the cake on either the side of the log's "trunk."

14. Spread the remaining Chocolate Filling evenly on the outside of the log and around each of the branches to secure them in place. To give the log a realistic look, carefully score the frosting with the tines of a fork, so it resembles the irregular texture of bark. Dust the "bark" with cocoa powder and then some confectioners' sugar to create "snow." If desired, decorate with candies and chocolates. Refrigerate until ready to serve.

15. To serve, cut the roll into slices and serve on dessert plates.

Apple–Walnut Cakes

"One rotten apple spoils the bunch" was more than just a saying in colonial days. Because apples were kept over the winter in large quantities, it was understood that a single bad apple would cause the entire harvest to rot. One way the colonists used their apples was in cakes like this one.

Makes eight 3 x 1½-inch (½ cup) ramekins; Serves 8

2 medium Macintosh or Granny Smith apples, peeled, cored,
  and chopped (about 2 cups)
½ cup B & B liqueur
1 cup packed light brown sugar
2 large eggs
1 cup all-purpose flour, sifted
1 tablespoon ground cinnamon
1 teaspoon baking soda
1 teaspoon freshly grated nutmeg
¾ cup vegetable oil
¾ cup walnuts, toasted and chopped (see Chef's Note)

1. In a medium bowl, combine the apples and liqueur, making sure apples are covered so they don't turn brown. Allow to marinate for 8 hours or overnight in the refrigerator.
2. When ready to bake the cake, preheat the oven to 350°F. Lightly coat eight ramekins with vegetable cooking spray and dust lightly with flour.
3. In the bowl of an electric mixer, beat the sugar, oil, and eggs on medium until just combined.
4. In a separate bowl, sift together the flour, cinnamon, baking soda, and nutmeg.
5. With the electric mixer on low, add dry ingredients to the sugar/oil mixture until combined.
6. With a rubber spatula, gently fold in the marinated apples and walnuts.
7. Divide the batter among the prepared ramekins and place them on a baking sheet.
8. Bake for 20 to 25 minutes until slightly puffed and golden-brown and a toothpick inserted in the center comes out clean.

Chef's Note

Toasting Nuts
Preheat oven to 350°F. Spread out the nuts in a single layer on a sheet pan. Bake for about 20 minutes, until golden brown. Let cool.

Orange–Ricotta Coffee Cake

Although oranges arrived regularly in Philadelphia aboard ships from Spain, these citrus fruits were expensive and largely a treat for the wealthy. When the oranges first arrived, they were decoratively displayed and when they were eaten, not a morsel was wasted. Even the orange peel was candied and used in cakes, such as this one.

Makes one 9-inch cake; Serves 8 to 10

¼ cup warm water (105° to 115°F)
1 package active dry yeast (¼ ounce)
½ cup granulated sugar
½ cup warm milk (105° to 115°F)
½ cup ricotta cheese
1 tablespoon grated orange rind
½ cup fresh orange juice, strained
1 large egg
½ teaspoon salt
3½ to 4 cups all-purpose flour
1 cup confectioners' sugar, sifted, for icing
2 tablespoons fresh orange juice, for icing

The word boule, pronounced BOOL, is French for ball. In baking, it usually refers to a round loaf of bread.

1. In the bowl of an electric mixer, beat the warm water and yeast on low until combined and the yeast is dissolved.
2. Slowly add in the granulated sugar, warm milk, ricotta cheese, orange rind and ½ cup juice, egg, and salt.
3. With the mixer on low, gradually add 2 cups flour, until the mixture starts to form a dough. Gradually add the remaining 1½ to 2 cups flour, adding only enough flour to make the dough stiff.
4. Turn the dough out onto lightly floured surface and knead with your hands for 5 minutes.
5. Place the dough in a large, greased bowl and cover loosely with damp towel.
6. Place the bowl in a warm area, such as on top of the oven, but away from drafts for about 1 to 1½ hours to allow the dough to rise; it should double in size. Punch it down.
7. Preheat oven to 350°F. Lightly coat one 9 x 2½-inch round cake or springform pan with vegetable cooking spray.
8. Shape dough into a *boule* and gently place in the pan. Bake 50 to 60 minutes until golden brown.
9. Cool cake in pan on wire rack for 10 minutes. Remove cake from pan. Completely cool.
10. For the icing, in a small bowl, combine the confectioners' sugar and orange juice and stir until smooth. Drizzle the icing over the top of the cooled cake in a decorative pattern. Serve.

Vanilla Cheesecake

Cheesecake has been popular for centuries, long before New York cheesecake became a staple on American menus—long before New York even existed, for that matter. The first mention in print of a dessert made with cream cheese or ricotta dates back to 1440. Flavoring cheesecake with a vanilla bean was a natural in early Philadelphia—vanilla beans were one of the many spices and seeds imported to American shores from the West Indies.

Makes one 9-inch cheesecake; Serves 12 to 14

1½ cups Graham Cracker Crust (see page 210)
16 ounces (two 8-ounce packages) cream cheese, softened
1 cup granulated sugar
3 large eggs
16 ounces (2 cups) sour cream
1 tablespoon vanilla extract
1 vanilla bean, scraped (see Chef's Note)
¼ teaspoon salt

1. Preheat the oven to 350°F.
2. Lightly coat a 9 x 3-inch springform pan with vegetable cooking spray. Wrap the bottom of the pan with aluminum foil to prevent water from seeping in around the side of the springform during the water bath.
3. Press the Graham Cracker Crust mixture onto the bottom and about 2 inches up the side of the pan. Set aside.
4. In the bowl of an electric mixer, beat the cream cheese and the remaining one cup of sugar on medium to high, until combined, scraping side of bowl often.
5. With the mixer on low, add in the eggs slowly. Mix until just incorporated.
6. Add in the sour cream, vanilla, scraped vanilla bean, and salt and mix until incorporated.
7. Pour the batter into the prepared pan.
8. Place the pan into a larger high-sided roasting pan and carefully pour boiling water into the roasting pan around the springform pan to a depth of 1½ inches. (This step reduces cracking.)
9. Bake for 30 to 35 minutes, until the middle of the cheesecake is nearly set when shaken and slightly puffy. Remove from oven and let cool on a wire rack.
10. Allow cakes to cool. Wrap and store the cake in a refrigerator for up to 5 days.

Chef's Note

Scraping Vanilla Beans
Cut the beans in half, lengthwise and scrape the tiny black seeds into your mixture. Discard the pods.

While in Philadelphia, Jefferson asked his French valet, Petit, to "bring a stock of macaroni, Parmesan cheese, figs of Marseilles, Brugnoles, raisins, almonds, mustard, vinaigre d'estragon, other good vinegar, oil and anchovies." He also asked for 50 vanilla beans, yet another flavor he introduced to the New World.

Hazelnut Cheesecake

Nuts, plentiful in the New World, were used to flavor everything from breads and pies to cakes, such as this satisfying cheesecake.

Makes one 9-inch cheesecake; Serves 12 to 14

1½ cups Graham Cracker Crust (see page 210)

16 ounces (two 8-ounce packages) cream cheese, softened

1 cup granulated sugar

3 large eggs

16 ounces (2 cups) sour cream

¼ teaspoon salt

½ cup hazelnuts, toasted, skined, and finely chopped (see Chef's Note)

¼ cup hazelnut-flavored liqueur

Toasting and Skinning Hazelnuts
Preheat oven to 350°F. Arrange whole hazelnuts in a baking pan and bake for 15 minutes until they are golden brown and you can smell them. Remove from the oven and let cool. When nuts are still warm, place them in a towel and roll back and forth to remove skins.

1. Preheat the oven to 350°F.
2. Lightly coat a 9 x 3-inch springform pan with vegetable cooking spray. Wrap the bottom of the pan with aluminum foil to prevent water from seeping in around the side of the springform during the water bath.
3. Press the Graham Cracker Crust mixture onto the bottom and about 2 inches up the side of the pan. Set aside.
4. In the bowl of an electric mixer, beat the cream cheese and sugar on medium to high, until combined, scraping the side of the bowl often.
5. With the mixer on low, slowly add the eggs and beat well.
6. Add the sour cream and salt and beat well.
7. Add the hazelnuts and the liqueur and beat well.
8. Pour the batter into the prepared pan.
9. Place the pan into a larger high-sided roasting pan and carefully pour boiling water into the roasting pan around the springform pan to a depth of 1½ inches. (This step reduces cracking.)
10. Bake for 30 to 35 minutes, until the middle of the cheesecake is nearly set when shaken and slightly puffy.
11. Remove from the oven and let cool on a wire rack. Refrigerate overnight. Carefully remove side of pan before serving.

Frangipane

This classic almond-flavored French pastry can be used to make pie shells or tarts, or it can be served alone, like a crisp cookie. Here, we prepare it as a layer cake frosted with Coffee Buttercream and garnished with luscious Chocolate Sauce. If you prefer a simpler version, serve this dessert plain with fresh fruit.

Makes one 15 x 10 cake; Serves 8 to 10

Cake

13 ounces (3 sticks plus 2 tablespoons) unsalted butter, softened
1⅓ cups (14 ounces) Almond Paste (see recipe, page 208) or use purchased
1¾ cups granulated sugar
¼ cup cake flour, sifted
9 large eggs

Coffee Buttercream   Makes about 3 cups

1¼ pounds (5⅝ cups) confectioners' sugar, sifted
1 cup (8 large) egg whites
1¼ pounds (5 sticks) unsalted butter, cubed and softened
½ cup very strong cold coffee

1 cup Chocolate Sauce (see page 146)

1. Prepare the Cake: Preheat the oven to 400°F. Lightly coat two 15 x 10 x 1-inch jelly-roll pan with vegetable cooking spray and line the bottoms with parchment paper.
2. In the bowl of an electric mixer on medium speed, begin creaming the butter. Add the Almond Paste in chunks gradually, until combined.
3. Add the sugar and beat well.
4. Add the flour, a little at a time.
5. Slowly add the eggs and continue beat well, scraping the side of the bowl often.
6. Evenly divide and spread the mixture into the prepared pans.
7. Bake for 10 to 20 minutes, until golden and cake pulls away from sides of pans.
8. Let cool 10 minutes on a wire rack. Peel off the parchment paper and let cakes cool completely. Turn the cake out of the pan onto the cooling racks.
9. Trim ½-inch off the edges of the cake on all sides. Reserve.
10. Prepare the Coffee Buttercream: In a 1-quart saucepan, bring 1 inch of water to a boil.
11. In a large bowl, combine the 1 cup of egg whites and sugar. Place the bowl over the saucepan of boiling water and whisk mixture until hot (about 160°F on a candy thermometer).
12. Remove the bowl from the heat and transfer the egg whites to a clean, dry bowl of an electric mixer. Beat on high speed until whites become stiff and the bowl is cool to the touch.
13. When the meringue is completely cool, add the softened butter a little at a time. Whisk until the mixture becomes slightly thick and fluffy.
14. Add the prepared coffee a little at a time to desired taste.
15. To assemble the cake, place the first layer of the cake on a large serving plate. Spread evenly with 1 to 1½ cups of the Coffee Buttercream. Top with the second layer. Frost the top, then the sides of the cake with the remaining buttercream. If desired, use any extra frosting to pipe a decorative border.
16. To serve, cut the cake into 3-inch squares and divide among dessert plates. Garnish each square with about 1 tablespoon of the prepared Chocolate Sauce.

Coconut and Macadamia Nut Tartlets

Coconut was introduced to the New World by sea captains who traveled to the West Indies before arriving in Philadelphia. Over the years, American cooks used it more and more in creations such as this. The trio of coconut, nuts, and chocolate in this tart is a winning combination. You can substitute hazelnuts for the macadamia nuts, if you prefer.

Makes eight 3¼ x ½-inch individual tartlets or one 9 x 1⅜-inch tart; Serves 8

Chocolate Shortbread Dough
½ pound (2 sticks) unsalted butter, cubed and softened
1 cup granulated sugar
2 cups all-purpose flour, sifted
1 cup unsweetened Dutch-processed cocoa powder, sifted
½ teaspoon salt
2 large eggs
2 large egg yolks

Filling
1¼ cups milk
2 large eggs
3 tablespoons granulated sugar

1 cup fresh or desiccated coconut flakes, lightly toasted
1 cup macadamia nuts, toasted and chopped (see Chef's Note, page 136)

1. Prepare the Chocolate Shortbread Dough: In a bowl with an electric mixer, cream the butter and sugar on medium to high, until light and fluffy.
2. In a separate bowl, combine the flour, cocoa, and salt.
3. With the electric mixer on low, slowly add the dry ingredients to the butter-sugar mixture and beat just until combined.
4. Add the eggs and yolks, and beat until dough just begins to hold together.
5. Wrap the dough in plastic wrap and chill in the refrigerator for at least 1 hour before using.
6. Preheat the oven to 400°F.
7. Prepare the Filling: In a medium bowl, whisk together the milk, eggs, and sugar until combined. Set aside.
8. Remove the dough from the refrigerator. Evenly divide the chilled dough into eight balls. On a lightly floured surface, roll each ball into a circle 6 inches in diameter. Ease pastry circles into 3¼ x ½-inch pans, being careful not to stretch the pastry. Gently press each round into the fluted side of the tart pan with removable bottoms. Trim pastry even with rim of pan. Place the tartlets on a baking sheet.
9. Line each pastry with a double thickness of foil, and fill with dry beans or pastry weights (see Chef's Note, page 152). Bake for 8 minutes. Remove foil. Bake for 4 to 5 minutes, until the dough is firm and set to the touch.
10. Reduce the oven temperature to 350°F. Sprinkle each tart shell with the coconut and nuts. Carefully pour the Filling into the shells.
11. Carefully transfer the baking sheet to the oven. Bake for 15 to 20 minutes, until a knife inserted near the center comes out clean.
12. Cool on a wire rack. Refrigerate within 2 hours; cover for longer storage.

Shortbread Triangles with Apple Chutney Filling

Shortbread is as British as Big Ben. This recipe is spiced up by grated fresh ginger.

Makes 18 triangles; Serves 6

Vanilla Shortbread

¾ pound (3 sticks) unsalted butter, softened
1 cup confectioners' sugar, sifted
½ teaspoon vanilla extract
3 cups all-purpose flour, sifted
½ teaspoon salt
1½ teaspoons granulated sugar, for garnish

Apple Chutney Filling

¼ pound (1 stick) unsalted butter, softened
½ cup packed dark brown sugar
¼ cup molasses
¼ teaspoon salt
2 sticks cinnamon
2 teaspoons grated fresh ginger
4 Granny Smith apples, peeled, cored, and cubed
1 tablespoon grated lime rind (about 1 medium lime)
2 tablespoons lime juice (about 1 medium lime), strained
½ cup raisins
½ cup walnuts, lightly toasted and chopped (see Chef's Note, page 136)

1. Prepare the Vanilla Shortbread: In the bowl of an electric mixer, cream the butter, confectioners' sugar, and vanilla on medium to high until light and fluffy.
2. In a separate bowl, combine the flour and salt.
3. With the mixer on low, slowly add the dry ingredients to the butter/sugar mixture, and beat just until the dough begins to hold together. Form the dough into a disc shape, wrap in plastic wrap, and chill in the refrigerator for at least 1 hour before using.
4. Prepare the Apple Chutney Filling: In a large sauté pan, melt the butter over medium heat. Stirring constantly, add the brown sugar, molasses, and salt.
5. Add the cinnamon sticks and ginger and bring the mixture to a boil.
6. Reduce the heat to low, and add the apples, lime rind, and lime juice. Cook just until the apples start to soften.
7. Add the raisins and walnuts, and remove from heat. Set aside.
8. Preheat the oven to 325°F. Line the baking sheet with parchment paper.
9. On a lightly floured surface, roll out the shortbread to ¼ inch thick.
10. Cut the dough into eighteen 3-inch triangle shapes and place them 1 inch apart on prepared baking sheets.
11. Sprinkle the sugar over the top of each triangle.
12. Bake for 15 to 20 minutes, until golden brown around the edges. Cool on a wire rack.
13. Assemble the triangles: When the triangles are cool, spoon ¼ cup of the warm Apple Chutney onto each of six triangles. Top each with another triangle and more chutney. Top with a third triangle. You should have a total of six, three-layer Apple Chutney triangles.
14. Dust the plate with confectioners' sugar and, if desired, serve with purchased caramel praline ice cream.

Almond and Raspberry Tart

Raspberries, brought over from Europe, quickly grew wild in the colonies, and were used in everything from jam and jelly to tarts such as this one.

Makes one 9-inch tart; Serves 8

½ pound (2 sticks) unsalted butter, softened
¾ cup granulated sugar
1 large egg
½ teaspoon vanilla extract
2 cups cake flour, sifted
1¼ cups sliced almonds, toasted and ground (see Chef's Note, page 136)
½ teaspoon ground cinnamon
¾ cup seedless red raspberry jam
¼ cup confectioners' sugar, sifted

1. Preheat the oven to 325°F. Lightly coat a 9 x 1⅜-inch tart pan with a removable bottom with vegetable cooking spray.
2. In the bowl of an electric mixer, cream the butter and sugar on medium to high, until light and fluffy.
3. Add the egg and vanilla and beat well.
4. In a separate bowl, combine the flour, ground almonds, and cinnamon. Add to the egg mixture and beat just until a soft dough forms. Wrap in plastic wrap and chill in the refrigerator for 30 minutes.
5. Roll 1½ to 2 cups of the dough mixture into a circle 11 inches in diameter. Ease pastry into pan, being careful not to stretch pastry. Gently press pastry into the fluted side of tart pan and trim the edges.
6. Spread the jam evenly over the bottom of pastry.
7. Roll the remaining dough into a 10 x 6-inch rectangle and cut into eight ¼-inch-thick by 1-inch-wide strips.
8. Weave the strips diagonally over the jam filling to create a lattice. Press ends of strips into rim of bottom crust, trimming ends as necessary.
9. Bake for 35 to 40 minutes, until the crust is golden brown.
10. Allow the tart to completely cool and dust with confectioners' sugar. Serve alone or, if desired, with good-quality purchased chocolate ice cream.

Lemon Curd Tart

Enhancing a typical French custard with lemon flavoring would have been something only found at the City Tavern in colonial Philadelphia, when lemons and limes were used and displayed as a symbol of affluence and sophistication. This versatile filling can also be used in cake, or served with warm scones.

Makes eight 3-inch tartlets; Serves 8

Lemon Curd Makes 4 cups
15 large egg yolks
2 cups fresh lemon juice (about 8 large lemons), strained
1¼ cups granulated sugar
½ pint (1 cup) heavy cream

Lemon Dough
2⅔ cups all-purpose flour
¼ cup granulated sugar
¼ teaspoon salt
7 ounces (1¾ stick) cold unsalted butter
¼ cup fresh lemon juice (about 1 large lemon), strained
2 large egg yolks

1. Prepare the curd: In a heavy-bottomed large saucepan (to prevent scorching), combine the 15 egg yolks, the 2 cups lemon juice, 1¼ cups sugar, and the cream.
2. Cook over medium heat, whisking continuously so that the mixture does not stick to the bottom.
3. When the mixture comes to a gentle boil, lower the heat and stir for 1 minute more.
4. Remove from the heat. Pour the mixture into a ovenproof bowl and let cool. Cover the surface with plastic wrap to prevent a "skin" from forming on the top.
5. Chill in the refrigerator overnight before using.
6. Preparing the dough: Place steel blade in processor bowl. Add the flour, sugar, and salt. Cover; process with on/off pulses, until the mixture is combined.
7. Add the butter. Process with on/off pulses, until most of the mixture crumbly.
8. With the processor running, quickly add the ¼ cup lemon juice and 2 yolks through the feed tube. Stop processor when all lemon juice and egg yolk is added; scrape down sides.
9. Process with two on/off pulses (mixture may not all be moistened). Remove the dough from the bowl. Form the dough into a disc shape, wrap in plastic wrap, and chill in the refrigerator for at least 1 hour before using.
10. Baking the tart: Preheat oven to 400°F. Set aside eight 3-inch tartlet pans. Roll out the dough on a lightly floured surface until it is ⅛ inch thick. Cut the dough into squares larger than tartlet pans. Gently place squares of dough loosely into the pans, and trim excess dough to ½ inch beyond the edges of the pans. Prick the dough on the bottoms of the pans in several places. Fold extra dough under and crimp edges.
11. Line each tartlet shell with a double thickness of foil. Fill with dried beans or pastry weights (see page 152). Bake for 15 minutes. Remove from oven and let cool.
12. When ready to serve, fill the baked and cooled tartlet shells with the lemon curd mixture.
13. Garnish with Chantilly Cream (see page 208), if desired.

Raspberry Trifle

America offered the early settlers a wide variety of wild raspberries, although European varieties were still imported for cultivation. Fruits from their precious harvests were used in delights such as this British dessert.

Fills one 3-quart (12 cups) trifle bowl; Serves 12

Yellow Cake
4 large eggs
½ cup granulated sugar
½ teaspoon vanilla extract
¼ teaspoon almond extract
⅔ cup all-purpose flour, sifted
3 tablespoons butter, melted and cooled

Cream Filling
2½ cups heavy cream
½ cup confectioners' sugar, sifted

1 cup brandy
1 cup raspberry preserves
4 cups Pastry Cream (see page 207; make two recipes)
1 pint (2 cups) fresh strawberries, hulled
1 pint (2 cups) fresh raspberries

1. Prepare the Yellow Cake: Preheat oven to 350°F. Lightly coat one 9-inch cake pan with vegetable cooking spray. Line the bottom of the pan with parchment paper circle and spray the top of the paper with the spray.
2. In a medium bowl set over a saucepan of simmering water, whisk the eggs and sugar until warm. Remove the bowl from the heat and whisk in the vanilla and almond extracts.
3. Transfer the warmed egg mixture to the bowl of an electric mixer. Beat on high until the mixture is pale yellow, thickened, and triples in volume.
4. Remove the bowl and sift ⅓ cup of the flour over top of the eggs, gently folding with a rubber spatula. Repeat sifting and folding with the remaining flour. Fold in the melted butter, being sure to scrape side of the bowl.
5. Pour mixture into prepared pan and bake for 20 to 25 minutes, until golden and a toothpick inserted in the center comes out clean. Cool the cakes on a wire rack for 10 minutes before removing from pan.
6. Using a serrated knife, cut the cake layer horizontally into two equal halves. Reserve.
7. Prepare the Cream Filling: In a chilled bowl of an electric mixer with chilled beaters, beat the heavy cream on low to medium, until soft peaks form. Add the confectioners' sugar and beat a few seconds more. Cover with plastic wrap and chill in the refrigerator until ready to use.
8. Assemble the trifle: Place one half of the cake layer into the bottom of a 10-inch glass bowl. Using a pastry brush, brush the cake with the brandy. With a spoon, spread half of the preserves over the cake layer. Spread half of the prepared Pastry Cream over the preserves.
9. Add the remaining half of the cake. Brush with the remaining brandy and spread the remaining preserves.
10. Spread the remaining Pastry Cream over the preserves.
11. Using a 12-inch decorator bag fitted with a star tip, transfer the reserved chilled filling into the bag, leaving enough room to close and twist the top of the bag. Pipe filling around the edges of the bowl. Fill the center with the strawberries and raspberries.
12. Chill in the refrigerator for 2 hours before serving.

Poached Pears with Chocolate Sauce

Although everyone raves over ultra-rich desserts, simple, poached fruit can be a satisfying—and guilt-free—postscript to a wonderful meal. Dessert pears have a juicy, white flesh that is slightly acidic, but also sweet. Poaching fruits in wine is a practice that originated in Burgundy, a province of France. In this recipe, Chocolate Sauce is the finishing touch.

Makes 6 poached pears; Serves 6

Pears

1 bottle (750 ml) red burgundy wine
1½ cups granulated sugar
4 sticks cinnamon
12 whole cloves
1 vanilla bean, split lengthwise
6 firm, ripe pears (such as Bosc or Bartlett), peeled and cored

Chocolate Sauce

3 cups granulated sugar
3 cups water
2 cups unsweetened Dutch-processed cocoa powder, sifted
1 pint (2 cups) heavy cream

1. Prepare the Pears: In a 5-quart stainless steel or enameled saucepan, bring the wine, the sugar, cinnamon, cloves, and vanilla bean to a boil, stirring occasionally
2. Cook the mixture for 15 minutes over high heat, stirring occasionally.
3. Lower the heat to medium. Carefully stand the pears upright in the saucepan. Cook, covered, for 15 to 20 minutes, until thickest part of the pear can be easily pierced with a wooden skewer. *Do not overcook.*
4. Cool the pears to room temperature. Using a slotted spoon, remove the pears from liquid. Set aside.
5. Prepare the Chocolate Sauce: In a 2-quart saucepan, combine the sugar, water, and cocoa. Whisk to combine.
6. Bring to a boil and remove from heat. Whisk in the heavy cream.
7. Set a fine wire sieve over a medium bowl. Strain the mixture through the sieve and let cool to room temperature.
8. To assemble the dessert, pour 2 tablespoons of the Chocolate Sauce on each dessert plate. Place a pear on each plate on top of the sauce. If desired, drizzle some of the remaining sauce over each pear and garnish with a with a purchased almond-flavored biscotti.

Cobblers, Crumbles, and Pies

Cobblers, crisps, and crumbles are perfect ways to use up fruits—camouflaging the looks of less-than-picture-perfect pieces—no doubt a benefit much appreciated by the colonial cook. When served at the Tavern, these baked fruit desserts reflect the fruits of the season. In May, strawberries are paired with rhubarb. Summer fruits take over during June, July, and August. During the colder months, apples are paired with cranberries. Pies simply use a pastry crust as the foundation for the same seasonal fruit fillings.

Blueberry Cobbler

Dried fruit is not a California invention—the Indians were drying blueberries when the Pilgrims first arrived on Plymouth's shores. This recipe uses fresh blueberries, although dried blueberries combined with apples would make a delicious winter version of this recipe.

Makes eight 3 x 1½-inch (½ cup) ramekins; Serves 8
4 pints (8 cups) fresh blueberries
1 cup granulated sugar
¼ cup cornstarch
2 tablespoons fresh lemon juice
4 cups Streusel Topping (see page 210)

1. Preheat oven to 350°F. Coat eight 3 x 1½-inch ramekins with vegetable cooking spray.
2. In a large bowl, combine the blueberries, sugar, cornstarch, and lemon juice. Gently toss together. Evenly divide the blueberry mixture among prepared ramekins. Top each with ½ cup of the Streusel Topping.
3. Place the ramekins on a baking sheet. Bake for 25 to 30 minutes, until the top is golden and the mixture starts to bubble.

Pear and Sour Cherry Cobbler

This fruit combination is just one of the many seasonal combos we make at the Tavern. Sour cherries, which are both smaller and more tart than their sweeter cousins, grew wild in early colonial days. Cherry trees have been cultivated for centuries. Sour cherries are available dried at health food stores and most large supermarkets.

Makes eight 3 x 1½-inch (½ cup) ramekins; Serves 8
1½ cup dried tart red cherries
½ cup brandy
8 pears, peeled, cored, and sliced
1 cup granulated sugar
3 tablespoons cornstarch
4 cups Streusel Topping (see page 210)

1. In a small bowl, combine the dried cherries and brandy and soak for 2 hours, until softened.
2. Preheat oven to 350°F. Coat eight 3 x 1½-inch ramekins with vegetable cooking spray.
3. In a large bowl, combine the pears, sugar, and cornstarch. Stir in the cherry mixture.
4. Gently toss together. Evenly divide the pear/cherry mixture among the prepared ramekins.
5. Top each with ½ cup of the Streusel Topping.
6. Place the ramekins on a baking sheet. Bake for 25 to 30 minutes, until the tops are golden and the mixture starts to bubble.

Apple–Cranberry Cobbler

Cranberries, a native American fruit, add a burst of flavor to this cold-weather cobbler. The early settlers found cranberries to be similar to lingonberries they found in their home countries, but in need of sweetening to tone down the red berry's natural tartness.

Makes eight 3 x 1½-inch (½ cup) ramekins; Serves 8
6 Granny Smith apples, peeled, cored, cut into 8 slices
2 cups whole fresh cranberries
¾ cup granulated sugar
2 tablespoons cornstarch
1 teaspoon ground cinnamon
2 cups Oat Topping (see page 210)

1. Preheat oven the to 375°F. Lightly coat eight 3 x 1½-inch ramekins with vegetable cooking spray.
2. In a large bowl, combine the apples, cranberries, sugar, cornstarch, and cinnamon.
3. Evenly divide the mixture among the prepared ramekins. Top each with 1¼ cup Oat Topping.
4. Place the ramekins on a baking sheet. Bake for 35 to 40 minutes, until the tops are golden brown and the mixture starts to bubble.

Apple-Fig Crumble

Figs, brought to America from Mediterranean shores, adapted well to the North American climate and terrain. When dried and stored in a cool, dark place, these fruits lasted almost indefinitely. This crumble made with dried figs is an ideal fall dessert.

Makes eight 3 x 1½-inch (½ cup) ramekins; Serves 8

1 bottle (750 ml) Madeira
1½ cups granulated sugar
15 dried figs, cubed
3 sticks cinnamon
1 vanilla bean, split lengthwise
8 Granny Smith apples, peeled, cored, and sliced
4 cups Streusel Topping (see page 210)
1½ cups Crème Anglaise (see page 209)

1. Preheat the oven to 350°F. Lightly coat the eight 3 x 1½-inch ramekins with vegetable cooking spray.
2. In a medium saucepan, bring the Madeira, granulated sugar, figs, cinnamon sticks, and vanilla bean to a boil.
3. Reduce heat to medium and cook for 20 to 30 minutes, until thickened and reduced by half. Place the apples in a medium, ovenproof bowl.
4. Remove the saucepan from the heat and pour the mixture over the apples.
5. Stir the mixture until well combined. Let cool. Discard the vanilla bean.
6. Evenly divide the apple-fig mixture among the prepared ramekins. Top each with ½ cup of the Streusel Topping.
7. Place the ramekins on a baking sheet. Bake for 25 to 30 minutes, until the tops are golden and the mixture starts to bubble.
8. Serve with Creme Anglaise or, if desired, a high-quality purchased vanilla ice cream.

Rhubarb–Strawberry Crisp

In the eighteenth century as today, this crisp would be served in May, when its primary ingredients were the most bountiful. Rhubarb was most likely introduced to America by the German settlers, who boiled and sweetened it for use in sauces, pies, preserves, wines, and fruit desserts, such as this easy-to-make crisp.

Makes eight 3 x 1½-inch (½ cup) ramekins or one 1½-quart baking dish; Serves 8

1½ pound fresh rhubarb, cleaned and diced
1 pint (2 cups) fresh strawberries, hulled and halved
¼ cup granulated sugar
¼ cup packed light brown sugar
2 tablespoons water
1 teaspoon fresh lemon juice
4 cups Streusel Topping (see page 210)

1. Preheat the oven to 375°F. Lightly coat eight 3 x 1½-inch ramekins or one 1½-quart shallow baking dish with vegetable cooking spray.
2. In a large bowl, combine the rhubarb and strawberries.
3. In a separate bowl, combine the granulated sugar, brown sugar, water, and lemon juice and mix well.
4. Pour the sugar mixture over the fruit. Gently toss together.
5. Evenly divide the mixture among the prepared ramekins.
6. Top each with ½ cup of the Streusel Topping.
7. Place the ramekins on a baking sheet. Bake for 25 to 30 minutes, until the tops are golden brown and the mixture starts to bubble.

Peach and Raspberry Crisp

Peaches were enjoyed by early Philadelphians in several ways—fresh, during the season, or sun-dried or made into sweet preserves for year-round consumption. In colonial times, this recipe could have used the fruit either fresh or as preserves.

Makes eight 3 x 1½-inch (½ cup) ramekins or one 2-quart baking dish; Serves 8

½ cup granulated sugar
⅓ cup sour cream
1 large egg
2 tablespoons all-purpose flour
1 teaspoon vanilla extract
5 ripe peaches, sliced, skin on
1 pint (2 cups) fresh raspberries
2 cups Oat Topping (see page 210)

1. Preheat the oven to 350°F. Lightly coat eight 3 x 1½-inch ramekins or one baking dish with vegetable cooking spray.
2. In a large bowl, combine the granulated sugar, sour cream, egg, flour, and vanilla.
3. Gently fold in the peaches and raspberries.
4. Evenly divide the fruit mixture among the prepared ramekins. Top each with ¼ cup Oat Topping.
5. Place ramekins on a baking sheet. Bake for 20 to 30 minutes, until tops are golden and the mixture starts to bubble.

Rhubarb-Strawberry Crumb Pie

Rhubarb and strawberries are a seasonal match made in heaven. While the pairing of the two in pie was not documented until the mid 1800s, strawberries were abundant in the New World and most certainly used in all types of colonial desserts. As early as 1607, Captain John Smith commented about the uncommonly large strawberries encountered on his expedition. This recipe would have been strictly seasonal, however. In the off-season, pies would have been made with fruit preserves.

Makes one 9-inch pie; Serves 8

2 pounds fresh rhubarb, cleaned and chopped (about 4 cups)

2 pints (4 cups) fresh strawberries, hulled and quartered

½ cup packed light brown sugar

¼ cup granulated sugar

¼ cup cold water

½ teaspoon fresh lemon juice

2 pounds Pâte Sucrée (see page 206)

4 cups Streusel Topping (see page 210)

1. Lightly coat one 9 x 1½-inch pie pan with vegetable cooking spray.
2. Preheat oven to 350°F.
3. In large bowl, combine the rhubarb, strawberries, brown sugar, granulated sugar, water, and lemon juice and mix well.
4. On a lightly floured surface, roll out the Pâte Sucrée into a circle about 10 inches in diameter. Ease the pastry into the prepared pie pan, being careful not to stretch pastry. Trim pastry to ½ inch beyond the edge of the pie pan. Fold under extra pastry. Crimp edge.
5. Transfer the fruit mixture to the pastry-lined pan. Top with the Streusel Topping.
6. Bake for 35 to 40 minutes, until the top is golden and the mixture starts to bubble. Cool on a wire rack.

Pumpkin Pie

Pumpkin pie is as American as apple pie, if not more so. Pumpkins were one of many squashes eaten by Native Americans, and introduced by them to the early settlers. In fact, pumpkin was served at the first Thanksgiving in 1623, and has been a traditional end note to the annual holiday ever since. Pumpkin pie is a mainstay at the Tavern.

Makes one 9-inch pie; Serves 8

2 pounds Pâte Sucrée (see page 206)
1¾ cups pumpkin purée (see Chef's Note, page 184)
    or about 15 ounces canned pumpkin
1½ cups whole milk
¾ cup granulated sugar
2 large eggs
2½ tablespoons all-purpose flour
1½ tablespoons unsalted butter, melted
½ teaspoon salt
½ teaspoon freshly ground allspice
½ teaspoon freshly grated ginger
1 teaspoon vanilla extract

1. Preheat the oven to 400°F.
2. On a lightly floured surface, roll out the Pâte Sucrée into a circle about 10 inches in diameter. Ease the pastry into a 9 x 1½-inch pie pan, being careful not to stretch the pastry. Trim pastry to ½ inch beyond the edge of the pie pan. Fold under extra pastry. Crimp edge.
3. Line pastry with a double thickness of aluminum foil. Fill with dried beans or pie weights. Bake for 15 minutes. Remove from oven and let cool. Reduce oven to 375°F. Carefully remove beans and foil. Set the baked pie shell aside.
4. In a large bowl, combine the pumpkin, milk, sugar, eggs, flour, butter, salt, allspice, ginger, and vanilla and mix well.
5. Carefully pour filling into the baked pie shell. To prevent over-browning, cover the edge of the pie with foil. Bake for about 40 minutes, until the filling is set. To test for doneness, touch the top of the pie; it should be firm but jiggle slightly.
6. Completely cool on a wire rack. Serve with Chantilly Cream (see page 208), if desired.

Baking "Blind"
Pre-baking a pie shell before adding the filling and baking it off is known as "blind baking," a term of English origin. This step usually involves placing aluminum foil carefully into an unbaked shell and adding pie weights to prevent the dough from puffing up while baking. If you don't have pie weights, dried beans or rice can be used for the same result.

Sweet Potato Pie

The sweet potato, a plant that was native to the tropical New World, was being cultivated as early as the mid-seventeenth century in North America. The sweet potato's versatility, in both sweet and savory dishes, has made it a favorite in Southern cooking, as well as a fixture on the Thanksgiving table.

Makes one 9-inch pie; Serves 8

2 pounds Pâte Sucrée (see page 206)
1½ cups cooked sweet potatoes, mashed
10 ounces (1¼ cups) sweetened condensed milk
¾ cup granulated sugar
3 large eggs
2 tablespoons unsalted butter, melted
1 teaspoon freshly ground allspice
1 teaspoon vanilla extract

1. Preheat the oven to 400°F.
2. On a lightly floured surface, roll out the Pâte Sucrée into a circle about 10 inches in diameter. Ease the pastry into the 9 x 1½-inch pie pan, being careful not to stretch the pastry. Trim pastry to ½ inch beyond the edge of the pie plate. Fold under extra pastry. Crimp edge.
3. Line pastry with a double thickness of aluminum foil. Fill with pie weights or dried beans. Bake for 15 minutes. Remove from oven and let cool. Reduce oven to 375°F. Carefully remove foil. Set the baked pie shell aside.
4. In a large bowl, combine the sweet potatoes, milk, sugar, eggs, butter, allspice, and vanilla and mix well.
5. Carefully pour the filling into the baked pie shell. To prevent over-browning, cover the edge of the pie with aluminum foil. Bake for 30 to 40 minutes, until the filling is set. To test for doneness, touch the top of the pie; it should be firm but jiggle slightly.
6. Completely cool on a wire rack. Serve with Chantilly Cream (see page 208), if desired.

Apple Pie

Apple pie was one of the few fruit pies that could be served year 'round on the colonial table. Apples wintered well, in fact, stored in root cellars, they lasted for months—to be enjoyed in a warm baked dessert in the dead of winter.

Make one 9-inch pie; Serves 8

5 Granny Smith apples, peeled, cored, and sliced (about 1½ pounds)
½ cup granulated sugar
1 teaspoon ground cinnamon
2 tablespoons unsalted butter, softened
2 pounds Pâte Sucrée (see page 206)

1. Preheat the oven to 375°F. Coat a 9 x 1½-inch pie pan with vegetable cooking spray.
2. In a large bowl, combine the apple slices, sugar, and cinnamon. Gently toss to coat. Add the softened butter. Set aside.
3. Divide the Pâte Sucrée in half. On a lightly floured surface, roll out each half of the pastry into a circle about 10 inches in diameter. Ease one circle of pastry into the prepared pie pan. Transfer the apple mixture to the pastry-lined pan.
4. Top with the remaining circle of pastry to cover the apple mixture. Trim pastry leaving ½-inch overhang. Fold under extra pastry. Crimp edge. Prick the top pastry with a fork to allow steam to escape.
5. Bake for 30 to 40 minutes, until the top turns golden and the filling starts to bubble.

Apple–Almond Crumb Pie

This easy dessert makes use of three staple ingredients available from the year-round colonial pantry—almonds, apples, and raisins.

Makes one 9-inch pie; Serves 8

1 pound (half recipe) Pâte Sucrée (see page 206)

Almond Crumb Topping
1¼ cups all-purpose flour
1 cup granulated sugar
9 tablespoons (1 stick plus 1 tablespoon) cold unsalted butter, cut into cubes
½ cup blanched almonds, chopped

Filling
5 Granny Smith apples, peeled, cored, and sliced (about 1½ pounds)
½ cup granulated sugar
½ cup raisins
3 tablespoons fresh lemon juice (about 1 medium lemon)
1 teaspoon ground cinnamon

1. Preheat the oven to 375°F. Coat a 9 x 1½-inch pie pan with vegetable cooking spray.
2. On a lightly floured surface, roll out the Pâte Sucrée into a circle about 10 inches in diameter. Ease the pastry into the prepared pie pan, being careful not to stretch the pastry. Trim pastry to ½ inch beyond the edge of the pie pan. Fold under extra pastry. Crimp edge.
3. Prepare the Almond Crumb Topping: In the bowl of a food processor combine the flour, sugar, butter, and almonds. Pulse until mixture becomes just crumbly. Set aside.
3. Prepare the Filling: In a large bowl, combine the apples, sugar, raisins, lemon juice, and cinnamon. Gently toss to coat.
5. Transfer the Filling into the pastry-lined pan. Top with the Almond Crumb Topping.
6. Bake for 40 to 45 minutes, until the top is golden and the filling starts to bubble.

Chocolate–Pecan Pie

Chocolate originally made its way to France from South America. Later, it was imported from France to the New World, a circuitous route, but necessary because there was no direct trade from South to North America. In colonial times, chocolate was very expensive and found only on the tables of the wealthy and at upscale eateries like City Tavern. As for pecans, Jefferson introduced the pecan tree to the eastern shores of Virginia, and even presented George Washington with some of the trees as a gift for Mount Vernon. Washington is said to have always had some pecans in his pocket.

Makes one 9-inch pie; Serves 8

Pastry
1⅓ cups all-purpose flour, sifted
1 tablespoon granulated sugar
½ teaspoon salt
6 tablespoons cold unsalted butter, cut into cubes
2 tablespoons cold vegetable shortening
1 large egg
3 tablespoons cold water

Filling
4 large eggs
1 cup light corn syrup
1 teaspoon vanilla extract
½ cup granulated sugar
½ cup packed light brown sugar
½ teaspoon salt
3 ounces (½ cup) semisweet chocolate chips
4 tablespoons unsalted butter, melted
2 cups pecans halves

1. Prepare the Pastry: Coat a 9 x 1½-inch pie pan with vegetable cooking spray.
2. In the bowl of an electric mixer beat the flour, sugar, and salt on low until combined.
3. Add the butter and shortening and beat until the mixture becomes crumbly.
4. Add the egg and beat just until combined.
5. Add the water and beat just until the dough begins to form. Wrap the dough in plastic wrap and chill in the refrigerator for at least 30 minutes before using.
6. On a lightly floured surface, roll out the pastry into a circle about 10 inches in diameter. Ease the pastry into the prepared pie pan, being careful not to stretch the pastry. Trim pastry to ½ inch beyond the edge of the pie plate. Fold under extra pastry. Crimp edge. Refrigerate the pie shell for at least 1 hour before using.
7. Prepare the Filling: Preheat the oven to 350°F.
8. In the bowl of an electric mixer, beat the eggs on medium to high until pale yellow and thickened. Add the syrup and vanilla. Beat well.
9. In a separate bowl, combine the ½ cup granulated sugar, brown sugar, salt, chocolate chips, and melted butter. Add to the egg mixture and mix well.
10. Spread the pecans over the bottom of the chilled pie shell. Carefully pour in the egg-chocolate mixture.
11. Bake for 40 to 45 minutes, until the pie puffs up slightly. To check for doneness, insert a knife into the center of the pie—it should come out clean. Completely cool on a wire rack.
12. Refrigerate within 2 hours; cover for longer storage.

Custards and Puddings

Puddings are generally attributed to the English and custards to the French.
No matter what they're called, it seems that every cuisine has egg-based desserts
that are very similar in ingredients and cooking technique. Our research
has indicated that custards, puddings, and flans were extremely
popular in the early colonies.

Rice Pudding

This colonial comfort food is simple but delicious. Rice played an important role in the early economy of the New World, where it became an important crop in South Carolina, which was exporting about 4,500 metric tons of rice annually as early as 1726. During the Revolution, when the British prevailed in Charleston, the entire rice crop was shipped to England, leaving no grain behind. Thomas Jefferson is said to have smuggled some Italian rice seed out of Europe in 1787, and brought it back to the Carolinas, where the industry eventually revived.

Makes one 2-quart baking dish; Serves 6

2 cups water
¾ cup uncooked long-grain white rice
2½ cups whole milk
½ cup granulated sugar
3 large eggs
1½ tablespoons unsalted butter, softened
1½ teaspoons vanilla extract
1 teaspoon ground cinnamon

1. Preheat the oven to 325°F.
2. In a 2-quart saucepan, bring the water to a boil and add the rice. Simmer, covered, for 15 to 20 minutes. Let stand, covered, for 5 minutes and drain, if necessary.
3. In a separate saucepan, bring the milk to a boil. Stir in drained rice and cook for 10 minutes more, until the grains are soft.
4. In a large bowl, whisk together the sugar, eggs, butter, vanilla, and cinnamon.
5. Gradually stir the hot rice mixture into the egg mixture.
6. Transfer to a 2-quart ovenproof glass or ceramic dish. Place the dish into a larger high-sided roasting pan and carefully pour boiling water into the roasting pan around the dish to a depth of 1½ inches. Bake, covered, for about 20 to 30 minutes, until a knife inserted near center comes out clean.
7. Sprinkle additional cinnamon on top as garnish.

Pear Flan

In colonial times, flans were made with any kind of available fruit, from pears to cherries to plums to peaches. This elegant custard makes wonderful use of late harvest pears such as Bosc or Anjou, and is a wonderful addition to the fall table.

Makes eight 3 x ½-inch (½ cup) ramekins or 6-ounce custard cups; Serves 8

2 cups granulated sugar

2 cups whole milk

2 cups (16 ounces) pear purée (available in most gourmet markets)

8 large eggs

4 large egg yolks

1. Preheat the oven to 325°F. Lightly coat the eight 3 x ½-inch ramekins or 6-ounce custard cups with vegetable cooking spray.

2. To caramelize the sugar, in a large sauté pan heat 1 cup of the sugar over medium heat, until it becomes syrupy and turns golden brown, watching closely so it doesn't burn and shaking the pan occasionally to heat the sugar evenly. *Do not stir.* Once the sugar starts to melt, reduce the heat to low and cook 5 minutes more, until all of the sugar is melted and golden, stirring as needed with a wooden spoon.

3. Immediately remove from the heat and pour 1 to 2 tablespoons of the caramelized sugar into the bottom of each ramekin or custard cup, being careful not to burn your skin with the caramelized sugar. Tilt each ramekin to coat the bottom evenly. Let stand 10 minutes.

4. Place the ramekins or custard cups in a large, high-sided roasting pan. Set aside.

5. To make the custard, in a large bowl, whisk together the milk, remaining 1 cup sugar, pear purée, eggs, and egg yolks.

6. Pour the custard into the prepared ramekins or custard cups. Add boiling water into the roasting pan around the ramekins or custard cups to a depth of ¼ inch (see Chef's Note).

7. Bake for 30 to 40 minutes, until set or until a knife inserted near the center comes out clean.

Custard Bread Pudding

Because making bread was such an involved process in colonial days, not a crust of bread was ever thrown away. Any scraps were saved up and used for bread pudding exactly like this one. For best results, soak the raisins overnight in rum or water to soften them. That way, they won't float to the top of the pudding, where they'll burn.

Makes one 10 x 3-inch round baking dish or 2-quart souffle dish; Serves 12

1 cup raisins

½ cup Jamaican rum

1 pound, 4 oz. white bread, crust trimmed, cut into 1-inch cubes
    (about 10 cups)

4 cups whole milk

15 large eggs

1½ cups granulated sugar

1 teaspoon ground cinnamon

½ teaspoon grated fresh nutmeg

1. In a small bowl, combine raisins in rum and soak for at least 2 hours.
2. Preheat oven to 350°F.
3. Lightly coat a 10 x 3-inch round baking dish or 2-quart soufflé dish with vegetable cooking spray.
4. Add the bread cubes to the dish and sprinkle the raisin/rum mixture on top.
5. In a large bowl, combine the milk, eggs, sugar, cinnamon, and nutmeg.
6. Stir the egg mixture into the bread/raisin mixture.
7. Cover with foil.
8. Place the baking dish in a larger, high-sided roasting pan. Add boiling water into the roasting pan around the baking dish to a depth of 2 inches.
9. Bake for 45 minutes. Remove the foil.
10. Continue baking, uncovered, for 5 minutes, until top is golden and the mixture is slightly puffed or until a knife inserted near the center comes out clean.
11. Cool slightly before serving. If desired, serve with Crème Anglaise (see page 209) flavored with rum to taste, if desired.

Plum Fool Parfait

This old English sweet dish is made by folding cooked, puréed seasonal fruit into whipped cream. The title "fool" perhaps derives from the French cooking term *foule*, which means to pulp. This parfait will look beautiful on your table, and is quite simple to make.

Makes 6 parfaits

9 Stanley or Rosa plums, pitted, and thinly sliced
½ cup red currant jelly
⅓ cup packed light brown sugar
2 teaspoons grated orange rind
1 stick cinnamon
1½ cups heavy cream
½ teaspoon vanilla extract
6 fresh mint sprigs, for garnish

1. In a 2-quart saucepan, cook the plums, jelly, sugar, orange rind, and cinnamon over medium heat for 20 to 30 minutes, until the plums are tender.
2. Remove the saucepan from the heat and let the mixture cool to room temperature. Remove and discard cinnamon stick.
3. In a chilled bowl of an electric mixer with chilled beaters, beat the heavy cream on high until soft peaks form. Add the vanilla and whip for a few seconds more.
4. In a parfait glass, alternately layer the plum mixture and whipped cream. Chill for 2 hours in the refrigerator before serving.
5. To serve, top each parfait with a fresh mint sprig for garnish.

Crème Caramel

Whether it's called crème caramel, flan, or baked custard, this traditional dessert is always a winner. Custard was a favorite of Thomas Jefferson, who discovered it on his first trip to France. He ate it, both hot and cold, with enough appetite to finish an entire recipe himself.

Makes six 3 x ½-inch (½ cup) ramekins or 6-ounce custard cups; Serves 6

1½ cups granulated sugar
5 large eggs
2 cups light cream
½ cup heavy cream
½ teaspoon vanilla extract

1. Preheat the oven to 325°F.
2. To caramelize the sugar, in a large sauté pan, heat 1 cup of the sugar over medium heat, until it becomes syrupy and turns golden brown, watching closely so it doesn't burn and shaking the pan occasionally to heat the sugar evenly. Do not stir. Once the sugar starts to melt, reduce the heat to low and cook 5 minutes more, until all of the sugar is melted and golden, stirring as needed with a wooden spoon.
3. Immediately remove from the heat and pour 1 to 2 tablespoons of the caramelized sugar into the bottom of each of six 3 x ½-inch ramekins or or six 6-ounce custard cups, being careful not to burn your skin with the caramelized sugar. Tilt each ramekin to coat the bottom evenly. Let stand 10 minutes.
4. Place the ramekins or custard cups in a large, high-sided roasting pan. Set aside.
5. To make the custard, in a large bowl, whisk together the eggs and the remaining ½ cup sugar.
6. In a small saucepan, bring the light cream, heavy cream, and vanilla to a boil.
7. Slowly pour 1 cup of the hot cream and vanilla mixture, whisking constantly, into the egg-sugar mixture. Whisk in the remaining hot cream and vanilla mixture. Strain the mixture through a fine wire sieve into a ovenproof bowl.
8. Pour the custard into the prepared ramekins or custard cups. Add boiling water into the roasting pan around the ramekins to a depth of ¼ inch.
9. Bake for 30 to 40 minutes until set or until a knife inserted near the center of each comes out clean.
10. Remove the custards from the water bath. Cool on a wire rack.
11. Cover and chill in the refrigerator for at least 1 hour before serving. Before serving, remove custards from refrigerator. Let stand at room temperature for 20 minutes. Turn each ramekin or custard cup over onto an individual dessert plate. (The caramel will create a syrupy sauce.) Serve immediately.

Cookies

Cookies have a long history in England and other parts of Europe.
They were popular because they stored and traveled well, could be served
on a moment's notice to guests, and were a staple of afternoon tea in England.
Naturally, the colonists brought such traditions—and recipes—with them to America.

Apricot Tea Cookies

The origins of these small, one-inch treats are found in Germany, and the recipe was brought over to America in the early 1700s. This recipe provides yet another use for the marmalades and preserves that were so much a part of the early American table. Although a favorite at holidays, apricot tea cookies would have marked special parties and events all year long.

Makes 3 dozen cookies

1 pound (4 sticks) unsalted butter, softened
¾ cup granulated sugar
2 large eggs
5 cups all-purpose flour, sifted
2 teaspoons baking powder
½ teaspoon salt
1 cup sliced almonds, toasted
½ cup apricot preserves
¼ cup flaked desiccated coconut, toasted
½ cup apricot jam

1. Preheat the oven to 350°F.
2. In the bowl of an electric mixer, cream the butter and sugar on medium to high, until light and fluffy, scraping side of bowl often.
3. Add eggs and beat well.
4. In a separate bowl, combine the flour, baking powder, and salt.
5. Add the almonds, preserves, and coconut and beat well.
6. Wrap the dough in plastic wrap and chill in the refrigerator for at least 1 hour, until easy to handle.
7. Shape the dough into 1-inch balls. Place 1 inch apart on an ungreased cookie sheet. Press your thumb into the center of each ball. Place ½ teaspoon jam in the center of each impression.
8. Bake for 12 to 15 minutes, until edges are lightly browned.
9. Transfer cookies to a wire rack and let cool.

Anise Biscotti

A biscotti, sometimes known as a rusk, is a slice of sweet bread that's baked until dry and golden brown. It has a terrific shelf life, and stores and transports well. Anise, which is actually a member of the parsley family, has a long history, dating back as early as 1500 B.C.—of perfuming and flavoring sweet as well as savory dishes. Anise seeds were brought over from Germany with other traditional Old World foodstuffs.

Makes about twenty-four 3 x ½-inch biscotti

1¾ cups granulated sugar
¾ cup vegetable oil
2 large eggs
½ cup sour cream
1 teaspoon vanilla extract
4½ cups all-purpose flour, sifted
1 teaspoon baking powder
1 teaspoon baking soda
½ teaspoon salt
½ teaspoon anise seed, crushed

1. Preheat oven to 350°F. Place parchment paper on a cookie sheet and lightly coat with vegetable cooking spray.
2. In the bowl of an electric mixer, beat the sugar, oil, and eggs on medium to high, until combined, scraping the side of the bowl often.
3. Add the sour cream and vanilla and beat well.
4. In a separate bowl, sift together the flour, baking powder, soda, and salt. Stir in the anise seed. With the mixer on low, slowly add the dry ingredients to the wet ingredients.
5. In the same bowl, knead the dough with your hands for 1 minute.
6. Shape the dough into a 12-inch roll, about 3 inches in diameter, and place the roll in the center of the prepared cookie sheet.
7. Bake for 20 to 25 minutes, until light golden brown.
8. Cool on the cookie sheet for about 25 minutes. Using a serrated-edge knife, cut the log into ½-inch-thick diagonal slices.
9. Place the slices, flat sides down, and put the cookie sheet back into the oven for 5 minutes. Turn each slice over and bake 5 minutes more, until biscotti are toasted. *Do not overbake.*
10. Transfer the biscotti to a wire rack and let cool. To store the biscotti, transfer them to a tightly covered container and store at room temperature.

Walnut–Orange Biscotti

This biscotti recipe combines two of the colonists' favorite flavors, orange and walnut.

Makes about twenty-four 3 x ½-inch biscotti

1¼ cups granulated sugar
6 ounces (1½ sticks) unsalted butter, softened
4 large eggs
2 tablespoons grated orange rind
1 teaspoon orange extract
3¾ cups all-purpose flour, sifted
¼ cup baking powder
1 teaspoon ground cinnamon
¼ teaspoon salt
1½ cups walnuts, chopped

1. Preheat the oven to 350°F. Place parchment paper on a cookie sheet and lightly coat with vegetable cooking spray.
2. In the bowl of an electric mixer, cream the sugar and butter on medium to high, until light and fluffy, scraping the side of bowl often.
3. Add the eggs, rind, and extract and beat well.
4. In a separate bowl, sift together the flour, baking powder, cinnamon, and salt.
5. With the mixer on low, slowly add the dry ingredients to the wet ingredients. Add the nuts and mix well.
6. Shape the dough into a 12-inch roll, about 3 inches in diameter.
7. Place the roll in the center of the prepared pan. Bake for 20 to 25 minutes, until light golden brown.
8. Remove from the oven. Cool on the cookie sheet for 1 hour, until cool to the touch. Using a serrated-edge knife, cut the roll into ½-inch-thick diagonal slices.
9. Place the slices, flat sides down, on the cookie sheet and put back into the oven for 5 minutes. Turn each slice over and bake for 5 minutes more, until biscotti are toasted. *Do not overbake.*
10. Transfer the biscotti to a wire rack and let cool. To store, transfer them to a tightly covered container and keep at room temperature.

Coconut Cookies

During colonial times, coconut was a versatile West Indian import. Its milk was used in sauces, and its flesh was eaten fresh or dried or desiccated for use in cakes and cookies like these tasty treats.

Makes 3 dozen cookies

1 cup granulated sugar
5 ounces (1 stick plus 2 tablespoons) unsalted butter, softened
1 large egg
1 cup all-purpose flour, sifted
1¼ cups flaked desiccated coconut, toasted

1. Preheat the oven to 375°F. Lightly coat cookie sheet with vegetable cooking spray.
2. In the bowl of an electric mixer, cream the butter and sugar on medium to high, until light and fluffy, scraping side of bowl often.
3. Add the egg and beat well.
4. Slowly add the flour and coconut and beat well, until the dough becomes stiff. Wrap in plastic wrap and refrigerate for 30 minutes, until chilled.
5. Shape the dough into 1-inch balls. Place them 1 inch apart on prepared cookie sheet.
6. Bake about 15 minutes, until edges are lightly browned.
7. Transfer cookies to a wire rack and let cool.

Spritz Cookies

Spritz, which means "squirt" in German, refers to a traditional butter cookie that is made with a cookie press. The dough for this spritz recipe also can be rolled into a log and cut into individual cookies for baking. Spritz are a really quick cookie to make. In fact, whenever my mother found out at the last minute that someone was coming by, she made these cookies. I remember that it took more time to prepare the fire in the stove than it did to bake these delicious, buttery treats.

Makes 1 dozen cookies

½ pound (2 sticks) unsalted butter, softened
¾ cup granulated sugar
2 large egg yolks
1 teaspoon vanilla extract
2½ cups all-purpose flour, sifted
2 teaspoons baking powder
½ teaspoon salt

1. Preheat the oven to 350°F.
2. In the bowl of an electric mixer, cream butter and sugar on medium to high until light and fluffy, scraping side of bowl often.
3. Add the yolks and vanilla and beat well.
4. With electric mixer on low, slowly add the flour, baking powder, and salt and beat well.
5. Shape the dough into 2-inch, finger-shaped logs. Place logs on ungreased cookie sheet 1 inch apart.
6. Bake for 15 minutes, until the edges are firm and golden but not brown.
7. Transfer the cookies to a wire rack and let cool.

Spice Cookies

This unassuming cookie makes use of three of what were considered exotic spices that regularly arrived in colonial Philadelphia from the West Indies—nutmeg, cinnamon, and ginger. I like the addition of the Lemon Glaze, which cuts the recipe's natural sweetness.

Makes about 36 cookies

½ pound (2 sticks) unsalted butter, softened

¾ cup granulated sugar

½ cup molasses

2 large egg yolks

1 teaspoon vanilla extract

2⅓ cups all-purpose flour, sifted

2 teaspoons ground cinnamon

1½ teaspoons ground ginger

½ teaspoon salt

¼ teaspoon freshly grated nutmeg

Lemon Glaze

1 cup confectioners' sugar, sifted

1½ tablespoons fresh lemon juice, strained

1. Preheat the oven to 350°F.
2. In the bowl of an electric mixer, cream butter and sugar on medium to high until light and fluffy, scraping down side of the bowl often.
3. Add the molasses, egg yolks, and vanilla and beat well.
4. In a separate bowl, sift together the flour, cinnamon, ginger, salt, and nutmeg.
5. With the electric mixer on low, add the dry ingredients to the wet ingredients.
6. Drop the dough in teaspoonfuls onto an ungreased a cookie sheet about 1 inch apart. Bake for 15 to 20 minutes, until golden.
7. Transfer the cookies to a wire rack and let cool about 15 minutes.
8. To make the glaze, in a small bowl, whisk together the confectioners' sugar and lemon juice until smooth.
9. When the cookies are cool, use a small spoon to drizzle the glaze over each cookie top.

Oatmeal–Raisin Cookies

This "comfort cookie" recipe features oatmeal and raisins, two staples in colonial days.

Makes about 14 cookies

6 ounces (1½ sticks) unsalted butter, softened
¾ cup granulated sugar
¾ cup packed light brown sugar
2 large eggs
2 teaspoons vanilla extract
2 cups old-fashioned rolled oats
1 cup all-purpose flour, sifted
½ teaspoon ground cinnamon
1 teaspoon baking soda
¼ teaspoon freshly grated nutmeg
1½ cups raisins

1. Preheat the oven to 375°F.
2. In the bowl of an electric mixer, cream the butter, granulated sugar, and brown sugar on medium to high until light and fluffy, scraping down side of the bowl often.
3. Add the eggs and vanilla and beat well.
4. In a separate bowl, combine the oats, flour, soda, cinnamon, and nutmeg.
5. With the mixer on low, gradually add the dry ingredients to the wet ingredients and beat well.
6. Add the raisins and beat well.
7. Using a 2-inch ice cream scoop, drop the dough onto an ungreased cookie sheet 2 inches apart. Bake about 15 minutes, until edges are golden.
8. Transfer the cookies to a wire rack and let cool.

Part 4: Beverages

Beverages, like eighteenth-century taverns themselves, played an integral role in the social life of the early Philadelphians and Founding Fathers. City Tavern, functioning as part town hall and part pub, posted notices, carried out social functions such as balls, and served up pints of ale and droughts of Madeira to thirsty patrons—who came to peruse newspapers from home and abroad, share ideas, buy and sell stocks and ship cargo, strike deals, and forge partnerships. In the wintertime, with only the heat from the fireplaces to keep them warm, patrons depended on hot beverages such as wassail and cider to thaw them out.

"But I do feel thirsty," said the poor lady, "and I think a glass of shrub would do my throat good; it's dreadful dry. Mr. Peckham, would you be so polite as to pass me a glass of shrub?" Silas Peckham bowed with great alacrity, and took from the table a small glass containing a fluid reddish in hue and sub-acid in taste. This was shrub, a beverage in local repute, of questionable nature, but suspected of owing its tints and sharpness to some kind of syrup derived from a maroon-colored fruit.

—Oliver Wendell Holmes, *The Event of the Season*

Rum or Cognac Shrub

The shrub, which Oliver Wendell Holmes refers to in his story, *The Event of the Season*, is a drink made from fruit juice vinegar sweetened with sugar and spiked with alcohol or fizzed with soda water. The base used to make shrubs contains fruit vinegars (in blueberry, cranberry, raspberry, strawberry, and apple flavors) sweetened with sugar, honey, or maple syrup and seasoned with spices. At today's City Tavern, like at the original City Tavern, we offer shrubs mixed with cognac, rum, or Champagne.

Makes about 16 ounces; Serves 2
Ice cubes
¼ cup shrub (see Resources, page 211)
½ cup dark rum or cognac
1 cup ginger ale

1. Fill a stemmed goblet two-thirds full with ice cubes.
2. Add the shrub and rum; pour in the ginger ale. Stir just to mix.
3. Serve at once.

Champagne Shrub

Makes 18 ounces; Serves 2
¼ cup shrub (see Resources, page 211)
1 cup Champagne or sparkling wine
1 cup ginger ale

1. Pour the shrub into a glass. Pour in the Champagne and ginger ale, stirring only if the Champagne fails to blend the ingredients thoroughly.
2. Serve at once.

The early Quakers of Philadelphia were not the somber, teetotalers of later generations. As a class, they were wealthy and enjoyed the good life—including wine and other spirits. Of all the wines in colonial Philadelphia, Madeira was the most fashionable and widely served.

Hot Cider

It's important to remember that centralized heating wasn't part of the early American lifestyle—when it was cold, people warmed up around a central fireplace, often with a hot beverage in their hands. I recommend applejack brandy as a wonderful flavor enhancer in this hot cider, but any brandy or rum will do the job.

Makes 18 ounces; Serves 2

2 cups fresh apple cider
2 sticks cinnamon
¼ cup applejack brandy or Jamaican rum

1. In a medium saucepan, bring the apple cider to a simmer over high heat.
2. Add the cinnamon sticks and simmer about 5 minutes to infuse the flavor of cinnamon into the liquid. Remove from heat.
3. Stir in the brandy or rum.
4. Serve hot in cups or mugs.

Wassail

Wassail dates back to the old English custom of wassailing during the Christmas and New Year's season. In those days, a big punch bowl was filled with this spiced drink and everyone gathered around the "wassail bowl" to toast the season. At City Tavern, we serve wassail all winter long, whenever there is a chill in the air.

Makes 24 ounces; Serves 6

2 tablespoons grated orange rind (about 1 medium orange)
2 teaspoons grated lemon rind (about 1 medium lemon)
10 whole cloves
5 sticks cinnamon
1 bottle (750 ml) red burgundy wine
¼ cup dark brown sugar
2 pinches freshly grated nutmeg

1. Place the orange and lemon rinds, cloves, and cinnamon sticks into a piece of 100% cotton cheesecloth. Tie up with kitchen twine to make a sachet.
2. Pour the wine into a saucepan.
3. Place the sugar and sachet in wine over low hear. Add the nutmeg.
4. Heat until wine is very warm. *Do not let boil* (boiling will burn off the alcohol content).
5. Remove and discard the sachet.
6. Serve in a fondue pot or an ovenproof punch bowl.

Wassail originates from the traditional Anglo-Saxon toast "Waes Nael," meaning to "be in good health." The spiced drink was always accompanied by the wassail song: "Here we come a-wassailing / Among the leaves so green, / Here we come a-wand'ring, / So fair to be seen, / Love and Joy come to you, / and to your wassail too, / And God bless you and send you a happy new year, / And God send you a happy new year."

Source: *Music Department of the Free Library of Philadelphia*

Hot Spiced Punch

This hot punch takes an item readily available during colonial times, freshly pressed apple cider, and marries it with the West Indian spices of nutmeg, cinnamon, and cloves. Hot punch made with cider is a favorite at today's City Tavern on a cold, winter's day.

Makes 34 ounces; Serves 8 to 10

4 cups (1 quart) fresh apple cider
¼ cup fresh lemon juice (about 1 large lemon), strained
4 sticks cinnamon
1 teaspoon whole cloves (about 6)
½ teaspoon freshly grated nutmeg

1. In a medium saucepan, bring the apple cider, lemon juice, and cinnamon sticks to a simmer over medium heat. Do not boil.
2. Place the cloves in a piece of 100% cheesecloth. Tie up with kitchen twine to make a sachet and add to the cider mixture. Simmer about 10 minutes, until spices have steeped into cider.
3. Remove and discard the sachet and cinnamon sticks. Add the nutmeg.
4. Serve hot in cups or mugs.

City Tavern Cooler

Although Madeira was the drink of choice in the City Tavern, rum from Jamaica, French brandy, and English whiskey were also consumed in healthy quantities. This recipe for a refreshing summer drink combines all three with another common beverage, apple cider.

Makes about 10 ounces; Serves 1

Ice cubes
2 tablespoons peach brandy
1 tablespoon Jamaican rum
1½ teaspoons whiskey
1 cup fresh apple cider

1. Fill in a 12-ounce highball glass half full with ice cubes.
2. Add the peach brandy, rum, and whiskey.
3. Add the apple cider.

City Tavern Eggnog

In February, 1796, Issac Weld wrote about a small entourage of travelers that stopped in Philadelphia for breakfast and enjoyed eggnog. This is the first time that the serving of eggnog was documented. This rich, filling drink of milk, eggs, rum, and sugar is as good today as it was back then. If you prefer not to serve raw eggs, use one quart of commercially prepared eggnog, which is pasteurized, as a substitute for the first four ingredients, then flavor with the remaining ingredients.

Makes about 48 ounces; Serves 10 to 12

7 large egg yolks
¾ cup granulated sugar
2 cups heavy cream
1 cup whole milk
¾ cup bourbon
¾ cup Jamaican rum
¼ cup brandy
Freshly grated nutmeg, for garnish

1. In the large bowl of an electric mixer, beat together the egg yolks and sugar on high speed about 5 minutes, until thick and pale yellow.
2. Gradually beat in the cream, milk, bourbon, rum, and brandy.
3. Cover and refrigerate until completely chilled.
4. Serve in cups or mugs. Garnish with the nutmeg.

Modern-day City Tavern staff swear there's a ghost in the restaurant—table settings are moved, dishes come crashing off the wall. Who knows? Maybe it's the nameless waiter murdered in the original City Tavern by Col. Craig on January 3, 1781, after a drunken brawl. The murderer was never prosecuted, some say because of the class differences that separated the two men.

George Washington's Beer Recipe

Beers, ales, and stouts were as popular in colonial days as they are today. It was over many a glass of ale that our country's forefathers hammered out the particulars of what was to be our country's constitution. City Tavern's George Washington Ale is based on the President's own personal recipe for beer. Our 1774 Beer is based on a recipe penned by Thomas Jefferson at Monticello. He made beer twice a year with the help of an English brewer.

If you attempt to brew this beer, please note that the alcohol level will be 11%, much higher than that of typical home-brewed or commercially prepared beer.

"To Make Small Beer:
Take a large siffer full of bran hops to your taste—Boil these 3 hours. Then strain out 30 gall n into a cooler put in 3 gall n molasses while the beer is scalding hot or rather draw the molasses into the cooler. Strain the beer on it while boiling hot, let this stand till it is little more than blood warm. Then put in a quart of ye[a]st if the weather is very cold cover it over with a blank[et] let it work in the cask— Leave the bung open till it is almost done working—Bottle it that day week it was brewed."

Source: *Precious Book Department, New York Library*

Part 5: Breads

Homemade bread was the culinary mortar of colonial life. Because bread was an absolute must for everyday dining, making bread was considered a vital skill. For this book, we have recreated historic recipes, including a recipe for sweet potato biscuits that Thomas Jefferson used at his home in Monticello, to give you the chance to recapture in your own kitchen the comforting tastes and smells of old-time homemade bread. At City Tavern, our basket of freshly baked breads and biscuits is one of our signature features. When I took over the Tavern, there was no bakery. I knew from my research that any restaurant concept true to the period couldn't do without a bakeshop—there was nowhere to buy the Sally Lunn and Anadama Bread that were the staples of the day. If we were to serve them, we would have to bake them ourselves.

Quick Breads

These recipes, just as the name implies, produce quick and delicious breads, perfect greeting for the unexpected guest or dinner party. Since the eighteenth-century cook was ruled by the season, these quick breads were ideal ways to use up an overabundance of ripe or harvested ingredients. In order to leaven the breads, colonists probably relied upon kitchen chemistry. The practice of mixing an acid with an alkali to create a leavening agent began in the eighteenth century with the many scientific developments that accompanied the Industrial Revolution; colonial cooks probably combined baking soda with sour milk or buttermilk, the acid content of the latter reacting with the soda to create a rising process for making quick breads. Commercial leaveners did not appear on the market until 1850, although a Boston company did produce baking powder before then, calling it "yeast powder."

Thomas Jefferson's Sweet Potato Biscuits

These biscuits, faithfully recreated every day at City Tavern, were adapted from Thomas Jefferson's food writings; unsuprisingly, they include one of Thomas Jefferson's favorite ingredients, pecans. In fact, three pecan trees, dating back to 1775, still grow at Monticello.

Makes about 2 dozen biscuits

5 cups all-purpose flour
1 cup packed light brown sugar
2 tablespoons baking powder
1½ teaspoons ground cinnamon
1 teaspoon salt
1 teaspoon ground ginger
½ teaspoon ground allspice
1 cup vegetable shortening
2 cups cooked, mashed, and cooled sweet potato
1 cup heavy cream
½ cup coarsely chopped pecans

1. Preheat oven to 350°F.
2. In a large mixing bowl, stir together the flour, brown sugar, baking powder, cinnamon, salt, ginger, and allspice.
3. Add the shortening and cut in with 2 knives until crumbly.
4. Add the sweet potatoes and mix well with a wooden spoon.
5. Add the cream and pecans and stir just until moistened.
6. Turn the dough out onto a lightly floured surface. Roll out the dough to 1½ inches thick. Cut out with a 2-inch floured biscuit cutter. Place biscuits 1 inch apart on ungreased baking sheets.
7. Bake for 25 to 30 minutes, until golden brown. Serve warm or let cool on a wire rack until room temperature.

Chef's Note

This biscuit dough freezes beautifully unbaked. Just layer the dough between wax paper and store, for up to three months. Defrost the dough, and follow baking directions. It pays to make a double batch of these biscuits and freeze half for later.

Lemon and Poppy Seed Bread

This sweet quick bread made excellent use of poppy seeds, the tiny, dried bluish-grey seeds that have been featured in savory and sweet bread recipes from central and eastern Europe. I recommend always using fresh lemon juice in this and other recipes, as the flavor of reconstituted juice isn't nearly as bright.

Makes two 8-inch loaves

1¼ pounds (5 sticks) unsalted butter, at room temperature
2 cups granulated sugar
9 large eggs
¼ cup fresh lemon juice (about 1 large lemon), strained
2 teaspoons grated lemon rind
1 teaspoon vanilla extract
4 cups all-purpose flour
2 tablespoons poppy seeds
2 teaspoons baking powder
1 teaspoon salt

1. Preheat the oven to 325°F. Coat two 8½ x 4½ x 2½-inch loaf pans with vegetable cooking spray.
2. In the bowl of an electric mixer, beat together the butter and sugar on medium about 2 to 3 minutes, until light and fluffy.
3. Beat in the eggs, one at a time. Add the lemon juice, lemon rind, and vanilla and beat until combined.
4. In a medium mixing bowl, stir together the flour, poppy seeds, baking powder, and salt. Add to the egg mixture and stir just until moistened.
5. Divide the batter between the prepared pans.
6. Bake about 1 hour, until golden brown and a toothpick inserted in the center comes out clean.
7. Cool in pans on wire racks for 10 minutes. To remove bread, flip pans on their sides and gently pull out bread. Serve warm or let cool to room temperature.

Lemons and oranges were symbols of wealth and affluence among the Philadelphia elite, who often prominently displayed the treasures in elaborate bowls in their homes. The fruits were imported from Spain because, at that time, no lemons or oranges grew in the Caribbean or North America. With only Europe as a source, the fruits were quite expensive in the colonies; in turn, serving anything prepared with citrus fruits was a coup and a status symbol. Both lemons and oranges were featured items on the trendy City Tavern menu. Every bit of the fruits, from the juice to the pulp to the peel, was used in sauces, salad dressings, cakes, and breads.

Almond–Buttermilk Biscuits

Buttermilk, the liquid that remained in the churn after making butter, has long been prized by bakers for the tangy taste it gives to breads and cakes. For these biscuits, buttermilk is teamed with crunchy almonds—another favored ingredient of the colonial period. For a special treat, serve these biscuits with Chantilly Cream (see page 208) and fresh berries.

Makes 12 biscuits
2¼ cups all-purpose flour
½ cup granulated sugar
1½ teaspoons baking powder
¾ teaspoon baking soda
¼ teaspoon salt
6 tablespoons unsalted butter
1¼ cups buttermilk
1 large egg yolk
1 teaspoon vanilla extract
1 cup sliced almonds

1. Preheat the oven to 425°F.
2. In a large mixing bowl, stir together the flour, sugar, baking powder, baking soda, and salt.
3. Add the butter and cut in with 2 knives until crumbly.
4. In a small mixing bowl, combine 1 cup of the buttermilk, the egg yolk, and vanilla.
5. Add to the dry ingredients and stir just until moistened.
6. Turn the dough out onto a lightly floured surface, roll out the dough until 1 to 1¼ inches thick.
7. Cut out with a 3-inch floured biscuit cutter. Place biscuits 1 inch apart on ungreased baking sheets.
8. Brush the tops of the biscuits with the remaining buttermilk and sprinkle with the sliced almonds.
9. Bake for 15 to 20 minutes, until golden brown.
10. Transfer to a wire rack and cool to room temperature. If desired, serve with Chantilly Cream and berries. If storing the biscuits, wrap in plastic wrap and keep at room temperature for up to 2 days.

Old-Fashioned Corn Bread

Corn bread was the settlers' fast food—it was quick to prepare, delicious, usually high in sugar, and packed with carbohydrates and fat, and served right out of the skillet. Readily available in later years, the cornmeal used to make the bread was a staple on the wagon trains heading west. Older recipes used bacon grease or lard rather than butter to make corn bread; some seasoned the dough with onions and bacon bits. Even though the original City Tavern was an upscale eatery, diners would still have requested corn bread. To them, a piece of warm corn bread along with a hearty rabbit stew was as appealing as caviar and *foie gras*.

Serves 10 to 12

2 cups cornmeal
2 cups all-purpose flour
½ cup granulated sugar
2 tablespoons baking powder
1 teaspoon salt
2 cups whole milk
¼ pound (1 stick) unsalted butter, melted
2 eggs, lightly beaten

1. Preheat the oven to 400°F. Coat a 12 x 7½ x 2-inch baking pan with vegetable cooking spray.
2. In a large mixing bowl, stir together the cornmeal, flour, sugar, baking powder, and salt.
3. In medium mixing bowl, combine the milk, butter, and eggs.
4. Add to the dry ingredients and stir just until moistened.
5. Pour the batter into the prepared pan. Bake for 30 to 35 minutes, until golden brown and a wooden toothpick inserted near the center comes out clean.
6. Let cool for 30 minutes (to prevent crumbling) and cut into 2-inch squares, or into desired shape, such as rectangles or rounds.

Cornmeal, unlike wheat flour, doesn't contain gluten-producing proteins (which, when combined with yeast, trap gases within batters and doughs, causing them to rise), and therefore, does not create a light and airy loaf of bread. Although they missed the traditional wheat breads of Europe, North American settlers came to depend on cornmeal out of necessity, mixing cornmeal with eggs and water to make fried corn bread and cake.

Blueberry Muffins

Blueberries are among the only fruits native to North America. As early as 1616, Samuel de Champlain found the Indians near Lake Huron gathering blueberries for the winter. "After drying the berries in the sun," he wrote in his journal, "the Indians beat them into powder and added this powder to parched meal to make a dish called 'Sautauthig.'" The settlers incorporated blueberries into desserts and breads to satisfy their renowned sweet tooth.

Makes 24 standard muffins

½ pound (2 sticks) unsalted butter, at room temperature
1¾ cups granulated sugar
5 large eggs
2 cups whole milk
1 teaspoon vanilla extract
3¾ cups all-purpose flour
3 tablespoons baking powder
½ teaspoon salt

1. Preheat the oven to 375°F. Coat twenty-four ½-cup muffin cups with vegetable cooking spray.
2. In the bowl of an electric mixer, beat together the butter and sugar on medium about 2 to 3 minutes, until light and fluffy.
3. Beat in the eggs, one at a time. Add the milk and vanilla and beat until combined.
4. In a medium mixing bowl, stir together the flour, baking powder, and salt. Add to the egg mixture and stir just until moistened.
5. Divide the batter among the prepared muffin cups, filling each cup about ⅔ full.
6. Bake for 20 to 30 minutes, until golden brown.
7. Cool on wire rack about 10 minutes. Remove from muffin cups and serve warm.

Lemon–Blueberry Bread

Blueberries were a seasonal fruit prevalent in the heavily wooded outskirts of Philadelphia. No doubt enterprising hucksters sold freshly picked berries at market and directly to inns and restaurants like City Tavern, during the summer months.

Makes one 8-inch loaf

Bread

1 cup granulated sugar
6 tablespoons unsalted butter, at room temperature
2 large eggs
2 teaspoons grated lemon rind
1½ cups all-purpose flour
1 teaspoon baking powder
¼ teaspoon salt
½ cup whole milk
1½ cups fresh blueberries

Lemon Glaze

⅓ cup granulated sugar
3 tablespoons fresh lemon juice, strained

1. Prepare the Bread: Preheat the oven to 325°F. Coat an 8½ x 4½ x 2½-inch loaf pan with vegetable cooking spray.
2. In the bowl of an electric mixer, beat together the sugar and butter on medium for 2 to 3 minutes, until light and fluffy.
3. Add the eggs and lemon rind and beat until combined.
4. In a small mixing bowl, stir together the flour, baking powder, and salt.
5. Fold the dry ingredients into the butter mixture in thirds, alternating with the milk.
6. Gently fold in the blueberries.
7. Pour the batter into the prepared pan and bake for 50 to 60 minutes, until golden brown and a toothpick inserted in the center comes out clean.
8. Cool in pan on wire rack for 10 minutes. To remove bread, flip pan on its side and gently pull out bread. Serve warm or let cool to room temperature on wire rack.
9. Prepare the Lemon Glaze: In a small saucepan, bring the sugar and lemon juice to a boil over high heat, stirring to dissolve the sugar. Remove from the heat. Drizzle over the cooled bread loaf.

Buttermilk Scones

Scones originated in England where they typically were served for afternoon tea. English settlers brought their recipes with them to the Colonies and continued to make the flaky morsels because they were easy to prepare from ingredients readily at hand.

Makes about 2 dozen

1 pound (4 sticks) unsalted butter, at room temperature
¾ cup granulated sugar
6 large egg yolks
5 cups cake flour, sifted
5 cups bread flour, sifted
4½ tablespoons baking powder
3 cups buttermilk
2 cups raisins

1. Preheat the oven to 375°F.
2. In the bowl of an electric mixer, beat together the butter and sugar on medium for 2 to 3 minutes, until light and fluffy.
3. Add the egg yolks slowly and beat until combined.
4. In a large mixing bowl, stir together the flours and baking powder.
5. Fold the dry ingredients into the butter mixture in thirds, alternating with the buttermilk.
6. Gently fold in the raisins.
7. Turn to dough out onto a lightly floured surface. Roll out the dough until 1½ inches thick.
8. Cut out with a 2-inch floured biscuit cutter. Place scones 2 inches apart on ungreased baking sheets.
9. Bake for 30 to 40 minutes, until golden brown.
10. Remove from baking sheets and cool on a wire rack for 10 to 15 minutes. Serve warm.

Cranberry Bread

When the pilgrims came to the New World, they found cranberry bogs extending from New England down to the shores of New Jersey. These seasonal berries were harvested for use in juice and relishes as well as to flavor breads such as this one.

Makes one 8-inch loaf

¾ cup granulated sugar

4½ ounces (1 stick plus 1 tablespoon) unsalted butter, at room temperature

4 large eggs

2⅓ cups cake flour, sifted

1 tablespoon baking powder

1 teaspoon salt

¾ cup whole milk

2 cups fresh cranberries

½ cup chopped pecans

2 teaspoons grated orange rind

1. Preheat the oven to 350°F. Coat an 8½ x 4½ x 2½-inch loaf pan with vegetable cooking spray.
2. In the bowl of an electric mixer, beat together the butter and sugar on medium for 2 to 3 minutes, until light and fluffy.
3. Add the eggs, one at a time, and beat until combined.
4. In a medium mixing bowl, stir together the flour, baking powder, and salt.
5. Fold the dry ingredients into the butter mixture in thirds, alternating with the milk.
6. In a medium mixing bowl, combine the orange rind, pecans, and cranberries. Gently fold into the batter.
7. Pour the batter into the prepared pan.
8. Bake about 1 hour, until golden brown and a toothpick inserted in the center comes out clean.
9. Remove pan from oven, let cool for 10 minutes. Flip pan on side and gently remove bread.

Zucchini–Nut Bread

This recipe is a modern adaptation because zucchini was not known in America until the twentieth century. Hardier varieties of squash, however, were grown and used to make moist, nutty quick breads. I prefer the delicate flavor of zucchini, however, which is why I made the change.

Makes two 8-inch loaves

3 large eggs
2½ cups grated zucchini
1¾ cups granulated sugar
1 cup vegetable oil
1 tablespoon vanilla extract
3 cups all-purpose flour
2 teaspoons ground cinnamon
1 teaspoon baking soda
½ teaspoon baking powder
¼ teaspoon salt
1 cup chopped walnuts, toasted (see Chef's Note, page 136)

1. Preheat the oven to 350°F. Coat two 8½ x 4½ x 2½-inch loaf pans with vegetable cooking spray.
2. In the bowl of an electric mixer, beat the eggs on medium until the yolks are broken. Add the zucchini, sugar, oil, and vanilla and beat until well combined.
3. In a medium mixing bowl, stir together the flour, cinnamon, baking soda, baking powder, and salt.
4. Fold the dry ingredients into the zucchini mixture.
5. Gently fold in the walnuts.
6. Divide the batter between prepared pans.
7. Bake about 1 hour, until golden brown and a toothpick inserted into the center comes out clean.
8. Cool in pans on wire rack for 10 minutes. To remove bread, flip pans on their sides and gently pull out bread. Serve warm or let cool to room temperature on wire racks.

Pumpkin–Raisin Bread

In colonial days, raisins were imported from Southern France and Germany by the barrel full and transported along with many other European foodstuffs to the New World. Raisins were a welcome addition to the early American pantry because their versatility was surpassed only by their long shelf life. A good source of sugar and vitamins, raisins were an imported treat until the late 1800s, when commercial raisin production was started in California.

Makes two 8-inch loaves

2 cups pumpkin purée (see Chef's Note)
1 cup vegetable oil
⅔ cup water
4 large eggs
3⅓ cups all-purpose flour, sifted
3 cups granulated sugar
2 teaspoons baking soda
1½ teaspoons salt
1 teaspoon ground nutmeg
1 teaspoon ground cinnamon
½ cup raisins

1. Preheat the oven to 350°F.
2. Coat two 8½ x 4½ x 2½-inch loaf pans with vegetable cooking spray.
3. In a medium mixing bowl, combine the pumpkin purée, oil, water, and eggs.
4. In a large mixing bowl, stir together the flour, sugar, baking soda, salt, nutmeg, and cinnamon. Fold the egg mixture into the dry ingredients.
5. Gently fold in the raisins.
6. Divide the batter between the prepared pans. Bake about 1 hour, until the top springs back when touched or pulls away from the sides of the pan and a toothpick inserted into the center comes out clean.
7. Cool in pans on wire racks for 10 minutes. To remove, flip pans on their sides and gently pull out the bread. Let cool to room temperature on wire racks. Slice when completely cool.

Puréeing Fresh Pumpkin
Preheat the oven to 400°F. Cut off the top of a medium pumpkin. Remove and the discard seeds. Cut the pumpkin in half and place both pieces, pulp sides down, on a baking sheet sprayed with vegetable cooking spray. Bake about 1 hour, until the inside is soft. Remove from the oven and cool. Remove the skin and place the pulp in a food mill or food processor bowl and purée until smooth.

Banana–Nut Muffins

Even though bananas were picked green, they frequently arrived here fully ripened aboard the ships that came from the West Indies. The average person, however, rarely ate tropical fruits. It was the elite, with plenty of money to spend, who enjoyed them in dishes at the original City Tavern.

Makes twelve 3 x 1½-inch muffins

2 cups all-purpose flour
¼ cup granulated sugar
1 tablespoon baking powder
½ teaspoon salt
1 cup whole milk
1 cup water
¾ cup mashed, ripe bananas (about 2 bananas)
⅓ cup vegetable oil
1 large egg
½ cup chopped walnuts, toasted (see Chef's Note, page 136)

1. Preheat the oven to 400°F. Coat twelve 3 x 1½-inch muffin cups with vegetable cooking spray.
2. In a large mixing bowl, stir together the flour, sugar, baking powder, and salt.
3. In a medium mixing bowl, combine the milk, water, bananas, oil, and egg. Add to the dry ingredients and stir just until moistened. Gently fold in the walnuts.
4. Divide the batter among the prepared muffin cups, filling each cup about half full.
5. Bake for 15 to 20 minutes, until golden brown.
6. Cool on a wire rack.

Ginger and Raisin Scones

In the eighteenth century, ginger was imported, along with cinnamon and allspice, from the nearby Spice Islands. Ginger was used freshly grated, candied, and ground as in these scones. There were no raisins grown in America until the late 1800s—they were all imported from Europe.

Makes eight 2-inch scones

2 cups all-purpose flour
⅓ cup packed dark brown sugar
1 tablespoon baking powder
¾ teaspoon ground cinnamon
½ teaspoon ground ginger
⅛ teaspoon ground cloves
6 tablespoons unsalted butter, at room temperature
¼ cup whole milk
3 tablespoons molasses
1 large egg
1 teaspoon vanilla extract
⅔ cup raisins

1. Preheat the oven to 400°F.
2. In a large mixing bowl, stir together the flour, brown sugar, baking powder, cinnamon, ginger, and cloves.
3. In a medium mixing bowl, combine the butter, milk, molasses, egg, and vanilla.
4. Add the egg mixture to the dry ingredients and stir just until moistened.
5. Gently fold in the raisins.
6. Turn the dough out onto a lightly floured surface. Roll out the dough to 1 to 1½ inches thick.
7. Cut out with a 2-inch floured biscuit cutter. Place 2 inches apart on an ungreased baking sheet.
8. Bake about 25 minutes, until golden brown.
9. If desired, serve warm with Chantilly Cream (see page 208) or butter.

Almond–Lemon Bread

Almonds could be stored over the winter in the pantry, offering a compact source of fat and protein. In the 1700s, these nuts grew in abundance in Pennsylvania, as did walnuts and hazelnuts.

Makes two 8-inch loaves

¾ pound (3 sticks) unsalted butter, at room temperature
2 cups granulated sugar
6 large egg yolks
¼ teaspoon ground cloves
1 teaspoon ground cinnamon
2 teaspoons grated lemon rind
1½ cups all-purpose flour
1½ cups cake flour
1½ cups sliced almonds, toasted (see Chef's Note, page 136)

1. Preheat the oven to 350°F.
2. Coat two 8½ x 4½ x 2½-inch loaf pans with vegetable cooking spray.
3. In the bowl of an electric mixer, beat together the butter and sugar on medium for 2 to 3 minutes, until light and fluffy.
4. Add the egg yolks, cloves, cinnamon, and lemon rind and beat until combined.
5. In a medium bowl, stir together the flours and almonds. Add to the butter mixture and stir just until moistened.
7. Divide the batter between the prepared pans.
8. Bake for 50 to 55 minutes, until the top springs back when touched and a toothpick inserted into the center comes out clean.
9. Remove pan from oven and let cool for 30 minutes. To remove, flip pan on side and gently remove the bread. Slice when completely cool.

Chocolate–Almond Swirl Bread

Chocolate was one of Thomas Jefferson's culinary passions. He cultivated his love of the treat while he was in Europe, where chocolate houses had become fashionable as early as 1657. As stated in *Chocolate: An Illustrated History*, Jefferson had predicted in the late 1750s that "the superiority of chocolate, both for health and nourishment, will soon give it the same preference over tea and coffee in America which it has in Spain."

Makes one 8-inch loaf

3 ounces semisweet chocolate pieces (½ cup)

½ pound (2 sticks) unsalted butter, at room temperature

1 cup Almond Paste (see page 208) or 10½ ounces purchased almond paste

6 large eggs

1½ teaspoons vanilla extract

½ cup all-purpose flour, sifted

1. Preheat the oven to 350°F. Coat one 8½ x 4½ x 2½-inch loaf pan with vegetable cooking spray.
2. In a small dry bowl set over barely simmering water, melt the chocolate. Reserve.
3. In the bowl of an electric mixer, beat together the butter and Almond Paste on medium, until light and fluffy.
4. Add the eggs and vanilla and beat until combined.
5. Add the flour and stir just until moistened.
6. Fold about one-third of the batter into the melted chocolate.
7. Pour the plain batter into the prepared pan. Spoon the chocolate batter over the top. Gently swirl the batter to marble.
8. Bake for 45 to 55 minutes, until the loaf is firm on top and pulls away from the sides of the pan and a toothpick inserted into the center comes out clean.
9. Cool in pan on a wire rack for 30 minutes. To remove bread, flip pan on its side and gently pull out bread. Slice and serve warm.

Apple–Walnut Bread

This sweet bread could be made all winter long, using apples stored in the root cellar and walnuts put up in the pantry with their shells intact.

Makes two 8-inch loaves

2 cups granulated sugar
1 cup vegetable shortening
4 large eggs
3¼ cups applesauce
4 cups all-purpose flour, sifted
2 teaspoons baking powder
2 teaspoons baking soda
1½ teaspoons ground allspice
1½ teaspoons ground cinnamon
1 teaspoon salt
½ teaspoon ground nutmeg
½ teaspoon ground cloves
½ cup whole milk
1½ cups chopped walnuts, lightly toasted (see Chef's Note, page 136)

1. Preheat the oven to 350°F.
2. Coat two 8½ x 4½ x 2½-inch loaf pans with vegetable cooking spray.
3. In the bowl of an electric mixer, beat together the sugar and shortening on medium for 2 to 3 minutes, until light and fluffy.
4. Beat in the eggs, one at a time. Add the applesauce and beat until combined.
5. In a large bowl, stir together the flour, baking powder, baking soda, allspice, cinnamon, salt, nutmeg, and cloves.
6. Fold the dry ingredients into the egg mixture in thirds, alternating with the milk.
7. Gently fold in the walnuts.
8. Divide the batter between the prepared pans.
9. Bake for 55 to 60 minutes, until the top springs back when touched and a toothpick inserted into the center comes out clean.
10. Cool in pan on a wire rack for 30 minutes. To remove bread, flip pan on its side and gently pull out bread. Slice and serve warm.

Popovers

Thomas Jefferson and other Francophiles would have eaten popovers, along with other French breads and pastries, on trips of state to Paris. This French recipe provides a quick, hot bread that is ideal for last-minute entertaining.

Makes 8

½ cup granulated sugar
1 cup whole milk
3 large eggs
3 tablespoons unsalted butter, melted
1 teaspoon extract (lemon, vanilla, or almond)
1 cup all-purpose flour
¼ teaspoon salt

1. Preheat the oven to 400°F. Coat a popover pan or muffin tin with vegetable cooking spray and dust the cups with the sugar, discarding any excess sugar.
2. In a blender container, combine the milk, eggs, melted butter, and extract and blend well.
3. Add the flour and salt and blend until smooth.
4. Divide the batter between the prepared cups, filling each cup three-fourths full.
5. Bake for 40 to 50 minutes, until puffed up and golden brown. Immediately after removing from oven, prick each popover.
6. Serve immediately with flavored butters and preserves.

Irish Soda Bread

The earliest Irish immigrants, who came to America with the British, brought this traditional recipe with them.

Makes one 9-inch round loaf

3½ cups all-purpose flour
2 tablespoons caraway seeds
1 teaspoon baking soda
¾ teaspoon salt
1⅔ cups buttermilk

Keep your baking powder in a dry place. If it is exposed to moisture, it will lose its potency.

1. Preheat the oven to 400°F.
2. In a large mixing bowl, stir together the flour, caraway seeds, baking soda, and salt.
3. Add the buttermilk to the dry ingredients stirring just until moistened.
4. Turn the dough out onto a lightly floured surface. Knead until dough holds together.
5. Shape the dough into a 9-inch circle, or *boule* (see Chef's Note, page 137), and cut an X on top of the bread. Place boule on a greased baking sheet.
6. Bake for 25 to 30 minutes, until golden brown and the bread sounds hollow when tapped on the bottom.
7. Remove from baking sheet and cool on wire rack for 15 minutes before slicing.

Yeast Breads

The yeast breads we make at City Tavern are faithful to the colonial model, freshly baked, every day. The only difference is in the size of the loaves. In eighteenth-century Philadelphia, the French and German immigrant bakers usually baked breads in oversized rounds and loaves, the same as they had in Europe. With the exception of our Sally Lunn Bread and Anadama Bread, we've adapted our baking proportions to create smaller, more individual-sized loaves.

Rosemary Bread

Rosemary was most likely brought to the New World by the French, who prized it for its therapeutic value—it was believed to relieve digestive ills—as well as for its symbolism—it was often used to represent a declaration of love. Rosemary bushes also were used in hedges to ward off garden pests. This recipe introduces the herb's distinctive flavor into a finely textured bread. If you don't have your own rosemary growing in the garden, the fresh herb is available at most supermarkets.

Makes one 12-inch-long loaf

2¼ teaspoons active dry yeast
2 cups warm water (110° to 115°F)
¼ cup vegetable oil
1 tablespoon finely chopped fresh rosemary or 2 teaspoons dried rosemary
1 teaspoon salt
5 cups bread flour

1. In a large mixing bowl, dissolve the yeast in the warm water. Let stand about 10 minutes, until foamy.
2. Stir in the oil, rosemary, and salt. Mix in the bread flour, 1 cup at a time, to make a soft dough.
3. Turn out the dough onto a lightly floured surface. Knead for 6 to 8 minutes, until smooth and elastic and adding only enough flour to prevent sticking.
4. Transfer the dough to a large buttered bowl or a bowl coated with vegetable cooking spray and turn dough to coat all surfaces.
5. Cover with a slightly damp towel. Let rise in a warm place, free from drafts, for 45 minutes to 1 hour, until doubled in size.
6. Punch down the dough. Turn out onto a lightly floured surface.
7. Knead for 3 more minutes, until smooth, then cover and let rest for 10 minutes.
8. Lightly coat a 15 x 10 x 1-inch baking sheet with vegetable cooking spray.
9. Preheat the oven to 375°F.
10. Roll the dough into a 12 x 8-inch rectangle. Starting at a long side, tightly roll up the dough jelly roll style. Pinch seam to seal. Taper the ends. Place the 12-inch loaf, smooth side up, on the prepared baking sheet.
11. Cover and let rise for 30 to 45 minutes, until almost doubled in size.
12. Bake the loaf for 20 to 25 minutes, until golden and the bread sounds hollow when tapped on bottom.
13. Remove from baking sheet and cool on wire rack for 10 to 15 minutes before serving.

Rye and Caraway Seed Bread

Rye and caraway seeds were believed by the English to promote digestion and "dissolve all windiness," according to John Gerrard's, *The Herball*, circa 1597. These flavorful ingredients also were favored by German and Eastern European cooks who would have brought them to the New World.

Makes 2 small loaves

2¼ teaspoons active dry yeast
2 cups warm water (110° to 115°F)
¼ pound (1 stick) unsalted butter, at room temperature
1 tablespoon caraway seeds
1 teaspoon salt
2 cups rye flour
3 cups bread flour
Cornmeal, to coat baking sheet

1. In a large mixing bowl, dissolve the yeast in the warm water. Let stand about 10 minutes, until foamy.
2. Using a wooden spoon, beat in the butter, caraway seeds, and salt. Mix in the rye flour, 1 cup at a time, followed by the bread flour, to make a moderately stiff dough.
3. Turn the dough out onto a lightly floured surface. Knead for 6 to 8 minutes, until smooth and elastic and adding only enough flour to prevent stickiness.
4. Transfer the dough to a large buttered bowl or a bowl coated with vegetable cooking spray and turn dough to coat all sides.
5. Cover with a slightly damp towel. Let rise in a warm place, free from drafts, for 45 minutes to 1 hour, until doubled in size.
6. Punch down the dough. Turn out onto a lightly floured surface.
7. Divide the dough in half. Cover and let rest for 10 minutes.
8. Preheat the oven to 375°F. Lightly grease a large baking sheet; sprinkle with cornmeal.
9. Shape each half of dough into a ball. Place the balls, smooth sides up, on the prepared baking sheet. Flatten each ball into a 6-inch round loaf.
10. Cover and let rise for 30 to 45 minutes, until almost doubled in size.
11. Bake for 35 to 40 minutes, until golden and bread sounds hollow when tapped on the bottom.
12. Remove from baking sheet and cool on wire racks. Stores well-wrapped for up to 2 days.

Sally Lunn Bread

This City Tavern favorite dates back to eighteenth-century England, where a young woman named Sally Lunn walked the streets of the spa city of Bath, selling her ware: the warm, crumbly bread that now bears her name. According to the *Oxford English Dictionary*, a "respectable baker and musician" bought her business and wrote a song about her. The song has since been forgotten, but Sally Lunn Bread, which was served in colonial America as a tea bread, remains popular even today. This bread was traditionally served with clotted cream (a traditional thick English cream made by heating unpasteurized milk); you can substitute Chantilly Cream (see page 208).

Makes one 9 x 5 x 3-inch mold

2¼ teaspoons active dry yeast
2 cups warm water (110° to 115°F)
½ cup granulated sugar
4 tablespoons unsalted butter, at room temperature
¼ cup whole milk
2 eggs, lightly beaten
1 teaspoon salt
6½ cups all-purpose flour

1. Generously butter or coat two turk's-head pans or two 7-cup tube molds with vegetable cooking spray. Reserve.
2. In a large bowl, dissolve the yeast in the warm water. Let stand about 10 minutes, until foamy.
3. Using a wooden spoon, beat in the sugar, butter, milk, eggs, and salt. Mix in the flour, 1 cup at a time, to make a soft dough.
4. Cover the dough with a slightly damp towel. Let rise in a warm place, free from drafts, for 45 minutes to 1 hour, until doubled in size.
5. Stir down the batter. Divide the dough between the prepared pans. Cover and let rise in a warm place 40 to 45 minutes, until almost doubled in size.
6. Preheat the oven to 375°F.
7. Bake for 30 to 35 minutes, until golden and the bread sounds hollow when tapped on the bottom.
8. Remove the bread from pans. Serve the bread warm or cooled and toasted.

Anadama Bread

This bread's name comes from a hand-me-down colonial story about a fisherman whose wife would send him off every morning with a breakfast of cold cornmeal-molasses porridge. One bitterly cold day when his wife wasn't there to serve him breakfast, he mixed some yeast and flour into his porridge and put it into a warm oven, creating a slightly sweet, deliciously filling bread. He exclaimed, "Damn you Anna!"—as in, "I could have been eating this all along." The name of this popular eighteenth-century bread has evolved into "Anadama."

Makes 2 loaves

2 packages active dry yeast (½ ounce)
2 cups warm water (110° to 115°F)
¾ cup cornmeal
½ cup molasses
6 tablespoons unsalted butter, at room temperature
1 teaspoon salt
5½ cups bread flour

1. In a large mixing bowl, dissolve the yeast in the warm water. Let stand about 10 minutes, until foamy.
2. Using a wooden spoon, beat in the cornmeal, molasses, butter, and salt. Mix in the flour, 1 cup at a time, to make a moderately stiff dough.
3. Turn the dough out onto a lightly floured surface. Knead for 6 to 8 minutes, until smooth and elastic, adding only enough flour to prevent sticking.
4. Transfer the dough to a large buttered bowl or a bowl coated with vegetable cooking spray and turn dough to coat all surfaces.
5. Cover with a slightly damp towel. Let rise in a warm place, free from drafts, for 1 to 1¼ hours, until doubled in size.
6. Punch down the dough. Turn out onto a lightly floured surface.
7. Divide the dough in half. Cover and let rest for 10 minutes.
8. Preheat the oven to 375°F. Lightly grease a large baking sheet; sprinkle with cornmeal.
9. Shape each half of dough into a ball. Place the balls, smooth sides up, on the prepared baking sheet. Flatten each ball into a 6-inch round loaf.
10. Cover and let rise for 30 to 45 minutes, until almost doubled in size.
11. Bake for 25 to 30 minutes, until golden and bread sounds hollow when tapped on the bottom.
12. Remove from baking sheet and cool on wire racks

Braided Easter Bread

The recipe for this traditional Easter sweet bread came across the ocean with the German and Eastern European immigrants who baked it to commemorate Christ's resurrection. They sometimes decorate it with a hard-cooked egg.

Makes two 14-inch braided loaves; Serves 10 to 12

2 packages active dry yeast (½ ounce)
2 cups warm water (110° or 115°F)
2 large eggs
2 teaspoons vegetable oil
1 teaspoon salt
7 to 8 cups all-purpose flour
2 eggs, lightly beaten, for washing

1. In a large mixing bowl, dissolve the yeast in the warm water. Let stand about 10 minutes, until foamy.
2. Using a wooden spoon, beat in the eggs, oil, and salt. Mix in the flour, 1 cup at a time, to make a soft dough.
3. Turn the dough out onto a lightly floured surface. Knead for 6 to 8 minutes, until smooth and elastic, adding only enough flour to prevent sticking.
4. Transfer the dough to a large buttered bowl or a bowl coated with vegetable cooking spray and turn dough to coat all surfaces.
5. Cover with a slightly damp towel. Let rise in a warm place, free from drafts, for 1 to 1½ hours, until doubled in size.
6. Punch down the dough. Turn out onto a lightly floured surface.
7. Divide the dough into sixths. Cover and let rest for 10 minutes.
8. Lightly grease two large baking sheets.
9. Preheat the oven to 375°F.
10. Shape each portion of dough into a 14-inch-long rope (6 ropes total).
11. Place 3 ropes on each prepared baking sheet 1 inch apart; braid ropes (see below).
12. Cover and let rise for 30 to 40 minutes, until almost doubled in size.
13. Brush braids with beaten eggs. Bake for 25 to 30 minutes, until golden and the bread sounds hollow when tapped on the bottom.
14. Remove from baking sheet and cool on wire rack.

BRAIDING DOUGH
TO AVOID OVERLY STRETCHING THE DOUGH:

1. Line up 3 ropes about 1 inch apart on a greased baking sheet.
2. Starting in the middle of the ropes, loosely braid by bringing the left rope under the center rope.
3. Next bring right rope under the new center rope. Repeat to the end.
4. On the other end, braid by bringing alternate ropes over center rope from center to end.
5. Pinch the ends together to seal; tuck under the loaf.

Orange Bread with Orange Glaze

This moist bread showcases the orange, one of the most prized fruits in the colonies. Unknown to average folks because of their premium price, oranges imported from Spain would have typically been on the City Tavern menu—remember, all the finest foods of the day were featured at the Tavern, the most upscale restaurant in the New World. But even at the Tavern food was never wasted, so in this recipe, where both the juice and the rind of the fruit is used.

Makes two 9-inch round loaves

Bread
2¼ teaspoons active dry yeast
2 cups warm whole milk (110° to 115°F)
4 tablespoons unsalted butter, at room temperature
4 tablespoons grated orange rind (about 2 medium oranges)
1 teaspoon salt
6 cups all-purpose flour
1 egg, lightly beaten, washing

Orange Glaze
2 cups confectioners' sugar, sifted
½ cup orange juice

1. Prepare the Bread: In a large mixing bowl, dissolve the yeast in the milk. Let stand about 10 minutes, until foamy.
2. Using a wooden spoon, beat in the butter, orange rind, and salt. Mix in the flour, 1 cup at a time, to make a soft dough.
3. Turn the dough out onto a lightly floured surface.
4. Knead for about 5 minutes, until elastic and smooth, adding only enough flour to prevent sticking.
5. Transfer the dough to a large buttered bowl or a bowl coated with vegetable cooking spray and turn dough to coat all surfaces. Cover with a slightly damp towel. Let rise in a warm place, free from drafts, for 45 to 50 minutes, until doubled in size.
6. Punch down the dough. Turn out onto a lightly floured surface. Divide the dough in half. Cover and let rest for 10 minutes.
7. Lightly grease two large baking sheets.
8. Preheat oven to 425°F.
9. Shape each half of dough into a ball. Place each ball on a prepared baking sheet. Flatten each ball into a 9-inch round loaf. Cover and let rise about 30 to 40 minutes, until almost doubled in size.
10. Brush the tops of the loaves with the lightly beaten egg.
11. Bake for 30 to 35 minutes, until golden and the bread sounds hollow when tapped on the bottom.
12. Remove from baking sheets and cool on wire racks.
13. Prepare the Orange Glaze: In a small bowl, stir together the confectioners' sugar and orange juice until smooth. If too thick, add a few drops of additional orange juice.
14. Drizzle the glaze decoratively over the tops of the loaves. Let stand for 30 minutes, until glaze is set.

Part 6: Pantry

When we think about the colonial pantry, it's important to remember that there was no electricity or refrigeration in those days. Food was purchased and prepared the same day, with only the winter cold providing any means for extended storage for fresh food. Everything was done by hand, from scratch, and even the very act of getting a fire started was an arduous process. The home cook in those days put much thought into preserving food, using methods such as pickling, sun and air drying, preserving, marinating, and salt curing. These items were stored either in the pantry—a dry, windowless room—or the naturally cool underground root cellar. The industrious cook would work diligently to stock her larder with jars of jams and preserves made from the bounty of the summer garden, sacks of ground cornmeal, rice, flour, dried peas and beans, barrels of pickles, and dried and smoked meats for use year 'round.

Stocks

At City Tavern, we make our stocks fresh every day the way the original Tavern chefs did. It's rare that today's home cook will take those steps, and realistically, it's not absolutely necessary for the success of the recipes in this book. You can come close to our results by using good-quality commercially prepared products (see Resources, page 211).

Beef Stock

Makes 4 cups (1 quart)

7 pounds meaty beef or veal bones (neck bones, shank crosscuts,
    short ribs, knuckles, or leg bones with marrow)
1 cup red burgundy wine
4 celery ribs, diced
2 carrots, diced
1 large white onion, chopped
1 garlic clove, chopped
2 tablespoons unsalted butter
12 cups (3 quarts) water
2 large ripe tomatoes, diced
1 teaspoon whole black peppercorns
1 bay leaf

1. Preheat the oven to 350°F.
2. In a high-sided roasting pan, arrange meaty bones. Roast for 1 to 1½ hours, until meat is well browned, turning the bones once.
3. Drain the fat from the roasting pan.
4. Add the wine to deglaze the pan, loosening any browned bits with a wooden spoon. Set aside.
5. In an 8-quart (2-gallon) stockpot, sauté the celery, carrots, onion, and garlic in hot butter over medium heat for 5 minutes, until the onions are translucent.
6. Add the water to the stockpot and bring to a boil. Add the tomatoes, peppercorns, bay leaf, and bone and wine mixture and bring to a boil.
7. Reduce the heat and simmer, uncovered, for 4 hours, until reduced to about 4 cups (1 quart) of liquid.
8. Line a large colander or sieve with 2 layers of 100% cotton cheesecloth. Set colander in a large heat-proof bowl, carefully pour hot mixture through it.
9. Set aside to cool.
10. Transfer the stock to a storage container, cover, and refrigerate or freeze until ready to use. Stock will keep in the refrigerator for up to 1 week and in the freezer for up to 1 month, if well sealed.

Vegetable Stock

Makes 8 cups (2 quarts)

16 cups (1 gallon) water
3 celery ribs, chopped
3 carrots, chopped
2 medium white onions, chopped
2 large ripe tomatoes
1 leek, cut lengthwise and rinsed thoroughly
1 bay leaf
1 garlic clove, chopped
1 teaspoon freshly ground black pepper

1. In an 8-quart (2-gallon) stockpot, combine all ingredients and bring to a boil.
2. Reduce the heat and simmer, uncovered, for 4 hours, until reduced to about 8 cups (2 quarts) of liquid.
3. Line a large colander or sieve with 2 layers of 100% cotton cheesecloth. Set colander in a large heat-proof bowl, carefully pour hot mixture through it.
4. Set aside to cool.
5. Transfer the stock to a storage container, cover, and refrigerate or freeze until ready to use. Stock will keep in the refrigerator for up to 1 week and in the freezer for up to 1 month, if well sealed.

Chicken Stock

Makes 10 cups (2½ quarts)

3 celery ribs, chopped
2 carrots, chopped
2 medium onions, chopped
1 tablespoon unsalted butter
40 cups (2½ gallons) water
1 stewing hen (about 4½ pounds), whole or cut into eight pieces
1 cup white wine
4 sprigs fresh thyme
½ teaspoon whole black peppercorns
1 bay leaf

1. In a 12-quart (3-gallon) stockpot, sauté the celery, carrots, and onions in the butter over medium heat for 10 minutes, until the onions are translucent.
2. Add the water, hen, and wine and bring to a boil.
3. Add the thyme, peppercorns, and bay leaf.
4. Reduce the heat and simmer, uncovered, for 2 hours, until reduced to about 5 quarts of liquid.
5. Line a large colander or sieve with 2 layers of 100% cotton cheesecloth. Set colander in a large heat-proof bowl, carefully pour hot mixture through it.
6. Return stock to stockpot.
7. Continue cooking the stock for 4 hours, until reduced to about 10 cups (2½ quarts) of liquid.
8. Transfer the stock to a storage container, cover, and refrigerate or freeze until ready to use. Stock will keep in the refrigerator for up to 1 week, and in the freezer for up to 1 month, if well sealed.

Lobster Stock

Makes 4 cups (1 quart)

16 cups (1 gallon) water
2 pounds lobster heads and bodies
3 celery ribs, chopped
1 medium white onion, chopped
1 large ripe tomato, chopped
1 tablespoon tomato paste
1 bay leaf

1. In an 8-quart (2-gallon) stockpot, combine all ingredients and bring to a boil.
2. Reduce heat and simmer, uncovered, for 6 hours, until reduced to about 4 cups (1 quart) of liquid.
3. Line a large colander or sieve with 2 layers of 100% cotton cheesecloth. Set colander in a large heat-proof bowl, carefully pour hot mixture through it.
4. Set aside to cool.
5. Transfer the stock to a storage container, cover, and refrigerate or freeze until ready to use. Stock will keep in the refrigerator for up to 1 week and in the freezer for up to 1 month if well sealed.

Court Bouillon

Makes 12 cups (3 quarts)

32 cups (2 gallons) water
1 cup white wine
1 cup diced celery
2 large carrots, diced
1 large onion, cut into quarters
½ cup sliced leeks, rinsed well
2 teaspoons salt
1 teaspoon whole black peppercorns
½ teaspoon cayenne pepper
1 large bay leaf
1 lemon, cut into wedges

1. In a 10-quart stockpot, place all of the ingredients and bring to a boil.
2. Reduce heat to medium and simmer uncovered for about 3 hours, until reduced by about half.
3. Line a large colander or sieve with 2 layers of 100% cotton cheesecloth. Set colander in a large heat-proof bowl, carefully strain hot mixture through it.
4. Set aside to cool.
5. Transfer to a storage container, cover, and refrigerage or freeze until ready to use. Stock will keep in the refrigerator for up to 1 week and in the freezer for up to 1 month, if well sealed.

Marinade for Beef, Pork, Rabbit, or Chicken

Because in colonial times meat wasn't as tender or as flavorful as the grain-fed product we're used to, marinating was used to tenderize meat cuts, which would then be slow-cooked until they attained a falling-off-the-bone consistency. This basic marinade can be used to flavor almost any fowl or meat. When marinating, be sure to work under sanitary conditions, using clean utensils and containers, and be sure to refrigerate meat during the marinating process.

Makes 4 cups (1 quart)
1 medium onion, thinly sliced
1 garlic clove, crushed
1 small carrot, thinly sliced
1 celery rib, chopped
2 tablespoons fresh parsley, chopped
3 whole black peppercorns
1 bay leaf
1 sprig fresh thyme
2 cups (16 ounces) red burgundy wine
½ cup red wine vinegar
½ cup brandy or cognac
1 tablespoon vegetable oil
Salt and freshly ground pepper to taste

Chef's Notes

• *For a more intense flavor, add rosemary or sage.*
• *Boil the marinade (to destroy any bacteria), if you want to include it to flavor a sauce.*

1. In a 4-quart stockpot, mix together all of the ingredients.
2. Add meat and marinate in the refrigerator overnight. Cook the meat as desired.
3. To use the marinade as a flavor-enhancer for sauces, bring it to a boil first. Otherwise, discard it.

Bouquet Garni

Makes 1 sachet
4 whole black peppercorns
3 sprigs fresh thyme
2 sprigs fresh parsley
2 medium garlic cloves
1 medium shallot
1 bay leaf

1. Place all ingredients in 100% cotton cheesecloth and tie with kitchen twine to make a sachet.
2. Place in stock or sauce as directed.

Sauces

These are the sauces that we use at City Tavern
to complement our main and side dishes.

Demi-glace

Demi-glace is the building block for any recipe that calls for a sauce, including stews and casseroles. At City Tavern, we make our demi-glace fresh from a rich veal or beef bone stock. The home cook may not have time for this, choosing instead to use a canned broth, or buy sauce base from the source listed in the Resources section (see page 211).

Makes 1½ cups

1 large shallot, chopped
1 teaspoon unsalted butter
1 cup red burgundy wine
1 bay leaf
1 whole black peppercorn
2 cups Beef Stock (see page 198)

1. In a 2-quart saucepan, sauté the shallot in hot butter over medium heat for 5 minutes, until golden brown and translucent.
2. Add the red wine, bay leaf, and peppercorn and bring to a boil. Reduce the heat and simmer, uncovered, for 8 to 10 minutes, until reduced to about ½ cup liquid.
3. Add the Beef Stock and continue cooking for about 30 minutes, until reduced to about 1½ cups.
4. Line a large colander or sieve with 2 layers of 100% cotton cheesecloth. Set colander in a large heat proof bowl, carefully pour hot mixture through it.
5. Set aside to cool.
6. Transfer the stock to a storage container, cover, and refrigerate or freeze until ready to use. Stock will keep in the refrigerator for up to 1 month, if well sealed. *Note:* Demi-glace may be made ahead of time and reheated. However, you must bring the temperature to 165°F for at least 15 seconds before serving.

Madeira Wine Sauce

This delicate sauce enhances chicken breast and roasted pork.

Makes 1 cup
½ cup Madeira
1 teaspoon cracked black peppercorns
1 cup Demi-glace (see opposite page)

1. In a medium saucepan, combine the Madeira and peppercorns and bring to a boil.
2. Add the Demi-glace. Reduce the heat and simmer, uncovered, for 10 minutes, until reduced to about 1 cup liquid.
3. Serve immediately. *Note:* Sauce may be made ahead of time and reheated. However, you must bring the temperature to 165°F for at least 15 seconds before serving.

Sherry Cream Sauce

We use this with salmon, shrimp, and almost any combination of seafood. This sauce adds great flavor to lighter entrées.

Makes 1¼ cups
1 large shallot, finely chopped
2 tablespoons unsalted butter
1 cup dry sherry
1 cup heavy cream
1 small bunch fresh chives, chopped (about 2 tablespoons)
Salt and freshly ground black pepper

1. In 2-quart saucepan, sauté the shallots in hot butter over medium heat for 3 minutes, until browned.
2. Add the sherry and continue cooking for 8 to 10 minutes, until reduced to ½ cup liquid. Add heavy cream and bring to a boil.
3. Reduce the heat and simmer for 5 to 10 minutes, until reduced to about 1¼ cups liquid.
4. Remove from heat. Stir in the chives. Season to taste with salt and pepper.
5. Serve immediately.

Sauce Béchamel

Sauce Béchamel is used for side dishes such as creamed corn, creamed spinach, and green beans.

Makes about 1½ cups

1½ cups whole milk
1 small onion, finely chopped
4 tablespoons plus 1 teaspoon unsalted butter
¼ cup all-purpose flour
1 teaspoon salt
1 whole clove
1 bay leaf
1 pinch ground nutmeg
Salt and freshly ground white pepper

1. In a small saucepan, bring the milk to a boil. Remove from heat and reserve in a warm place.
2. In a 2-quart saucepan, sauté the onion in the hot butter over medium heat for 5 minutes, until the onion is translucent.
3. Slowly whisk in the flour until well-combined.
4. Slowly whisk in the reserved, warm milk and bring the mixture to a boil. Add the 1 teaspoon salt, clove, bay leaf, and nutmeg.
5. Reduce the heat and simmer, uncovered, for 20 minutes, until desired thickness.
6. Season with salt and pepper to taste.
7. Strain the mixture through a fine wire sieve into a heat-proof container.
8. Serve immediately.

Mustard Sauce

This thick and creamy sauce is used in appetizers such as Mustard Eggs (see page 23), cold poached salmon, and steamed shrimp.

Makes 1½ cups

2 medium onions, finely chopped
3 medium shallots, finely chopped
3 tablespoons unsalted butter
1 tablespoon vegetable oil
1 tablespoon all-purpose flour
2 cups white wine
½ cup cider vinegar
2 tablespoons tomato paste
2 tablespoons Dijon mustard
Salt and freshly ground white pepper
2 tablespoons finely chopped fresh parsley, for serving

1. In a 2-quart saucepan, sauté the onions and shallots in the hot butter and oil over medium heat for 3 minutes, until translucent.
2. Sprinkle the flour over the onion mixture and cook, stirring frequently, until well combined.
3. Stir in the wine, vinegar, tomato paste, and mustard. Reduce the heat and simmer, uncovered, for 30 minutes, until reduced by one fourth.
4. Season with salt and pepper to taste.
5. Keep warm until ready to serve. Before serving, stir in the parsley.

Homemade Mayonnaise

This is a recipe for classic mayonnaise. If you prefer a lighter version, or one that doesn't call for raw egg yolks, you can use a store-bought variety with reasonably good results.

Makes about 1 cup

1 egg yolk
1 teaspoon lemon juice
1 tablespoon white wine vinegar
1 teaspoon granulated sugar
1 cup vegetable oil
Salt and freshly ground white pepper

1. In a blender or food processor bowl, combine all ingredients, except the vegetable oil. Cover.
2. With the blender or food processor on high, slowly drizzle in oil through feed tube.
3. Pour the dressing into a bowl, cover with plastic wrap and store in the refrigerator for up to 3 days.

Pastry

These are the pantry items we use at City Tavern
in our pastry shop.

Pâte Brisée (Basic Pie Dough)

This traditional French pastry is ideal for all kinds of pies, both sweet and savory.

Makes 12 ounces; enough for one 9-inch pie crust

1⅓ cups all-purpose flour, sifted
¼ teaspoon salt
4 tablespoons cold unsalted butter, cubed
¼ cup cold vegetable shortening, cubed
4 to 5 tablespoons ice-cold water

1. In a medium bowl, stir together the flour and salt. Using a pastry cutter or 2 knives, cut in the butter and shortening until the mixture resembles coarse crumbs.
2. Sprinkle the water, 1 tablespoon at a time, over flour mixture and toss together with a fork, until a dough starts to form. It will be a little sticky or tacky.
3. Form the dough into a disk shape, wrap in plastic wrap, and chill in the refrigerator for at least 30 minutes before using.

Pâte Sucrée (Rich Pie Dough)

We use this rich pie dough with our traditional Apple Pie and Pumpkin Pie for a perfectly flaky crust.

Makes 2 pounds; enough for one 9-inch double-crust pie

3 cups all-purpose flour, sifted
¼ cup granulated sugar
½ pound (2 sticks) cold unsalted butter, cubed
2 large eggs

1. Place steel blade in food processor bowl. Add the flour and sugar. Cover, process with on/off pulses, until the mixture is combined.
2. Add the butter. Process with on/off pulses until most of the mixture is crumbly.
3. With the processor running, quickly add the eggs through the feed tube. Stop processor when all eggs are added and scrape down side of the bowl.
4. Process with 2 more on/off pulses (mixture may not all be moistened).
5. Remove the dough from the bowl. Form the dough into a disk shape, wrap in plastic wrap, and chill in the refrigerator for at least 1 hour before using.

Quick Puff Pastry

Although we do everything from scratch at City Tavern, the truth is, there is virtually no difference in taste between commercial puff pastry, available in most supermarkets, and this recipe. If you are going to make puff pastry yourself, be sure to follow the directions exactly to ensure the best results.

Makes 3 pounds; enough for 12 meat turnovers or potpie lids

4 cups all-purpose flour, sifted
2 teaspoons salt
7 tablespoons unsalted butter, melted
1 cup ice-cold water
1 pound (4 sticks) cold unsalted butter, cubed

1. In the bowl of an electric mixer, beat the flour and salt on low until combined. Add the 7 tablespoons melted butter and beat well.
2. While still beating, slowly add the ice-cold water.
3. When the dough starts to form, add the pound of cubed butter and beat just until combined. (You should see small specks of butter embedded in the dough—essential for forming a layered effect in the dough. As you roll or shape the dough, these butter specks will blend in.)
4. Remove the dough from bowl, form into a disk shape, wrap in plastic wrap, and chill in the refrigerator for at least 30 minutes before using.

Pastry Cream

This pastry cream is ideal for filling everything from fruit tarts to layer cakes and cream puffs. It is a traditional French recipe, which no doubt accompanied French pastry chefs to the New World.

Makes 3 cups

2 cups whole milk
½ cup granulated sugar
¼ cup all-purpose flour
¼ cup cornstarch
3 large eggs
½ teaspoon vanilla extract
2 tablespoons unsalted butter, softened

1. In a 2-quart heavy saucepan, bring the milk and ¼ cup of the sugar to a boil over medium heat, stirring occasionally.
2. In a large bowl, whisk together the flour, cornstarch, eggs, vanilla, and remaining ¼ cup sugar.
3. Slowly pour the hot milk into the egg mixture, whisking continuously, until thickened.
4. Pour the mixture back into the saucepan and cook, stirring constantly, over a low heat until mixture thickens and just comes to a boil.
5. Remove from the heat. Pour the mixture into a heat-proof bowl and stir in the butter. Cover the surface with plastic wrap to prevent a "skin" from forming on the top, and let cool at room temperature for 30 minutes.
6. Chill in the refrigerator for at least 1 hour before using. Pastry Cream will keep in the refrigerator 4 to 5 days if sealed in an airtight container.

Chantilly Cream

This classic sweetened whipped cream is the perfect topping for our Almond-Buttermilk Biscuits (see page 177), as well as many of our desserts and tea breads.

Makes 4 cups

2 cups heavy cream
½ cup confectioners' sugar, sifted

1. In a clean, dry bowl of an electric mixer, whip together the cream and sugar, until soft peaks form. Refrigerate until ready to serve.

Almond Paste

Almond paste was—and remains—a dominant ingredient in all kinds of French pastry, where it is used to fill tortes, cookies, and other sweets. French pastry chefs in the eighteenth century, as well as today, consider it a fundamental building block of their craft.

Makes 14 ounces (1⅓ cups)

1 cup granulated sugar
1 cup water
10 ounces (3 cups) dry, blanched almonds
2¼ cups confectioners' sugar

1. In a small saucepan, combine the sugar and water and bring to boil, stirring often, until the sugar dissolves. Remove from heat and let cool. Set aside.
2. In a food processor bowl, add the almonds and grind to a fine, powder-like consistency. Stop the processor and scrape down the sides of the bowl.
3. Add the confectioner's sugar and process with on/off pulses for 30 seconds. Scrape down the sides of the bowl.
4. With the processor running, gradually add the cooled sugar syrup through the feed tube, until the mixture forms a paste. (The amount of syrup needed will vary depending on how dry the almonds are.)
5. Remove the Almond Paste from the bowl.
6. If not used immediately, wrap the Almond Paste tightly in plastic wrap and chill in refrigerator until ready to use. Almond paste will keep in the refrigerator for up to 4 weeks if well sealed.

Crème Anglaise (Vanilla Custard Sauce)

This classic French custard sauce can be served hot or cold, over cake, poached fruit, or other desserts, such as our famous bread pudding. It adds a sophisticated finish to elegant desserts—such as those that have been on the City Tavern menu since the eighteenth century.

Makes 1½ cups

2 cups whole milk
¼ cup granulated sugar
1 vanilla bean, scraped (see Chef's Note, page 138)
4 large egg yolks
2 tablespoons Jamaican rum

1. In a 2-quart heavy saucepan bring 2 cups of the milk, 2 tablespoons of the sugar, and the scraped vanilla bean to a boil over medium heat.
2. In a large bowl, whisk together the egg yolks and remaining 2 tablespoons of sugar.
3. Slowly pour 1 cup of the hot milk mixture, whisking constantly, into the egg yolk-sugar mixture. (*Do not pour the entire yolk-sugar mixture into the boiling milk mixture, as it will curdle the eggs.*)
4. Pour the milk-yolk mixture into the saucepan and cook over medium heat, stirring constantly, until the mixture coats the back of a spoon. *Do not boil.*
5. Remove from the heat and stir in rum.
6. Strain the mixture though a fine wire sieve into a heat-proof bowl. Place the sauce in an ice bath (see Chef's Note).
7. When cool, transfer the sauce to a bowl. Cover the surface with plastic wrap and chill in the refrigerator, until ready to use. Sauce will keep in the refrigerator for 4 to 5 days if well sealed.

Making an Ice Bath
If a custard mixture is not iced, the eggs will continue to cook and then scramble, making the mixture unusable. To make an ice bath, fill a large bowl with ice cubes. Insert a smaller heat-proof bowl within the large bowl. Arrange the ice cubes around the bowl. Pour the custard into the smaller bowl and stir continuously —to allow heat to escape—until the mixture has cooled.

Graham Cracker Crust

We use this no-fail crust recipe for all our cheesecakes.

Makes 1¾ cups; enough for one 9-inch cheesecake crust

1½ cups finely crushed graham crackers (about 22)
¼ pound (1 stick) unsalted butter, melted
¼ cup granulated sugar

1. In a large bowl, thoroughly combine the graham crackers, butter, and sugar. Reserve.

Streusel Topping

This traditional German topping is used for cobblers, coffeecakes, and pies.

Makes 4 cups

1 cup all-purpose flour
1 cup packed light brown sugar
¾ cup granulated sugar
1 tablespoon ground cinnamon
6 ounces (1½ sticks) cold unsalted butter, cut into cubes
2 cups chopped walnuts

1. In the bowl of an electric mixer, mix the flour, brown sugar, granulated sugar, and cinnamon on medium speed until combined.
2. Add the butter and mix well, until the texture becomes crumbly. Stir in the walnuts.
3. Use immediately or transfer to a covered container and store in the refrigerator for up to 1 month.

Oat Topping

This variation of German streusel incorporates oats, a readily available eighteenth-century ingredient. The texture is wonderfully crunchy.

Makes 2 cups

½ cup all-purpose flour
½ cup old-fashioned oats
½ cup packed light brown sugar
½ cup chopped walnuts
4 tablespoons cold unsalted butter, cut into cubes

1. In a medium bowl, combine the flour, oats, and brown sugar.
2. Cut in the butter with 2 knives or place in a food processor bowl and process until the texture becomes crumbly. Stir in the walnuts.
3. Use immediately or store in a covered container in the refrigerator for up to 1 month.

Resources

D'Artagnan
280 Wilson Ave.
Newark, NJ 07105
1-800-327-8246
973-344-0565

Fresh and exotic selection of game and fowl including venison, pheasant, Cornish game hen and duck. National delivery available.

North Country Smokehouse
P.O. Box 1415
Airport Road
Claremont, NH 03743
1-800-258-4304

One-of-a-kind superior quality sausages including duck sausage, apple-smoked bacon and hams. National delivery available.

More Than Gourmet
115 West Bartges Street
Akron, OH 44311
330-762-6652

Chef-quality demi-glace and all-natural reduction sauces sold in small portions for home use. National delivery available.

Tait Farms
RR 1
Box 329
Centre Hall, PA 16828
1-800-787-2716
814-466-2386

A refreshing selection of shrubs offered in a variety of flavors, essential in the traditional eighteenth century shrub drinks. National delivery available.

❧

Illustration Credits

Front jacket photograph: © William Deering

Front cover illustration: © Concepts By Staib, Ltd.

Back flap photograph: © Courtney Grant Winston

Wood cuts: *Old English Cuts and Illustrations* by Bowles and Carver, Dover Publications, 1970. Originally published in the late-1780s and early-1790s by the firm of Bowles and Carver.

Courtesy of Independence National Historical Park:

Endpapers: Detail from map of Philadelphia, inscribed: To Thomas Mifflin, Governor and Commander in Chief of the State of Pennsylvania, This Plan of the City and Suburbs of Philadelphia is respectfully inscribed by The Editor, 1794.

Back jacket and pp. 1, 15: Detail from engraving, *Bank of Pennsylvania, South Second Street*, Philadelphia, by William Birch, c. 1800.

p. 4: Detail from engraving, *New Market, in South Second Street*, Philadelphia, by William Birch, 1799.

p. 10: Detail from engraving, *Arch Street Ferry, Philadelphia,* by William Birch, 1800.

p. 14: Detail from engraving, *Second Street North from Market Street with Christ Church.* Philadelphia, by William Birch, 1799.

p. 16: City Tavern, East Elevation, drawing #0603–9, by Denise Rabzak. Courtesy of National Park Service, Independence National Historical Park. Historic Architect's Office. Scaled Drawings, Plans and Elevations, 1985–1986. Accession #3895.

p. 17: City Tavern, West Elevation, drawing #0603–11, by Denise Rabzak. Courtesy of National Park Service, Independence National Historical Park. Historic Architect's Office. Scaled Drawings, Plans and Elevations, 1985–1986. Accession #3895.

p. 18: Detail from engraving, *The City and Port of Philadelphia, on the River Delaware from Kensington*, by William Birch, 1800.

p. 65: Detail from engraving, *Back of the State House, Philadelphia*, by William Birch, 1799.

p. 128: Detail from engraving, *High Street, [viewed] from the Country Market-place Philadelphia: with the procession in commemoration of the Death of General George Washington, December 26th 1799*, by William Birch, 1800.

p. 168: Detail from engraving, *Arch Street, with the Second Presbyterian Church. Philadelphia*, by William Birch, 1799.

p. 174: Detail from engraving, *View in Third Street, from Spruce Street Philadelphia*, by William Birch, c. 1800.

p. 197: Detail from engraving, *High Street, from Ninth Street, Philadelphia*, by William Birch, 1799.

✒

Selected Bibliography

Bailey, Adrian, ed. *Cook's Ingredients*. Pleasantville, NY: The Readers Digest Association Inc., 1990.

Chalmers, Irene. *The Great Food Almanac*. San Francisco: Collins Publishing, 1994.

Glasse, Hannah. *The Art of Cookery Made Plain and Easy*. Rev. ed. Schenectady, NY: United States Historical Research Service, 1796.

Herbst, Sharon Tyler. *The New Food Lover's Companion*. 2nd. ed. Hauppauge, NY: Barron's Educational Series, Inc. 1995.

Hess, Karen. *Martha Washington's Booke of Cookery*. New York: Columbia University Press, 1981.

Hines, Mary Anne; Gordon Marshall; and William Woys Weaver. *The Larder Invaded: Reflections on Three Centuries of Philadelphia Food and Drink*. Philadelphia: The Winchester Company, 1987.

Johnson, Sylvia. *Tomatoes, Potatoes, Corn and Beans*. New York: Athetheum Books for Young Readers, 1997.

Marsh and Frederic Morton. *Chocolate: An Illustrated History*. New York City: Crown Publishers, 1986.

Platt, John D.R. *Historic Research Study, The City Tavern, Independence National Historic Park*

Toussaint-Samat, Maguelonne. *History of Food*. Translated by Anthea Bell. Cambridge, MA: Blackwell Publishers, 1987.

Index

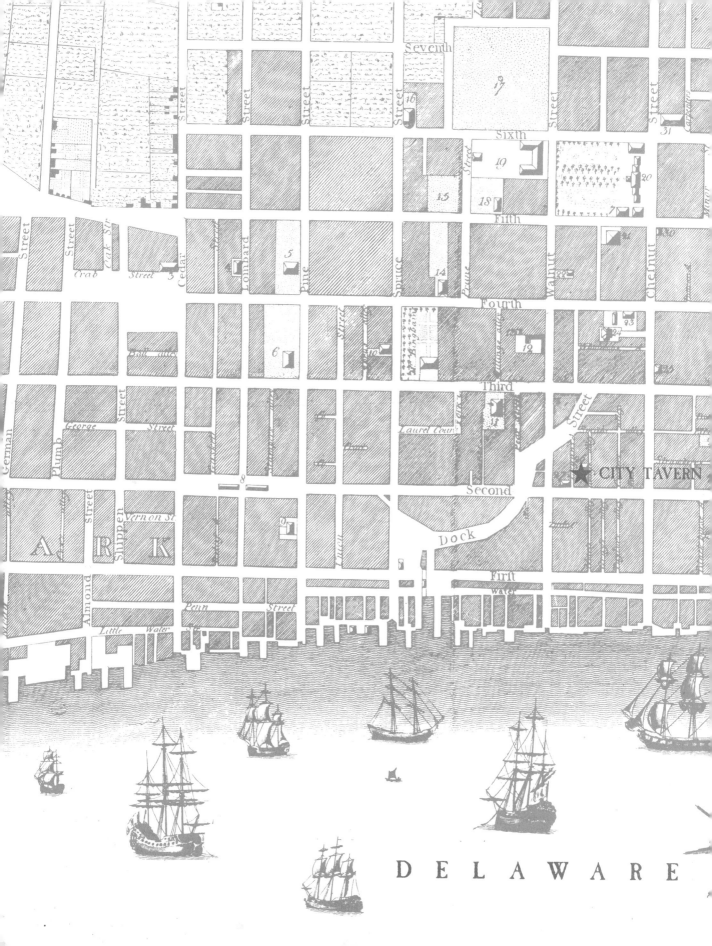

Seventh

Street

17

16

Street

Sixth

Street

Street

19

Street

20

15

18

7

31

Fifth

Street

Street

Oak Str

5

Lombard

Pine

Spruce

14

Walnut

Chesnut

Street

Street

Street

Crab

Street

Cedar

Street

3

Prune

Fourth

22

24

30

Street

Street

6

Street

10

Longlane

12

23

24

German

Plumb

Shippen

George

Street

Street

Third

Laurel Court

11

Vernon St

CITY TAVERN

★

8

Second

9

Dock

A   R   K

Third

Almond

Penn

Street

Little   Water

First

Water

DELAWARE